HEBREW ILLUMINATED MANUSCRIPTS

HEBREW ILLUMINATED MANUSCRIPTS

by BEZALEL NARKISS

Foreword by
CECIL ROTH

Copyright © 1992 by Keter Publishing House Ltd., Jerusalem

All rights reserved. No part of this book may be reproduced or transmitted in any form or by any means, electronic or mechanical, including photocopying, recording or by any information storage and retrieval system, without permission in writing from the Publisher.

Cat. No. 896035

Library of Congress Catalog Card Number: 72–90254
ISBN Number: 8148–0593–0

First printing, 1969
Second printing, 1974
Third printing, 1978
Fourth printing 1992

Printed by Keterpress Enterprises
Printed in Israel

Publisher's Note

The present volume of reproductions of Hebrew illuminated manuscripts is the first of a series of publications in various spheres of Judaica which the Publishers are issuing in advance of the *Encyclopaedia Judaica* now in preparation. This volume is both an independent contribution to Art History and an example of the production standards of the *Encyclopaedia Judaica*; illustrations will be a major feature of the Encyclopaedia, and special care is being devoted to the color plates.

The book contains sixty Hebrew illuminated manuscripts in full color. Two of the world's experts on Hebrew illumination have been associated with this publication: the idea of publishing such a book was suggested by the Encyclopaedia's Editor-in-Chief, Professor Cecil Roth, who participated in the selection of the manuscripts and wrote the Foreword; the Introduction and the description of each of the manuscripts are the work of Dr. Bezalel Narkiss, Senior Lecturer in History of Medieval Art at the Hebrew University, Jerusalem, and Illustrations Consultant to the *Encyclopaedia Judaica*.

It is our pleasant duty to thank the libraries and collectors in many countries who have permitted us to reproduce the manuscripts: a full list appears on the following page.

Special mention must be made of the Trustees of the British Museum, who afforded us generous facilities, and Dr. J. Rosenwasser, of the Department of Oriental Printed Books and Manuscripts, for his guidance. Dr. Luisella Mortara Ottolenghi of Milan helped us with her special competence. Generous assistance was given by: Dr. Manuel dos Santos Estevaes and Miss Isabel Cepeda, Portugal, and by M. Bernard Blumenkranz in Paris; Mrs. T. and Dr. M. Metzger of Strasbourg for measurements and folio number of plate 6; the Institute of Paleography who permitted us to consult some of the dated manuscripts which they have described.

Miss Avalon Krukin deserves special thanks for her help in obtaining at the last moment some illustrations of special significance.

Thanks are due also to Dr. Bernhard Baer of Ganymed Press, London, who acted as our color printing consultant; to Mrs. Genya Yarkoni, Mr. David Harris who did the color photography in Israel; to the color printers, E. Lewin-Epstein and United Artists.

Last but not least, we wish to thank a small group of devoted editors, typesetters and proofreaders, who made it possible to produce this book according to plan: Daniel Furman, Miss Nadine Habousha, Miss Gloria Hillel, Miss Moira Paterson, Miss Devorah Seton, Moshe Shalvi, and Miss Lois Skolnick.

The publication of the work received great impetus from the Encyclopaedia Judaica Research Foundation, and from the vision and generosity of Mr. and Mrs. Ludwig Jesselson of New York, as well as the gracious contributions of his friends, Dr. and Mrs. Adolfo Blum, Mr. and Mrs. Esteban Felsenstein and Mr. Hermann C. Starck. Mr. Starck's contribution was made in memory of Mrs. Klari Starck, West Berlin, whose understanding and feeling for books, especially Judaica, was outstanding.

Names which appear in the Bible are rendered according to the translation of the Jewish Publication Society of America. Post-biblical names and modern places in Israel are rendered according to the rules of transliteration given below. All other geographical names are given according to the *Columbia Lippincott Gazetteer of the World*, (1962). A glossary will be found at the end of the book.

TABLE OF HEBREW TRANSLITERATION

א	not transliterated	ל	l	◌ָ	a	◌ֶ	e
בּ	b	מ	m	◌ַ	a	◌ִ	i
ב	v	נ	n	◌ֹ, וֹ	o	◌ֵ	e
ג גּ	g	ס	s	◌ֻ, וּ	u	◌ֱ	e
ד דּ	d	ע	not transliterated	◌ָ קמץ	o	◌ֳ	o
ה	h	פּ	p	◌ֵי	ei	◌ֲ	a
ו	v	פ	f				
ז	z	צ	ẓ				
ח	ḥ	ק	k				
ט	t	ר	r				
י	y	שׁ	sh				
כּ	k	שׂ	s				
כ	kh	ת, תּ	t				

vocal *sheva* —e

silent *sheva* —not transliterated

Acknowledgments

We wish to express our thanks to the Libraries, Museums, and Collections who have provided us with photographs and granted us their permission to reproduce their works.

DENMARK
Det Kongelige Bibliotek, Copenhagen

FRANCE
Bibliothèque Nationale de Paris

GERMANY
Badische Landesbibliothek, Karlsruhe
Mit Genehmigung der Hessischen Landes- und Hochschulbibliothek, Darmstadt
Leipzig University Library
Orientalische Abteilung der Staatsbibliothek Preussischer Kulturbesitz, Berlin
Staats- und Universitätsbibliothek, Hamburg

GREAT BRITAIN
By courtesy of the Curators of the Bodleian Library, Oxford
British Museum, London
By courtesy of Cambridge University Library
By courtesy of the Master and Fellows of Emmanuel College, Cambridge
By permission of the Governors of the John Rylands Library, Manchester
S. D. Sassoon Collection, Letchworth

HUNGARY
Library of the Hungarian Academy of Sciences, Kaufmann Collection, Budapest

ISRAEL
Israel Museum, Jerusalem
Jewish National and University Library, Jerusalem
Schocken Library, Jerusalem

ITALY
Accademia Dei Concordi Di Rovigo
Courtesy of the Biblioteca Ambrosiana, Milan
Biblioteca Palatina, Parma
University Library of Bologna
Biblioteca Apostolica Vaticana, Vatican City
Seminario Vescovile, Vercelli

PORTUGAL
Lisbon National Library

UNITED STATES
Library of Congress
Courtesy of Library, Hebrew Union College, Jewish Institute of Religion, Cincinnati
The Library of the Hispanic Society of America, New York
The Library, Jewish Theological Seminary, New York
Private Collection, New York

U.S.S.R.
Leningrad Public Library

YUGOSLAVIA
National Museum, Sarajevo

COLOR SEPARATIONS :
E. Lewin-Epstein Ltd. dust jacket, and plates : 1, 2, 5, 6, 13, 14, 16, 17, 20, 21, 27, 30, 32, 34, 35, 38, 41, 42, 46, 47, 48, 49, 50, 54, 56, 57, 58, 60.
United Artists Ltd. plates : 3, 4, 7, 8, 9, 10, 11, 12, 15, 18, 19, 22, 23, 24, 25, 26, 28, 29, 31, 33, 36, 37, 39, 40, 43, 44, 45, 51, 52, 53, 55, 59.

Foreword

It is impossible to state with any degree of certainty how far back in history the tradition of the illuminated Hebrew manuscripts began. The oldest extant specimens belong to the Arab environment, in the period corresponding to the European Dark Ages. But it is out of the question that the practice began at this period; and indications are not lacking which suggest a longer history. It may well be, in fact, that the illumination of Hebrew manuscripts goes back even as far as the classical period, although no specimens have survived.

During recent years, archeological discoveries have revealed that it was the practice in the Roman period to adorn synagogues in Palestine with mosaic floors which embodied not only decorative features and animal figures but also graphic representations of Biblical scenes and personalities; while the walls might be covered with frescoes depicting in great detail entire cycles of Bible history, with possibly some special symbolic significance, such as have survived at Dura Europos on the Euphrates.

If this was considered legitimate in the actual place of worship, notwithstanding the ostensibly stringent Biblical prohibition of "Graven Images," it is hardly possible that a greater degree of anti-iconic strictness was observed as regards objects such as manuscripts, which were intended for domestic use. According to some, the Dura Europos frescoes referred to above were based on versions which adorned manuscript texts of the Bible.

The earliest extant Christian Bible illuminated manuscripts are, as it happens, of Old Testament books, such as the so-called Vienna Genesis, and are conjectured by some scholars to have been based on Jewish prototypes. It is significant too that the favorite topics for early Christian religious art were based on "Old" rather than "New" Testament subjects (the sacrifice of Isaac, the story of Jonah, and so on) again perhaps suggesting Jewish prototypes: and it is noteworthy that precisely these subjects reemerge (rather than emerge) as favorite topics in the Jewish manuscript and religious art of the Middle Ages. Christian illuminated Bible manuscripts in the medieval heyday often elaborate the plain narrative with materials reflecting rabbinic legend; and it is a moot point whether this resulted from an antecedent Jewish art or from the common store of medieval religious folklore.

Finally, there are certain motifs in the illuminated medieval Hebrew Bibles—the tradition which goes back to the 10th or 11th century—which seem to carry on the tradition of very remote antiquity, reflected both in the early Jewish monuments of the classical period on the one hand, and in Christian illuminated codices on the other. The outstanding example of this is the conventional representation of the Sanctuary and its vessels which we see also in the Latin Codex Amiatinus (of the 6th/8th century)—confessedly based on an Oriental prototype—and in early Jewish monumental art. There are indications that the conventional figure of the Evangelist prefixed to early Latin and Greek texts of the Gospels may also have a Jewish antecedent: indeed, the parallel figure in the Codex Amiatinus shows not an Evangelist but Ezra the scribe, apparently wearing the Jewish phylactery—a feature hardly imaginable in a Christian archetype.

The treatment of this subject in detail would require an entire volume: but enough has been said to indicate that the tradition of Jewish manuscript art of illumination may go back for many centuries before the earliest extant specimens. Jewish wanderings, coupled with the wholesale destruction of Hebrew books by Christian censors, may be responsible for the disappearance of the entire body of evidence. But another adverse element was the periodic triumph among the Jews of anti-iconic principles. The recent rediscovery of elements which demonstrate that representational art among the Jews goes back far longer in time than was previously imagined, must not blind us to the fact that there were periods when the opposite tendency prevailed. One of these was presumably at the period of the iconoclastic reaction in Byzantium; another probably at the period of the triumph of Islam: for it was obviously impossible for the Jews—custodians of Holy Writ and the classical opponents of images and image-worship—to be less rigorous in this respect than their neighbors.

The earliest extant illuminated Hebrew manuscripts date, in fact, from this period and environment, and are rigorously non-representational. They concentrate indeed on Bible manuscripts, — but even so the sacred text is kept plain, with only the barest marginal decoration, sometimes embossed in gold.

The artistic work has concentrated however in a series of decorative pages at the beginning (or the beginning and the close) of the volume, consisting of intricate geometric patterns and abstract designs —sometimes curiously modern in feeling—which embodied auspicious verses, or, later on, a rendering in a miniscule hand of work (e.g., a masoretic treatise, or a vocabulary) with some sort of bearing, however remote, on the Bible. Naturally this does not apply to the Scroll of the Law used in synagogal reading, in which no extraneous element of any sort was permitted.

Hebrew illuminated manuscripts in the fullest sense (i.e., embodying representations of the human figure) emerge for the first time in the Franco-German area in the 13th century. It must be re-emphasized that those known to us are merely the earliest to be preserved, not the earliest to be executed: for obviously, they are not revolutionary innovations, and their very existence presupposes an antecedent tradition, which conceivably (one cannot go further) links up with that of the late classical period. The texts illuminated now in the Franco-German orbit included prayer books, ritual codes and so on.

Contrary to what might have been expected, Italy apparently enters into account, in this connection, relatively late. At the period of the Renaissance, however, the small circle of affluent and highly educated Jewish loan bankers—admirably assimilated to their environment in a cultural sense—imitated their non-Jewish neighbors in their eagerness to have their libraries filled with books written on the finest parchment by the most expert scribes, and decorated artistically without regard to expense. This interest extended to every category of literature—Bible texts, ritual codices, liturgies, philosophical classics, even medical works. However, not all such Hebrew codices were necessarily produced for Jewish bibliophiles. In this remarkable age, when Hebrew too was considered one of the languages of humanism, non-Jewish patrons of literature also considered it a point of pride to incorporate into their libraries Hebrew codices, some of which were illuminated as a matter of course. A case in point is a Bible in the Laurenziana Library in Florence (Cod. Plut. I. 31), executed for one of the Medici and superbly illuminated in a markedly Christological fashion by none other than Francesco d'Antonio del Chierico: and there is reason for believing that similar non-Jewish patronage was responsible for other illuminated manuscripts of first quality.

It is natural to ask oneself whether the illuminators of these manuscripts were Jews. In some cases the answer is clear, for the artist-scribe identifies himself as a Jew in uncompromising fashion. In others, to be sure, the Christian artist can be identified with virtual certainty on stylistic grounds. There remains, however, some degree of uncertainty in the large proportion of border line cases which are anonymous. As regards these, there is no need to assume automatically, as was once the case, that those of first quality were necessarily of non-Jewish authorship. We know that in Italy, Jews were sometimes admitted as members of the Guild of Illuminators, as happened in a couple of cases in Perugia in 1507–08, while a Portuguese Jew, Abraham ibn Ḥayyim, composed probably in the mid-15th century a remarkable treatise on the art of illumination. Moreover, in some of even the finest illuminated manuscripts the artist shows an awareness of Jewish legend, practice and tradition which suggests Jewish origin or—even more significantly—makes the pictorial narrative proceed not as in Christian codices from left to right, but from right to left, in the order of the written Hebrew text. Non-Jews were in any case not so eager to work for Jews, nor Jews to employ gentiles for religious purposes: and in the light of recent researches it is more logical to assume that even the most sumptuous Hebrew manuscripts were as likely as not to have been illuminated as well as written by Jews.

The art of the illuminated manuscript reached its climax in the Renaissance, but received a fatal blow with the advent of the printed book at this same period: yet it survived for certain formal purposes. In the Jewish world it showed, perhaps, a greater vitality. One reason may have been that the relatively small Jewish populations did not make it easy to publish printed books lavishly illustrated with engravings, except in the case of the ever-popular Passover *Haggadah* and handbooks of religious usage (*minhagim*). However, it became usual among Jews to commission small ritual handbooks which were given to be illuminated, whether by the scribe or by some other hand. It was in Germany, in the 17th and 18th centuries, that this practice reached its apogee, as seen in a succession of illuminated volumes, some of them based in the last instance on printed texts, produced in Eastern and Central Europe at this period by a succession of gifted artists—the precursors of those of a later generation who participated so eagerly in the School of Paris.

CONTENTS

FRENCH

GERMAN

ITALIAN

Introduction

THE JEWISH ATTITUDE TO ART

It is generally assumed that Jews have an aversion to figurative art. This assumption is, in a way, true since Jewish life, in accordance with the *halakhah*, has been directed toward belief and righteous behavior, with a verbal rather than visual expression of its tenets. However, artistic expression, far from being prohibited, was actually encouraged, either for educational purposes or for what is known as *hiddur mitzvah*, that is, adornment of the implements involved in performing rituals. Once these reasons were established, a place for artistic expression was found in Judaism. Gradually, the art gathered momentum. Embellishing biblical, ritual, legal, or even secular Hebrew books and manuscripts was one of the most important ways in which the Jew could express his devotion to the written word.

Contrary to general belief, in biblical Judaism there was no prohibition of artistic expression. The Second Commandment, "You shall not make for yourself a sculptured image, or any likeness. . .," defines itself as a law against idol worshiping by adding "You shall not bow down to them or serve them" (Ex. 20:4, 5). No fear of idolatry can be detected in the detailed instructions given by God to Moses on how to build the Tabernacle and its implements, including the specification to adorn the ark with two winged cherubim, between whom God dwelt (Ex. 25:18–22). This evidence would indicate that, from early days, the law of the Israelites prohibited idol worship, but not all forms of artistic representation.

Art was valued throughout the Israelite period, and although idolatry still prevailed among the Israelites, King Solomon, for instance, did not consider it wrong to rest his "molten sea" of the Temple on twelve bronze statues of oxen (I Kings 7:23–26). The earliest conscious abstention on the part of the Jew from making any "sculptured image" came into force, it seems, during the early Hellenistic period when, after the death of Alexander the Great, Ereẓ Israel fell into the hands of the Syrian Seleucid kings, who tried to impose Hellenistic religious practices upon their empire. Their command to adorn and worship statues of Greek gods evoked Jewish rebellion, reinforcing the monotheistic belief in an invisible God. During the period of the Second Temple, Judaism matured and crystalized into a monotheistic universal religion, no longer fearing idolatry.[1] This was the beginning of the age of the Mishnah, when Greek culture greatly influenced the Hebrew language and Jewish theology, law, and artistic concepts.

The attitude of the heads of the Sanhedrin during the second century C.E. toward art, and even toward pagan images, proves the lack of fear of image making. A story is told about Rabban Gamaliel II, who went to a bath in Acre dedicated to Aphrodite.

In answer to a gentile's query as to why he attended a place containing an idol he said, "The bath was not built in honor of Aphrodite, but rather, Aphrodite's statue was put there to beautify the bath" (Av. Zar. 44b).

This objective attitude toward works of art is further illustrated by the fact that the same Rabban Gamaliel had representations of the moon in his office, to help ignorant witnesses identify the shape of the New Moon, in spite of the fact that the moon was regarded as the symbol of a Greek goddess (RH 24a). In such an environment, a system of pictorial representations pertaining mainly to the Bible might well have developed. Biblical scenes in Jewish monumental and minor art of the early centuries C.E. have survived to this day. A painting probably representing the judgment of Solomon was found on one of the surviving walls in Pompeii.[2] The battle between David and Goliath is depicted on a clay lamp of the second or third century from Alexandria.[3] Representations of the sacrifice of Isaac can be found in numerous artifacts as early as the third century.

The existence of the mid-third century synagogue in Dura Europos[4] on the Euphrates, which had its entire wall covered with frescoes of biblical episodes, is most important. The paintings, which are not depicted in the correct biblical sequence, portray episodes from the lives of the patriarchs, prophets, and kings. Although these pictures are significant for their symbolic, rather than narrative, character, some narrative elements indicate that by the third century there must have been a cycle of biblical pictures, possibly in an illuminated manuscript, which the artists used as a model.[5]

It is interesting to note that many of these illustrations are based on legendary or midrashic, rather than the actual biblical, episodes. In the Dura Synagogue there is a scene of the finding of Moses in which Jochebed and Miriam are identified with Shiphrah and Puah, the two midwives. This is derived from the Aramaic translation of Exodus 1:15.[6] Such Midrashim date from early Hellenistic times, although there are no extant illuminated manuscripts from this period. The facts that Old Testament subjects are prominent in Early Christian art and that these depictions also contain Jewish midrashic episodes, suggest that the Early Christian artists used Jewish pictorial material as models. These Early Christian biblical representations appear in catacomb wall paintings, on sarcophagi, on ivory and metal boxes, and in illuminated Greek and Latin manuscripts. It is, therefore, not surprising that most of the Christian illuminated manuscripts are Bibles. An illustration in the seventh century Latin *Ashburnham Pentateuch* shows Rebekah visiting the school of Shem and Eber on Mount Moriah to inquire about her suffering during pregnancy.[7] The earliest extant examples of Hebrew biblical manuscripts are at least as early as the first century C.E., originating in the Dead Sea area. These manuscripts are in scroll form and contain no illuminations. According to the Talmud (Shab. 103b) ". . .if one writes the [Divine] Name in gold, they [the scrolls] must be hidden." This prohibition suggests that Torah scrolls decorated in this fashion did exist. The tractate *Soferim* (1:8) mentions an instance of a Torah scroll belonging to the Alexandrians in which the Names of God were written in gold throughout. The matter was brought before the sages, who prohibited its use and ordered the copy to be "hidden" in a *genizah*.[8] Aristeas' letter describing the translation of the Bible into Greek by the seventy sages (the Septuagint) states that among the gifts brought to King Ptolemy was a scroll of the law written entirely in gold. While there is no conclusive evidence for the existence of Hebrew illuminated manuscripts during the Hellenistic period,[9] there is definite indication of their existence in the East during the Middle Ages, although the exact dates of their origin are not known. The influence of oriental motifs is evident in all succeeding schools of Hebrew illumination. In Europe, the earliest surviving Hebrew illuminated manuscripts stem from 13th century Germany. There are a considerably larger number from the 14th century, while their existence during the 15th century is evenly spread throughout Europe. By the end of the 15th century, the invention of printing caused the decline of all manuscript illumination, including Hebrew. Thereafter, only a few schools of Hebrew illumination appeared, the most important of them in Central Europe in the 18th century.[10]

HEBREW MANUSCRIPT ILLUMINATION[11]

Throughout its history, the style of Hebrew illuminated manuscripts was basically dependent on contemporary schools of illumination in each region. Thus, the oriental school is similar to the Muslim, Persian, or Egyptian schools in style as well as motifs, while each of the European regional schools has stylistic and decorative elements directly influenced by the Latin or Greek illumination of the period. However, particular elements became traditional in Hebrew illumination and survived in Europe despite the change in general style during the late Middle Ages. As a result, the style of Hebrew illuminated manuscripts, particularly those executed by minor artists who tended to follow their models more closely, was often outmoded.[12] Although more accomplished artists might use traditional Jewish motifs in their illuminations, they tried to conform to the latest fashion of contemporary styles. Thus it is most difficult to define a Jewish style in any of these schools, even where distinctively Jewish motifs can be found.

Undoubtedly most of the illuminators of Hebrew books were Jewish. A few of their names are known to us from their colophons, such as Joseph ha-Ẓarefati, the artist of the 1300 C.E. *Cervera Bible* (pl. 6), who painted a zoomorphic colophon at the end of the manuscript.[13] Others appear in contracts for book illuminations. In one such example, from Palma de Majorca in 1335, Asher Bonnim Maymo undertakes to copy and illuminate a Bible and two books by Maimonides for David Isaac Cohen.[14] Furthermore, the evidence of Jewish *halakhah*, customs, and legendary material in the illustration may indicate a Jewish artist's acquaintance with earlier Jewish models.

As mentioned earlier, the Second Commandment, prohibiting the making of "sculptured images" for idolatry, did not restrain Hebrew illumination during the Middle Ages. Since late classical times there had been no fear of idolatry in Judaism regarding figured paintings. In fact, whenever Jewish illuminators opposed representational art during the Middle Ages, it was mainly due to the stricter attitude of their general environment. For instance, the Jews in Muslim countries refrained from depicting human figures in sacred books because of the Muslims' prohibition against such illustrations. Since this prohibition was based on the biblical Second Commandment, the Jews could not let themselves appear less observant than their Muslim compatriots. In the Byzantine Empire, during the period of iconoclasm (726–843), Jewish artists may also have completely abstained from illuminating Hebrew manuscripts. A further example of restricted representation of the human form developed in Germany during the 13th century. Under the influence of the ascetic Christian movement in the south of Germany and northern Italy during the 12th and 13th centuries, similar Jewish asceticism developed. This caused Jewish illuminators to introduce a new motif into their art, indicating their iconophobic tendency by depicting distorted figures, such as human bodies with animal heads,[15] several of which are reproduced here (pls. 25–28, 33, 34). Although pagan, Christian, or Muslim in origin, animal-headed figures became one of the main Jewish motifs in South-German Hebrew illumination of the 13th and 14th centuries.[16] However, R. Meir of Rothenburg, the leader of the Jewish communities in Germany at the end of the 13th century, disapproved of illustrating prayer-books because of the distraction the illustrations might cause the reader, rather than because of the Second Commandment's prohibition.[17]

Another characteristic aspect in Hebrew illuminated manuscripts was a direct outcome of the absence of capital letters in the Hebrew script. Since initials did not lend themselves to decoration, they were replaced by decorated "initial words," or sometimes whole decorated verses, as in illuminated Arabic Korans. This characteristic survived throughout the Middle Ages in Europe as well as in the East. Where illuminated initial letters did develop in Europe, they were influenced directly by Latin illumination. The page reproduced here from the *Darmstadt Haggadah* (pl. 43) is a good example of these latinized initials.

The square Hebrew script is in itself very ornamental. The constantly recurring shapes of letters give the page a pleasant rhythm.[18] This is sometimes deliberately broken by decorated monumental script using elongated ascenders and descenders. Some Hebrew letters, such as the *lamed*, have long ascenders; others, like the *kof* and final *kaf*, *nun*, *pe* and *ẓadi*, have extended descenders. It was common for Hebrew calligraphers in the East, as well as in Europe, to use these extensions as part of the decoration of the page or initial word panels. Impressive examples are found in the *Hamilton Siddur* (pl. 7), or the *Rylands Spanish Haggadah* (pl. 13).

Another element peculiar to Jewish illumination was the use of micrography (minute script) to form geometrical or floral designs surrounding a page of conventional script or to form a whole carpet page. The most common examples are the marginal lists of irregularities in writing, spelling, and reading the Bible which constitute the so-called masorah magna. In oriental and Spanish Bibles, the masorah is written in micrography in decorated carpet pages, and masoretic micrography outlines the design. Examples included in this volume are the oriental *Second Leningrad Bible* (pl. 2), the *Damascus Keter* from Spain (pl. 5), and the *Lisbon Bible* from Portugal (pl. 20). In Ashkenazi Bibles the masoretic micrography decorates initial-word panels and also the margins of text pages. Unlike oriental and Spanish Bibles, the micrographic decorations contain animals and grotesques and sometimes text illustrations; e.g., the 13th century *Reuchlin Bible* (Karlsruhe, Bad. Land., Cod. Reuchlin 1). In accordance with tradition, the masorah apparatus, though not necessarily legible or comprehensible, had to be written in the Bible codices.

In subject matter, too, Jewish illumination had its peculiar characteristics. The main inspiration of the Jewish illuminator was in the Bible, and therefore he tended to choose biblical episodes as subject-matter for illumination in manuscripts of every description. An important supplement to the biblical sources were legendary episodes based on midrashic commentaries found in all European schools as early as the 13th century. Some of these episodes, e.g., Abraham being thrown into the fire of the Chaldeans by order of King Nimrod, appear simultaneously in far removed areas, as in the *Golden Haggadah* from Spain and the *Leipzig Maḥzor* from Germany (Leipzig University Library, MS. V. 1102), indicating the existence of an earlier common European prototype.[19]

Iconographically, some subjects are treated in a specifically Jewish manner, as distinct from the general Christian or Muslim representations. For instance, in Christian art, a picture of the creation of the world will include the image of the Creator; in a Jewish work, however, only the hand of God or rays will indicate the existence of the Supreme Power, as for instance in the *Sarajevo Haggadah*.[20]

Jewish customs and rituals, both domestic and synagogal, are depicted in most liturgical manuscripts, as can be seen in many pages reproduced here (e.g., pls. 12, 14, 37, 38, 41–43, 45, 50, 53, 59). These illustrations must have been created by Jewish artists.

Since Hebrew illumination is directly related in style to the general schools of illumination, it serves as an important link with the history of non-Hebrew illuminated manuscripts. Moreover, in areas where the only dated illuminated manuscripts are Hebrew, this may become important evidence for dating and placing a certain style. For example, the date (1348) of the Copenhagen *Moreh Nevukhim* (pl. 18) helps in dating other manuscripts and paintings from Catalonia where it was executed.[21]

MATERIALS AND TECHNIQUES IN HEBREW MANUSCRIPTS[22]

While most Hebrew manuscripts were written on sheepskin parchment, the skins of other animals were also used: sometimes cowhide for large manuscripts, both in Europe and in the East; goatskins were used in the East; calfskin vellum, of which the finest, called "uterine vellum," came from embryos and still-born calves, was more expensive and therefore used only for costly manuscripts, such as the *Rothschild Miscellany*, (pl. 56).[23] The simplified process of parchment production in Europe during the 13th century enabled the scribes to use cheaper skins. All parchments were chalked before use, the Italian parchments the most thickly, with the result that they have a greater stiffness. In most manuscripts, the text was written on both sides of the parchment, save for the full-page miniatures, for which artists tended to use the flesh side, leaving the hair side blank. This practice prevailed mainly in Spain. Paper was also used for writing and decorating, but, since it is not as durable as parchment, only few examples have survived. Since paper is more absorbent, it was inferior to parchment as a medium for painting. Most quires are of four to ten conjoint leaves. Many have a catchword at the bottom left hand corner of the *verso* of the quire's last leaf to help binders arrange them in their correct sequence. Pagination is rare; where it exists, it is indicated in the top left hand corner of the *recto* of each leaf.

Writing habits differed from one region to another, producing a regional variance in the types of script. Obvious paleographic differences result from the use of a reed pen by oriental and most Sephardi scribes, while Ashkenazi and Italian scribes used mainly a quill. The Sephardi (e.g., pl. 5) and oriental (e.g., pl. 3) script has vertical and horizontal strokes of the same width, due to the scribe's having to turn the reed in its width while changing direction. The Ashkenazi script (e.g., pls. 22 and 28), on the other hand, has thinning vertical lines, resulting from the greater flexibility of the quill.[24]

The inks used by the scribes and artists differed according to the materials available to them in their respective countries. Most of the inks were prepared from a mixture of charcoal and water, with other natural extracts sometimes added. The color of the ink depended on the elements mixed. Acorn charcoal, for instance, produced very dark black ink, while iron compounds produced a reddish-brown color. Silvery ink normally oxydized and in due course made holes in the parchment.[25]

Most of the colors were extracted from natural compounds, and the more durable ones were a mixture of well-pounded minerals or colored stones. The binding material might be a mixture of gypsum, sometimes egg, in solution with water. Gold was applied in two ways: either pounded and mixed with ocher or yellow, painted with a brush; or in the form of gold leaf, applied on a base of gypsum mixed with minium and then burnished. The volume and texture of colors differed from one school to the other and from one period to the next, generally reflecting the local school of illumination in the same way as did the style.[26]

Horizontal ruling and vertical margination, often indicated by lines drawn by a stylus or lead pencil, were common in most regional schools of Hebrew manuscripts. The script usually hangs from these lines, rather than standing on them. In France and Germany, scribes tried to write between two horizontal lines.

Some of the basic decorations of the page were done by the scribes themselves. In addition to planning the layout of the page, the scribe was responsible for placing of the illustration, the initial word panels, and linear decorations. Other craftsmen were assigned the rest of the decoration. The vocalizer was in most cases the copyist of the masorah in Bibles, or the commentary in other texts, and was therefore responsible for most micrography decoration.[27] The illuminator illustrated the manuscripts according to the chief scribe's directions, using sketch books from his workshop or other illuminated manuscripts as models. The final process, the addition of color and gold, was carried out by an apprentice. The scribe was responsible for the entire manuscript and was therefore, in most cases, the only craftsman mentioned in the colophon. The vocalizer sometimes added his name in the margin or inserted it in some part of the decoration. The illuminator, regarded as the minor craftsman, hardly ever signed his name.

ORIENTAL SCHOOL

The earliest known school of surviving oriental Hebrew illuminated manuscripts dates from the ninth century and probably originated in Mesopotamia, later spreading to Syria, Palestine, and Egypt. An offshoot of this school developed in Yemen during the 15th century. Most of the Hebrew illuminated manuscripts originating in the East between the ninth and the thirteenth centuries have survived through the Cairo *Genizah*. A *genizah*, usually located in a synagogue, is a repository for old or mutilated manuscripts or documents which contain the name of God and must therefore not be destroyed. The hoard of thousands of fragmentary manuscripts discovered at the end of the 19th century in a synagogue in Fostat, Old Cairo,[28] is at present dispersed among many collections and libraries all over the world.

Examples of the various oriental styles from the ninth to the thirteenth centuries exist in Hebrew manuscripts. In most cases of dated manuscripts, the style corresponds to general Muslim art of the same period. The geometrical interlacing interwoven with foliage scrolls and palmettes, typical of Persian, Syrian, or Egyptian Arabic Koran illumination, may also be found in the Hebrew Bible manuscripts. In the tenth century, the delicately gold-tinted open flowers seen from above, arranged one next to the other within undulating scrolls to form a rhythmic pattern, are the most typical decoration in carpet pages of Korans and Bibles alike. Light blue, green, and red, which fill the background of the palmette motifs, are similarly common, e.g., the two carpet pages in a tenth-century fragment of a Hebrew Pentateuch written in Arabic characters (B.M. MS. Or. 2540).[29] In the 11th and 12th centuries, dark outlines were applied to the interlacings and flowers, usually on a panel of gold background decorated with deeper colors, as may be seen clearly in the 1008 or 1010 *Second Leningrad Bible* (pl. 2). During the 13th century, Persian floral motifs penetrated into the decoration of most schools of art throughout the Muslim empires. The cartouche and palmette motifs in illuminated Bibles such as the *Second Gaster Bible*[30] are good examples of this kind of decoration. By the 14th century, there was a decline in the art of Hebrew illumination in the Eastern schools of Persia, Syria, Palestine, and Egypt, although the Arabic schools continued to flourish.

The Yemenite school, surviving examples of which date from the end of the 14th century and later, developed to its fullest capacity only in the second half of the 15th century. Biblical manuscripts from Yemen were produced in three separate volumes: the first contained the Pentateuch, with the addition of a grammatical treatise (usually *Mahberet ha-Tigan*,[31] by an unknown author); the second, the Prophets; and the third, the Hagiographa. Yemenite Bibles were embellished with floral carpet pages and micrography in geometrical forms (see British Museum, MS. Or. 2350 of 1408, 2348 of 1469, and 2346 of 1469). These Bibles contain no text illustrations, but the decorations on the text pages are similar to, and probably derived from, the earlier oriental type. Roundels bearing palmette motifs and other floral designs were used as fillers for incomplete lines or as section indicators (pl. 4; see British Museum, MS. Or. 2348 of 1469). Oriental illumination has some peculiar identifying features. First, there is a complete lack of human figures and a paucity of text illustrations. The oriental type of floral and geometrical decoration in carpet pages and panels is the most definitive indication of Hebrew illuminated manuscripts from the East. Although the motifs and the idea of carpet pages in

Hebrew Bibles may derive from Islamic illumination, the Jewish workshops developed their own characteristically Jewish version. This, in turn, influenced other schools of illumination in Europe.

BIBLES

Most of the illuminated manuscripts of oriental origin are Bibles, although there are also some children's textbooks, decorated marriage contracts (*ketubbot*), and a few fragments of liturgical and scientific books.

Of the illuminated Bibles, only very few are complete manuscripts; and these sometimes contain colophons giving the date and place of execution, the name of the scribe, and the patron for whom they were made, as in the *Second Leningrad Bible* (pl. 2). In most cases, these sumptuously decorated Bibles belonged to the Karaite communities in Palestine and Egypt; many of them boast a direct relation to the most accurate Bible texts of Aaron b. Moses b. Asher, the last of a tenth-century family of masoretes from Tiberias, whom some scholars have thought to be a Karaite.[32]

The earliest Hebrew illuminated biblical manuscript, dated 895 C.E., contains the Latter Prophets and is still preserved in the Karaite synagogue in Cairo.[33] Its decoration includes several carpet pages, some with geometric motifs only, while other carpet pages combine both geometric motifs and micrography. Other decorations occur in the three framed colophons and also at the end of each of the books of the Prophets. Their style is oriental and may be either Mesopotamian or Palestinian.

Similar decorations occur in other oriental Bibles. Their carpet pages may be divided into two types. The first contains geometrical and floral interlacings in gold, green, red, and blue, with a large decorated motif, usually a palmette, on its outer border. Such pages are usually placed at the beginning and end of the Bible, like the Koran carpet pages of the same period.[34] The origin of this type of carpet page is unknown, but similar types can be found in eighth-century Christian sacred books of Hiberno-Saxon and Northumbrian origin, such as the Lindisfarne Gospels. Other possible derivations are floor mosaics of the early Middle Ages and decorated book covers which used the palmette motif as a closing device.[35]

The second type of carpet page in oriental Bibles also contains floral and geometric patterns, but in addition it has masoretic micrography patterned in various forms. As early as the ninth century, scribes used the masorah for decoration, devising ornamental forms instead of writing it in simple lines or diagonal columns. Carpet pages of both types can be found in oriental Bibles up to the 13th century, by which time their production had decreased.

Another kind of full-page decoration in oriental Bibles is composed of the Tabernacle implements. In the *First Leningrad Bible* of 929 C.E. (Leningrad Public Library, MS. II 17), there are two pages (one of which is reproduced in pl. 1A) containing stylized expositions of the Tabernacle. The most prominent object on both pages is the seven-branched *menorah*, with its traditional knops, flowers, and candles. Above the *menorah* is the Ark of the Covenant, containing the two Tablets of the Law and flanked by stylized leaf-like cherubim. At the sides are the incense altar, the jar of manna, the laver and its stand, Aaron's flowering rod, and other vessels. The implements are framed by what seems to be the fence around the Tabernacle, with a triple-gate facade.

The exposition of the *menorah*, the Ark, the jar of manna, and the triple-gate facade of the conventional temple probably originated in late Hellenistic tradition. All these elements appear on minor Jewish art objects of the first to the third centuries, such as clay oil lamps, painted gold-leaf glasses, and coins, as well as in monumental wall paintings in synagogues and catacombs and in later synagogal floor mosaics. As will be shown later, this tradition of decorating a Bible with implements of the Tabernacle was followed in both Sephardi and Ashkenazi Bibles. Apparently, the Bible became a substitute for the destroyed Temple, *Mikdashyah* ("God's Temple") becoming one of its appellations.

The text of oriental Bibles, traditionally written in three columns, was only partially decorated. At the end of each book of the Bible the number of verses in the book is usually given and is sometimes framed by an ornamental border. Colophons and dedicatory inscriptions are framed in the same way. The beginning of each book may have a decorative bar at its upper margin, similar to decorated panels at the openings of the *suras* of the Koran. The *parashot* are indicated by a decorative motif, usually a roundel with a palmette, similar to *sajdahs* and *'ashiras* in Korans. In some Bibles, the margins are decorated with scrolls and palmettes, which serve to fill out an incomplete line. The Song of Moses (Ex. 15), traditionally written in a distinct verse form (a page of three columns arranged in a brick-like pattern, with lines of three sections alternating with lines of two sections), was sometimes framed by decorative geometrical and floral bands.[36]

Of the few existing examples of oriental Bibles that contain text illustrations, two are 12th-century Persian Pentateuchs. One has pictures of sacred vessels between the text columns of the page, illustrating the text's description of the Princes' gifts to the Tabernacle in the desert (Num. 7:1).[37] The other has an illustration of the two Tablets of the Law, inscribed with the opening words of each Commandment next to the text of the Ten Commandments (Ex. 20:2–17).[38]

SINGLE PARASHOT, CODICES, AND CHILDREN'S BOOKS

Decorative elements similar to those in Bibles adorned small booklets containing single *parashot* of the Pentateuch. There is evidence that these booklets may have been fashionable as bar mitzvah and wedding gifts. The *Parashat Shelaḥ Lekha*[39] manuscript of 1106–07, part of which is reproduced here (pl. 3), is the most complete example of such a booklet.

From the tenth to the thirteenth centuries, textbooks for teaching children the alphabet were also decorated. The letters were outlined in ink and filled with different colors. After the colored and vocalized letters, there followed a section of the Pentateuch, usually Leviticus 1:1–7, which was regarded as the most suitable text for a child's initial study. An opening carpet page was usually added to these books, denoting their distinct relation to the Bible (see Cambridge University Library, T.-S.K.5.13 for a fragment of such a school book).

KETTUBOT

Apart from Bibles, the most common illuminations from the East are the *ketubbot* (marriage contracts). These single-page documents normally have decorative opening words, written in the large elegant letters characteristic of oriental script. Serifs or ascenders and descenders of letters were extended and supplemented by linear foliage scrolls and micrography, forming a decorative area. At times, the entire page was framed by a wide arcaded border as in the tenth or eleventh-century *Barka Ketubbah.*[40] By contrast, the marriage contract itself was usually written in a simple, sometimes crude, script.

OTHER BOOKS

Liturgical books were also decorated in the East. Some prayer books have decorated monumental scripts similar to those of the *ketubbot*, or outlined, colored, bold script. The *Haggadah*, recited on Passover Eve at the ritual meal in the Jewish home, conventionally had illustrations of the round *mazzah* wafer and the *maror.*[41] Initial words were written in a special way, as in the *piyyut* of "*Dayyeinu*" ("It Would Have Sufficed"), in which the repeated initial word in each verse is written one beneath the other to form a decorative column (Camb. U.L., T.-S., 324).

Some fragments of decorated scientific books originating in the East have survived; they have geometrical and floral motifs, with colored roundels, squares, foliage scrolls, and ornamental script used as section headings and line fillers (Camb. U.L., T.-S., Arab. 11/31).

SPANISH ILLUMINATION

The Spanish and Provençal schools of Hebrew illumination were greatly influenced by oriental decoration. These schools reached their peak during the 14th century, but became virtually extinct after the destruction of many Spanish Jewish communities in 1391. However, with the revival of Jewish life in the western part of the Iberian Peninsula during the 15th century, new schools developed.

The style and iconography of the Spanish school derive from both the Orient and the Occident. The existing Sephardi illuminated manuscripts belong to the Christian Conquest period and reveal a strong link with the oriental type of illumination. Spanish Bibles, like oriental ones, have mainly Egyptian decorative elements, such as carpet pages, the Tabernacle implements, micrography, decorated masorah *parashot* indicators and, at the end of each book, decorated frames indicating the number of verses. There is a theory that these elements were assembled and modified from the eighth to the thirteenth centuries in Hebrew manuscripts of Muslim Spain. Since no Spanish Hebrew illuminated manuscripts of this period have survived, this assumption cannot be verified.

The few existing dated Hebrew manuscripts from the Iberian Peninsula are mainly Bibles. They are stylistically so different from the *Haggadot* and from the non-illustrated liturgical, legal, and scientific books that it is very difficult to make a comparative study.

The northern Spanish school, directly related to Provence and influenced by the northern French school, is the earliest Spanish style of which we have a record. The work of this school is characterized by Bibles of a large format. In them the foliage decoration, comprised of interlacing scrolls, is reminiscent of Muslim arabesques (see Paris, Bib. Nat., Cod. héb. 1314, fol. 3v). The typical *mudejar* (Arabs under Christian rule) filigree ornament of thin, elegant, undulating scrolls, with paisley and round flower designs, remained in fashion in other Spanish schools up to the 15th century.[42]

The Catalan and Castilian schools of Hebrew illumination in the 14th century were probably directly influenced by the traditional elements of local Spanish and northern-French style. Italian influence was more pronounced in the Kingdom of Majorca and in Catalonia. It is evident in the use of darker colors, Byzantine modeling, and fleshy leaves, in Bibles, *Haggadot*, and other Hebrew illuminated manuscripts. The Byzantine and Italianate elements are evident in the coffered ceilings of the miniatures in the *Golden Haggadah*, as well as in the style of the figures in its "Sister."[43] The combination of French and Italian gothic style in the *Golden Hagaddah* resembles the style of the miniatures in a Catalan legal manuscript (c.1320) now to be found in Paris.[44] The Italianate style of Catalonia can be seen in the 14th-century *Copenhagen Moreh Nevukhim* from Barcelona (pl. 18). The highlights and shadows of the figures, as well as the crispness of the multicolored leaves entwining the stem, are two of the Italianate elements. The penetration of Italian elements to Castile came a generation later, and the traditional French gothic style prevailed even in the middle of the 14th century. The *Rashba Bible* of 1383 (from Cervera) in the Sassoon collection (MS. 16), has typical Franco-Spanish decoration in the frames of the carpet pages and arcades, though it has delicate Italianate scrolls as *parashot* indicators and book openings. The style of figures and decorative motifs of the undated

Haggadot can be related directly to the dated Bibles. The zoo- and anthropomorphic letters of the *Hamilton Siddur* (pl. 7) are somewhat similar to those of the *Cervera Bible* of c. 1300, while the linear filigree work within the letters of the *Hamilton Siddur* may, like its bright colors, indicate an even earlier date. The *Sassoon Spanish Haggadah* and the *Barcelona Haggadah* are somewhat related to the *Golden Haggadah* and to the Catalan Bibles of the first quarter of the 14th century. The *Rylands Spanish Haggadah* and its "Brother" are, like the *Kaufmann Haggadah*, more Italianate, and must therefore be of the second half of the 14th century. The *Sarajevo Haggadah*, retaining some French-gothic elements, may be of Catalan origin dating from the middle of the 14th century. The *Farḥi Bible* of 1383–86 serves as evidence that the Hispano-Provençal school still existed in the 14th century. Its scores of arabesque carpet pages are still Spanish-gothic style, though the fleshy foliage motif extending from the corners is more Italianate.

The destruction of most of the Jewish communities in the Kingdoms of Castile and Aragon in 1391 brought to an end some of the most important schools of Hebrew illumination in these areas, and many illuminated manuscripts were destroyed. During the 15th century, however, new schools developed—some in the above-mentioned kingdoms, though in different population centers. One of these new centers was Seville, in the south. Two Bibles from the middle of the 15th century, in the Sassoon collection, are good examples of this school. The earlier one, from 1415,[45] is only barely decorated with micrography. The later one, from 1468,[46] has many micrographic decorations of full pages, panels, arcades, and borders. Though most of the motifs are traditional, the predominant southern-Spanish Muslim feeling prevails. A Bible from Berlanga of 1455,[47] is also related in decoration to the south Spanish school of the mid-15th century. In Corunna, northern Spain, the *First Kennicott Bible* of 1476 was probably not a unique example. Similar in style is a Pentateuch from 1479, now in Dublin.[48]

The most important school in the Iberian Peninsula at the end of the 15th century was the Portuguese. Most of the manuscripts of this school are Bibles, though it also produced a few prayer books like the *siddur* (from Lisbon) of 1484,[49] and some copies of Maimonides' *Mishneh Torah*. An interesting fact about the Bibles is that most of them are not complete, but, like many Ashkenazi manuscripts, contain only Pentateuchs, the five *Megillot* (Song of Songs, Ruth, Lamentations, Ecclesiastes, and Esther) and *haftarot*. The manuscripts of the Portuguese school, which had its center in Lisbon, are decorated with wide border frames on their opening pages, grammatical treatises, and masoretic variations. Initial words are mainly written in gold within very large panels that are decorated with *mudejar* filigree work. The elaborate frames consist mainly of three areas, one surrounding the other, with different motifs presented in alternation. The filigree motif, which is a background to the monumental gold script, is framed by floral and foliage ornamentation. The foliage border is decorated with birds, grotesques, dragons and flower pots. The two most important manuscripts of this school are the *British Museum Mishneh Torah* of 1472 (pl. 19) and the *Lisbon Bible* of 1483 (pl. 20). Most of the Portuguese manuscripts have no text illustrations.[50]

The *Bible of the Hispanic Society of America*[51] (pl. 21) has no colophon, and may have been written in Castile. It can be attributed to the Portuguese school because of the typical decorative motifs in the frames of the opening pages of books. The expulsion of the Jews from the United Kingdom of Spain in 1492 and from Portugal in 1496–97 caused the spread of the Jewish population throughout Europe and into North Africa. The Spanish Jews brought their illuminated manuscripts to all these areas. In style, and especially in the system of illumination, the Spanish schools influenced Hebrew illuminated manuscripts in Italy, Turkey, Tunisia, and Yemen. Despite the invention of printing, some examples from these countries are extant from as late as the beginning of the 16th century.

BIBLES

The earliest recognizable Spanish school of Bible illustration developed in Castile during the second half of the 13th century. Examples of illuminated Bibles from this school indicate an oriental origin in both the type of decoration and the main floral, geometrical, and micrographic motifs. The carpet page from the *Damascus Keter*, a Bible copied in Burgos by Menahem b. Abraham ibn Malik in 1260, is a good example of the Spanish style.[52] (pl. 5). The oriental flavor of the foliage scroll, outlined by micrography, is somewhat subdued by the Western touch of a burnished-gold filling and magenta-brown background.

Other Bibles from Castile, such as the 14th-century one from Cervera, near Toledo[53] (pl. 6), reveal more Westernized taste, and were probably influenced by the south French schools of illumination. Areas such as Roussillon, adjoining the Pyrenees in the south of France, should be regarded both culturally and socially as part of the north Spanish schools. A Bible copied in Perpignan in 1299[54] contains one of the earliest full-page expositions of the implements of the Tabernacle. The implements are arranged arbitrarily within frames. The first page (fol. 12v) shows the seven-branched *menorah* and its tongs and fire pans, with two step-like stones on either side of the base; the jar of manna; the staff of Moses and Aaron's flowering rod; the ark with the Tablets of the Law deposited in it; the two winged cherubim over the ark-cover; and the table, with the showbread—two rows of six loaves—above which are two incense ladles. On the second page (fol. 13) are the gold incense altar, silver trumpets, the horn, the sacrificial altar with a leaning ramp, the laver on its stand, vessels, basins, pans, shovels, and forks.[55]

Most of the Spanish and Provençal Bibles of the 13th–15th centuries included at least two full pages as described above, with implements of the Tabernacle arranged at random (i.e., not according to the Tabernacle plan). This symbolic arrangement of implements connotes national redemption, and the rebuilding of the Temple. The iconographical details of each of the implements and vessels are very similar to those in the *First Leningrad Bible* of 929 (pl. 1A). For instance, although the *menorah* in Spanish Bibles is less stylized, it has the same flowers, knops, cups, and candles, but with round branches. In fact, a similar arrangement of Tabernacle implements, with a *menorah* of round branches depicted in its center, is found on another decorated page of the *First Leningrad Bible*.[56]

A tree on top of the Mount of Olives is sometimes found on the pages depicting the implements. Since the Mount of Olives is traditionally regarded as the place where the Messiah will appear, signaling the Redemption, such a picture undoubtedly expresses the hope that the Temple will be rebuilt.[57] The only other non-biblical representations on the implement pages are the two stepping stones that enable the high priest to reach the top of the *menorah* and light it. One of the most elaborately decorated Spanish Bibles is the *Farḥi Bible* (pl. 16), executed by Elisha b. Abraham Crescas in Provence between 1366 and 1382.[58] Instead of the usual two pages of implements, the *Farḥi Bible* contains four, in addition to which it also has a stylized plan of the Tabernacle.

Plans of the Temple also exist in Spanish illumination. One early example is attached to the 1306 *First Ibn Merwas Bible* (Toledo, 1306).[59] A larger fragment, executed by Joshua b. Abraham ibn Gaon in Soria (1306), is bound together with the *Second Kennicott Bible*.[60] It contains all the implements and vessels of the Second Temple arranged in ground-plan form, unlike the more common random arrangement.

Most Spanish Bibles contain carpet pages composed of micrography or painted motifs similar to the oriental ones. The *Damascus Keter* from Burgos (1260), mentioned above, has 14 such carpet pages preceding each of the main divisions of the Bible (pl. 5). In another Spanish

Bible from the Bibliothèque Nationale of the early 14th century,[61] the carpet pages contain delicate interlacings outlined in micrography. The *Farhi Bible* is by far the most elaborate example of this style as it contains 29 carpet pages, each with a different pattern of arabesque.[62] Two novel features appear in the carpet pages of Spanish Bibles. One is the calendar page, which provided a perpetual count according to the 12 lunar months of the Jewish year and allowing for seven leap-years (i.e., with 13 months) within the 19-year solar cycle. Most of the calendars are circular, similar to the zodiac form; some, such as that in the *First Joshua Ibn Gaon Bible* of 1301,[63] consist of movable disks. Contemporary calendars were also added, usually beginning with the year in which the manuscript was written. Joshua b. Abraham ibn Gaon, referred to above, was both a masorete and an illuminator who specialized in calendars and carpet pages, as he stated in the frame on the first of an illuminated quire of a Bible.[64] The second novelty in the Spanish Bibles was the series of decorated pages of linguistic expositions on the text. These expositions were either comparative tables of masoretic variations between the texts of Ben Asher and Ben Naphtali or grammatical treatises and dictionaries, such as David Kimḥi's *Sefer Mikhlol*.[65] The comparative tables use the same masoretic material as the oriental Bibles, but arrange them in vertical columns within decorated arcades, similar to the Christian Canon Tables. The *Bibliothèque Nationale Bible* mentioned earlier,[66] has some carpet pages which contain two arcades with masoretic comparisons. The grammatical treatises are also arranged within arcades or a single elaborately-framed column.

Arcades and frames became increasingly elaborate during the 15th century. The 1483 three-volume Bible from Lisbon[67] has dozens of elegantly framed pages containing lists of variations (pl. 20). The Bible owned by the Hispanic Society of America[68] contains similar arrangements of framed texts (pl. 21).

The *Cervera Bible* (1300), written by Samuel b. Abraham ibn Nathan and illuminated by Joseph ha-Ẓarefati ("the Frenchman"),[69] has many framed pages containing Kimḥi's grammatical treatise. The decorations in these frames are never illustrations of the text. Fanciful manifestations of the artist's imagination, they portray grotesque animals and court or rural scenes. A falconer and an archer standing within a fortified town and an eagle carrying off one of a flock of chickens are but two examples.[70]

Other decorated full pages in the *Cervera Bible* are the colophons of the scribe and the artist (see pl. 6). Joseph ibn Ḥayyim, the artist of the *Kennicott Bible* (Corunna, 1476), followed the Cervera model so closely that he used the same phrasing, painting each letter in a similar fashion within a full page.[71] He also modeled his decorations of Kimḥi's grammatical treatise (pl. 17) on those in the *Cervera Bible*.

The text pages of Spanish Bibles are, like oriental, rarely illustrated. Such marginal illustrations as there are may have been influenced by the French illuminated Bibles[72] for, as will be shown later, the Franco-German Bibles were the only ones with extensive illustrations on the text pages. In the Spanish school, some decorative indicators for the *parashot* and book openings illustrate the text. Thus, in the *Damascus Keter* (Burgos, 1260), there are two indicators which may have been intended to illustrate the text. One, depicting the head of a man, may have been intended as the young David (I Sam. 16:18), while another, depicting a walled city, apparently represents Jerusalem (Jer. 29:7).

The *Cervera Bible* has several more obvious text illustrations. The indicator for *Parashat Ki-Tavo* (Deut. 26) displays a basket of fruit, illustrating the offerings of the first fruit in the Temple; above it are an elephant and castle, which are not illustrative of the text but which may allude to the royal arms of Castile. At the end of the book of Exodus, there is a panel showing the *menorah* (fol. 60). A stag is painted alongside Psalm 42 (fol. 326), and a lamenting grotesque decorates the book of Lamentations (fol. 371v). The book of Zechariah (fol. 316v) is illustrated by his vision of the two olive trees providing oil for the *menorah* (chap. 4). The book of Jonah (fol. 304) opens with a picture of a ship with sailors, under which the prophet is being swallowed head first by a whale—a not uncommon scene in illuminated Spanish Bibles.

A similar picture of a sailing vessel is found at the beginning of the book of Jonah in a Bible written in Soria (1312) by Shem Tov b. Abraham ibn Gaon, probably a brother of Joshua ibn Gaon.[73]

Further resemblances between the *Shem Tov Bible* and the *Cervera Bible*, such as the grammatical and masoretic treatises written within columns and the crouching lions at the bases of arcades,[74] suggest that they are based on a common model. These two manuscripts are also related in artistic style.

Careful scrutiny reveals further similarities between several Bibles of the early 14th century. One of these, a Bible containing the Latter Prophets and Hagiographa, in Trinity College, Dublin,[75] is decorated mainly with animals, such as the locust at the opening of the book of Joel (fol. 68v). The numerous text illustrations in the margins and between the columns of the *First Joshua Ibn Gaon Bible* of 1301[76] include Noah's ark (fol. 13), the dove holding an olive branch (fol. 14), Hagar's water jug (fol. 20), Abraham's sacrificial knife (fol. 20v), the goblet of Pharaoh's butler (fol. 133), David's sling with Goliath's sword, and the bear and lion killed by David (fol. 170).

Of all the 15th century Bibles, the *First Kennicott Bible* has by far the largest number of text illustrations. At the opening of the book of Jonah (fol. 305), the traditional picture of the prophet being swallowed head first by a whale, beneath a decorated ship, is depicted in a way similar to that in the *Cervera Bible*.[77] The use of many details from the *Cervera Bible* by the Kennicott artist, working 175 years later, is curious, as the interim period produced many other styles of Bible illumination. However, since the *Cervera Bible* is known to have been owned by a certain Don David Mordecai of Corunna in 1376, we may assume that the manuscript was still in the same place a hundred years later and that the patron of the *Kennicott Bible*, Isaac b. Don Solomon de Braga, saw and coveted it; unable to acquire it, he commissioned another codex with even richer decorations along the same lines from two superbly competent artist-craftsmen.[78] Certainly Joseph ibn Ḥayyim, the illuminator of the *Kennicott Bible*, used a Bible similar to the *Cervera Bible* as one of his models.

Masorah magna and parva, written in micrography in the outer margins and between the text columns of Spanish Bibles, frequently take floral and geometrical forms; the most elaborate ones form candelabra-like trees.[79] As in the oriental Bibles, the "Songs of Moses" are framed by elaborate bands of floral and geometrical decorations, sometimes executed in micrography.[80]

HAGGADOT

During the 13th and 14th centuries, the Passover *Haggadah* was one of the most popular illuminated manuscripts to be found in the Jewish communities. Using biblical and midrashic texts, it stresses the relationship between Israel's past and its present. It is read in the course of a ritual meal, the structure of which was based on a Greek symposium—where food, wine, and appetizing herbs stimulate discussion on the subject of Exodus.

The text of the *Haggadah* went through several recensions during the Middle Ages. Only in the 13th century did the text of the *Haggadah* crystallize to form a book separate from the *siddur* (the daily prayerbook), though simultaneously remaining part of it. Some additions and variations, however, were introduced into the text of the *Haggadah* at an even later date. As the Passover *seder* was the most important domestic ritual, when the entire family gathered around the table, the *Haggadah*, more than any other sacred book, allowed the artist freedom to express his personal tastes. Furthermore, the interest of scribes and artists in the production and illumination of this comparatively small book was encouraged by the development of European book production during the 13th century. At this period the economic and social development of town life and consequently the founding of universities encouraged an increasing number of secular workshops for book production. These workshops supplemented or replaced the monastic scriptorium and introduced the new craft of the "illuminator", who was to embellish and brighten the page at the request of wealthy clients. Simultaneously, new techniques in the preparation of parchments, inks, colors, gold leaf, and other materials gradually made illuminated books for domestic use accessible to most citizens.

Although not every Jewish household could afford an illuminated *Haggadah*, the richer Jews, who sometimes served princes or courtiers and were acquainted with beautifully illuminated codices, tried to imitate these fashions by ordering the illumination of Hebrew books. Traditional Jewish subjects, motifs, and iconography were fused with the more fashionable styles and layouts of contemporary Christian illumination according to the personal taste of the artist and the patron.

While some features are common to all schools of Hebrew illumination, each of the regional schools has some local trait peculiar to its *Haggadah*. The illumination of *Haggadot* was, of course, dependent on its contents, which may be roughly divided into four categories: textual, ritual, biblical, and eschatological. This rule is true of all Ashkenazi, Sephardi, and Italian *Haggadot* from the 13th to the 15th centuries.

The rich Spanish *Haggadah* is usually composed of three parts: the text of the *Haggadah*, full-page biblical miniatures, and a collection of *piyyutim* recited in the synagogue during Passover week and on the Sabbath before Passover. Whereas the text of the Spanish *Haggadah* is very sparsely illustrated, mainly with textual and ritual representations, and the section of the *piyyutim* is hardly decorated at all, the most significant artistic section is that of the full-page miniatures. The best known of about a dozen surviving specimens of this rich type of Spanish *Haggadah* are the *Sarajevo*, the *Kaufmann*, and the *Golden Haggadah*. Full-page biblical miniatures that preceded the Spanish *Haggadot* may have been derived from the manner of illuminating the Latin Psalter in England and France during the later Middle Ages,[81] which in its turn is based on the "Aristocratic" type of Greek Psalter illumination of earlier Byzantine schools.[82]

The most common text illustrations of the Spanish, as of other, *Haggadot* are the main elements of the Passover Feast, according to Rabban Gamaliel: *Pesaḥ* (paschal lamb), *mazzah* (unleavened bread), and *maror* (bitter herb). In the Spanish *Haggadot*, the last two are elaborately illuminated, sometimes filling a full page (not the first, since the paschal lamb sacrifice in the Temple is only symbolically represented at the *seder* ceremony). The examples reproduced here are the *mazzah* from the *Barcelona Haggadah* (pl. 12) and the artichoke-like *maror*, being held by two men, from the "Brother" to the *Rylands Spanish Haggadah* (pl. 14). Rabban Gamaliel and his pupils, as well as other rabbis mentioned in the text, are frequently portrayed. Other text illustrations include the "four sons" and the decorative structure of the poem "*Dayyeinu*" (pl. 13), as found in the oriental *Haggadot*. Some are literal illustrations of the Hebrew text (cf. man leaving prison in the *Sassoon Spanish Haggadah* (pl. 11) and the tongueless dog in the *Kaufmann Haggadah* (pl. 15)).

The ritual illustrations are for the most part instructional, beginning with the preparations for Passover—the baking of the *mazzot*, the sacrifice of the paschal lamb, and the cleaning of the house and the dishes. Other illustrations show people reciting the *Haggadah* in the synagogue (pl. 9)—a custom which was known in Spain[83]—or leaving the synagogue; the family sitting around the *seder* table; the washing of the hands; the pouring, lifting, or drinking of the four cups of wine; the hiding and finding of the *afikoman*; and the eating of the various herbs.

These *genre* scenes of medieval Jewish life depict the customs of various European communities by portraying their daily and festive dress, household utensils, furniture, and buildings.

Those Spanish *Haggadot* which have no text illustrations are nevertheless decorated by initial words and letters in the traditional manner of zoo- and anthropomorphic letters with elongated ascenders and descenders as in the page from the *Hamilton Siddur* (pl. 7). The biblical pictures, mainly painted as a series of full-page miniatures either preceding or following the text, constitute the most sumptuous aspect of the few surviving Spanish *Haggadot*. They probably originated as textual illustrations in earlier French, German, or Italian illuminations.[84] The Exodus story was the most frequent subject, sometimes preceded by the history of the Patriarchs, as in the *Golden Haggadah* (pl. 8). At times, as in the *Sarajevo Haggadah* (pl. 10), the cycle was broadened, ranging from the Creation of the World to Moses' blessing of the Israelites before his death. Most of the biblical series of miniatures are followed by pictures of the ritual preparations for Passover. At times the biblical and ritual illustrations become confused. In one example, in the *Rylands Spanish Haggadah*, the smearing of the lintel with blood was incorporated into a preparatory cycle. Many legendary episodes derived from the Midrash are included in the biblical cycle: Joseph meeting an angel on his way to his brothers in Dothan,[85] Joseph's coffin being thrown into the Nile by the Egyptians,[86] and the test of Moses with gold and live coal.[87]

In the eschatological illustrations there are references to the ultimate destiny of the Jewish nation—the reestablishment of the state, and the rebuilding of the Temple in Jerusalem. A schematic picture of the Temple facade in the *Sarajevo Haggadah* is one example (pl. 10A). The passage, "Pour out Thy wrath upon the gentiles, who do not recognize Thee" (Psalm 79:6), was a frequent inspiration for literal illustration. In the *Kaufmann Haggadah*, the hand of God is depicted pouring from a cup over a group of people.

Some prayer books are decorated with initial-word panels, but text illustrations in *siddurim* are very rare and occur mainly in the *Haggadah* section of the prayer book[88] where they are mainly limited to the *mazzot*, bitter herbs, and the rabbis mentioned in the text. The *Bologna Siddur*, however, contains a cycle of full-page biblical miniatures.[89]

OTHER BOOKS

Legal books, the most common of which was Maimonides' *Mishneh Torah*, were also illuminated in Spain.[90] This treatise usually has an entire framed page at the beginning of each of its 14 books. Text illustrations in the *Mishneh Torah* appear only in Book Eight, accompanying the description of the Temple and its implements. Most *Mishneh Torah* manuscripts, in Spain as well as in Germany and Italy, have a diagram of the Temple that indicates the proper position of each of the implements. The *British Museum Mishneh Torah* (Portugal, 1472) is one of the most elaborately and delicately decorated examples of Spanish illumination (pl. 19). Maimonides' philosophical treatise, *Moreh Nevukhim* ("The Guide of the Perplexed") was another popular choice for illumination.[91] Divided into three parts, it has only title page decorations and infrequent illustrations. The *Copenhagen Moreh Nevukhim* (Barcelona, 1348) is an exception (pl. 18), as the initial-word panels of each of the three parts contain an illustration related to the text.[92] Other philosophical treatises, such as Levi b. Gershom's *Sefer Milḥamot Adonai* of 1391,[93] contain decorated title pages. Some scientific treatises have diagrammatic or instructional paintings. The Hebrew translation from the Arabic of the astronomical text *Almagest* by Ptolemy, in the Sassoon collection (MS. 699), has hundreds of diagrams as well as painted panels. Another astronomical manuscript in the Sassoon collection (MS. 823) contains treatises by many authors. The part composed by Ptolemy has pictures of the heavenly constellations, signs of the zodiac, and cosmological diagrams. Jews were the expert astronomers in Spain, constructing astrolabes and preparing many nautical maps. The famous *Catalan Atlas* (from Majorca) of 1375[94] is the work of a Majorcan Jew, Abraham Ḥisdai Crescas (Cresques) and his son Judah. The suffering and, in due course, extinction of the French Jewish community during the 13th and 14th centuries ended this school of illumination, destroying thousands of books, many of which were perhaps illuminated. The burning of the Talmud in Paris in 1240 included many other manuscripts. The expulsion of the Jews from England in 1290, and from France in 1306 and again in 1321, are landmarks in their history of persecution. Nor was the situation in Germany any better. Since the Crusaders had begun their march through Europe, they had successfully employed accusations of blood libel to incite the newly established urban communities to massacre the Jews. Nevertheless, while very few Hebrew manuscripts survive from France, and more from England, a fair number of illuminated manuscripts are extant from Germany, mainly from the Rhine area.

FRENCH SCHOOL

Side by side with the Sephardi culture, which developed in Spain, Provence and, later, in North Africa, the Ashkenazi culture spread through Germany, northern France, England and the Low countries. It reached Italy in the 15th century, when German Jews entered northern Italy. By that time the Ashkenazi influence was prevalent in Eastern Europe. Italy, however, retained a somewhat special vitality.

The northern French school of Hebrew illumination seems to have been one of the most important in the Ashkenazi communities. It was apparently closely related in style and iconography to the English and German Hebrew schools. Of the few surviving illuminated French manuscripts most are sparsely decorated. However, some are sumptuous and reveal the high quality and sophistication of French illumination. The *British Museum Miscellany* (possibly from Troyes, c. 1280; pl. 23), is one of the best examples. The text contains scores of books and treatises, including the entire Bible and liturgy for the whole year. Almost every page is illuminated with floral, animal, and grotesque motifs, but the *Haggadah* is the only comprehensively illustrated text. The most significant are the four groups of full-page miniatures, which are not altogether an integral part of the manuscript, and some of which may even have been later random additions. The lack of uniformity and the repetition of certain subjects, such as Aaron lighting the *menorah* (fols. 114 and 522v), indicate that they are not the work of one artist. It appears that Benjamin, the scribe of the manuscript—who had his name illuminated in several places (e.g. 142v, 306v)—gave directions to the illuminator in the lower margins of some pages. In one instance (fol. 219v), the scribe wrote *shalshelet* ("chain") in the lower part of the page and the artist accordingly decorated the side margin near the text with an undulating chain ornamented with animal grotesques. Most of the full-page miniatures are biblical, others are midrashic or eschatological.[95] Among the less usual subjects depicted in the miniatures are the cherubim guarding the Tree of Life (122); Solomon's molten sea (121v); Moses' copper serpent (742v); Samuel beheading Agag (526); the food of the Righteous in Paradise—Leviathan (318v), the Behemoth (319), and the mythical bird *Bar Yokhani* (also known as *ziz*) (517v); a town being swallowed in the jaws of a dragon (740v); a chiromantic hand (115); and a diagram of zodiacal signs (548).

HAGGADOT

The *Haggadah* in the *British Museum Miscellany* (fols. 205ff.) is illustrated by pictures of the family at the *seder* table (fol. 205); the washing of hands, the Egyptian taskmasters (fol. 205v), the bondage of the Israelites (fol. 206v); a lamb being turned on a spit (fol. 207v) and (twice) with the lifting of a wine cup (fol. 208). The choice of these illustrations is closely connected with the German illuminated *Haggadot*, which are discussed below. There were probably examples of manuscripts containing only *Haggadot* from the French area also. A crude example of a 13th century *Haggadah* which survived from France, is the *Dragon Haggadah* (pl. 22).

BIBLES

Very few illuminated Hebrew Bibles from France have survived. A small Bible, bound in Maimonides "Guide of the Perplexed," in the Cambridge University Library (Add. MS. 468), is possibly of French origin. The manuscript, which lacks two opening folios and is torn in many places, has some text illustrations in the margins and between the two text columns. These include Noah's ark (fol. 4v), the dove bearing an olive leaf (fol. 5v), the rainbow (fol. 6), Abraham and Lot's shepherds fighting (8v), and Lot's daughters with their father (12v). Text illustrations in French Bibles may have been the source of biblical illustrations in Spanish and German illuminated manuscripts, although too few French manuscripts, survive to prove this point.

A typical Ashkenazi Pentateuch, which also contains the five *Megillot*, the *haftarot*, and the book of Job, was written and illuminated in 1300 in Poligny, in the Jura region of eastern France.[96] Decorated with floral and grotesque masorah in micrography, it has only one illustration (pl. 24).

Small manuscripts containing the Psalter were also common in the northern French Jewish communities. Most of these are merely decorated.[97] One Psalter opens with a half-length representation of David playing the harp.[98] This manuscript also has French and Latin translations and glossaries interlining the Hebrew.

OTHER BOOKS

Legal books of French origin are primarily copies of Moses of Coucy's *Sefer Mitzvot Gadol*, and R. Isaac of Corbeil's *Sefer Mitzvot Katan;*[99] mainly decorated, they contain hardly any illustrations.

From the end of the 14th century, some illumination developed in southern France (properly Provence) where the Jews were allowed to remain after the expulsion. Bibles,[100] prayer books,[101] philosophical treatises, such as Levi b. Gershom's *Sefer Milḥamot Adonai*[102] and scientific treatises[103] have survived. Southern French illumination of this period is closer in style to Italian and Spanish schools than to those of northern France.

GERMAN SCHOOL

The earliest surviving European Hebrew manuscripts are from Germany. A manuscript containing the biblical commentary by Rashi (R. Solomon Yiẓḥaki), written by Solomon b. Samuel of Würzburg in 1233 (Munich, Cod. Heb. 5), is the earliest dated of these illuminated manuscripts. Heading each *Parashah* and at the beginning of each book are initial-word panels containing text illustrations. These include Abraham being led by angels to the Land of Canaan (Vol. I, fol. 9v); Jacob blessing Ephraim and Manasseh (fol. 40v); and Job, seated naked on the dung heap, being visited by his three friends (Vol. II, fol. 183). The artistic style of the manuscript, which is directly related to the south German School of Latin illumination, shows no specifically Jewish characteristics save for the featureless human faces.

While the reason for this is not definitely known, it may have a connection with other means of distorting the human form common in southern Germany during the 13th century, such as covering human faces with crowns, wreaths, kerchiefs, or helmets; depicting them from behind; or replacing them with animal or bird heads. All of these devices are employed in the *Ambrosian Bible* (pl. 25) of the south German school, like the Rashi commentary of

Munich. Various means are used to distort the human figure in the text illustrations within the panel. For example, although a naked Adam and Eve are viewed from the front, their heads are turned backward (fol. 1v); the angel in the sacrifice of Isaac has a blank face (fol. 102v); Pharaoh's head is covered by a large crown (fol. 56v); the Righteous in Paradise, all have crowned animal heads. Z. Ameisenowa has suggested that people with animal heads designate holy men, righteous people, evangelists, deacons, or the stars in heaven. This practice, which may have originated in Muslim and Persian motifs, was borrowed by Christian as well as Jewish artists. The Jewish school of illumination in southern Germany adopted this motif and used it not only for righteous people and angels, but also sometimes to portray gentiles. Since there was no direct official prohibition against the depiction of the human form in illuminated manuscripts, it would appear that the south German Jews imposed this restriction upon themselves out of some iconophobic notion that may have developed here in the 12th century from the pietistic movement headed by Judah and Samuel "the Pious". This hasidic movement in Germany was ascetic, restricting embellishments in private or public life and forbidding any sort of decoration in manuscripts, even to the extent of prohibiting decoration with micrographic masorah. From the responsa of the German rabbis of the 13th century it seems that their aversion to illustrating manuscripts stemmed not from fear of idolatry, but rather to avoid distraction during prayer.

STYLISTIC DEVELOPMENT OF GERMAN MANUSCRIPTS

Although generalization omits some of the more subtle distinctions, it may help to divide the large quantity of surviving Ashkenazi manuscripts into groups. Generally speaking, the illuminated Bibles were the first to develop in the south of Germany during the first half of the 13th century. Pentateuchs supplemented with *Megillot* and *haftarot* for use in the synagogue were developed in the second half of the century and were in fashion around 1300. Large illuminated *mahzorim* existed for about one hundred years, from the middle of the 13th to the middle of the 14th century. Illuminated *Haggadot* were prominent during the 15th century, although their format was fashioned in the 13th century.

The south German school of illumination was the most prominent and prolific of the Ashkenazi schools. It is also probably the most closely related in style to the local south German contemporary Latin illumination. From the beginning, the only Jewish motif in Hebrew illumination from southern Germany was the distortion of the human face. The soft undulating drapery, bright colors with dark outlines, expressive gestures, and acorn scrolls with large leaves and open composite flowers seen from above are but a few of the south German stylistic features to be found in Hebrew as well as in Latin illumination of the 13th and 14th centuries.[104] This school survived during the 14th century. A good example is the *ketubbah* from 1392, (Vienna, Nat. Lib. Cod. Heb. 218), the style of which is similar to that of the *Erna Michael Haggadah* of about 1400 (pl. 38).

The mid-Rhenish school of illumination was influenced in style by south German as well as by the northern French illumination. Thus, the *Hamburg Miscellany* from Mainz (pl. 41) reflects both of these elements. The lower Rhine area is the most "frenchified" of all German schools, as can be seen from the *Kaufmann Mishneh Torah*. During the 15th century, Italian influence is evident in manuscripts executed in southern as well as central Germany, such as the *Darmstadt Haggadah* and the *Siddur of the Rabbi of Ruzhin*.

Very few names of artists from medieval Germany are known. Joel b. Simeon sometimes called Feibush Ashkenazi, is famous because he signed so many manuscripts executed in his workshop. Active in Germany and Italy in the second half of the 15th century, he was of German origin, probably from Cologne or Bonn, but established a workshop in northern

Italy. In his signed manuscripts he referred to himself as a *sofer* ("scribe"), *livlar* ("scrivener"), and a *ẓayar* ("limner"). It is unlikely that he copied and illuminated all the manuscripts signed by him, but was probably the head of an atelier with several craftsmen at his service. (For a complete list of manuscripts signed by or attributed to him, see bibliography to plate 42). It was no doubt due to the influence of the Italian Renaissance that the artist felt secure enough to sign his name not only as a scribe, but also as an illuminator. Other names found on illuminated manuscripts are mainly of the scribes. A scribe who signed his name as Ḥayyim was active around 1300 in southern Germany. His script and signature can be found in the *Schocken Bible* (pl. 31) and in the *Duke of Sussex Pentateuch* (pl. 32), as well as in the *Tripartite Maḥzor* (pl. 33 and 34). A scribe called Menahem copied both the *Birds' Head Haggadah* (pl. 28) and the *Leipzig Maḥzor*, although no illuminator's name is mentioned. The *nakdanim* ("punctuators"), who were also the masoretes of Bibles, were responsible for all the pen drawings and micrographic decorations in Ashkenazi manuscripts. Of these, as well, only a few names are known.

BIBLES

Hebrew Bibles of the German school fall into two categories: one consists of complete Bibles, mostly in large, even giant, format, such as the *Ambrosian Bible*, written in large script, with Aramaic translation incorporated into the text after each verse; the other, designed for use in the synagogue on the Sabbath and on festivals, contains the Pentateuch, with its Aramaic translation, the five *Megillot*, *haftarot*, parts of Job, and sometimes the "passages of doom" in Jeremiah (2:29–3:12; 9:24–10:16). German Bibles are illuminated differently from the oriental and Spanish ones. Most are decorated by the punctuator-masorete in micrography and pen drawing, either in large initial-word panels or in the margins of the text area.

Painted initial-word panels also exist and sometimes extend to a full page, as in the *Duke of Sussex Pentateuch* (pl. 32) and the opening page of the *Schocken Bible* (pl. 31). Sometimes these painted panels illustrate the text, but a few are merely decorative. The 46 medallions of the frontispiece to Genesis in the *Schocken Bible* depict episodes from the entire Pentateuch. The micrography within the text sometimes also illustrates the text. An illustration in the *Duke of Sussex Pentateuch* shows the ram caught in a thicket alongside the text of the sacrifice of Isaac (fol. 28). A Bible in the British Museum (Add. MS. 21160, c. 1300), has some interesting examples of such illustrative micrography; e.g., Joseph riding a horse (fol. 192), Pharaoh's baker carrying a triple basket on his head (fol. 43), the four beasts of Ezekiel's vision (fol. 285), and Jonah being spewed from the mouth of the whale and seated under a tree (fol. 292–292v). However, most of the masoretic variations surrounding the text form grotesques.

What sometimes appears like a carpet page in a German Bible is in fact an excess of masoretic material copied in decorative shapes, either at the beginning or the end of books of the Bible.[105] Implements of the Temple, so often found in Spanish Bibles, are very rare. One example occurs in the *Regensburg Pentateuch* of about 1300, now in the Israel Museum (pl. 29), which has an exposition of the Tabernacle implements, including Aaron in his robes extending his arm to light a very large *menorah*, which is set alone on the facing page.

Ashkenazi Pentateuchs of the second half of the 14th century are smaller and illustrated in a manner differing from that of the earlier period. The *Coburg Pentateuch* of 1396, is an example of this later type.

MAḤZORIM

The most important innovation of the German school of Hebrew illumination is in its *maḥzorim*. While the *siddur* contains the daily and personal prayers, both for home and synagogue, the *maḥzor* (literally "cycle") contains the synagogal communal prayers for the festivals and the seven "Special Sabbaths" of the Jewish year. In the Italian rite, the term *maḥzor* embraced both the daily and the festival prayers. Primarily intended for the use of the *hazzan*, the German *maḥzorim* are usually large—written in clear, bold letters—and contain a large selection of *piyyutim* ("liturgical poems") for each festival, offering the cantor a variety of choice.

A large number of German *maḥzorim* are illuminated with initial-word panels and with illustrations of a ritual and textual nature. These *maḥzorim* were executed over a period of some 100 years, from the mid-13th to the mid-14th century. The finest examples, all of which originated in south Germany, are the *Worms Maḥzor* of 1272, (pl. 26); the *Laud Maḥzor* of about 1290 (pl. 27); the *Leipzig Maḥzor* of about 1300; the *Tripartite Maḥzor* of about 1320 (pl. 33–34); and the *Darmstadt Maḥzor* of 1340.[106] These *maḥzorim* illustrate both the development of style in southern Germany and the use of special Jewish motifs. An example of both such development and of motif is found in the distortion of human figures. In all manuscripts before 1300, the use of animal-headed people is consistent; in the *Leipzig Maḥzor*, people have birds' beaks instead of a nose and mouth; but the artists of the later *Tripartite Maḥzor* did not understand the reason for such distortions, and painted all the male figures with ordinary human heads and all the females with animal heads.

Southern German *maḥzorim* have a very wide range of text illustrations. Most of them begin with the prayers for the four "Special Sabbaths" before Passover, continuing with Passover, the Feast of Weeks, the New Year, the Day of Atonement, and the Feast of Tabernacles. Four of the *Megillot* ("scrolls") are also usually included in the *maḥzor*—sometimes placed together, at other times appended to the particular celebrations with which they were associated. The book of Esther was usually written separately on a scroll, to be read at the festival of Purim.

The *Leipzig Maḥzor* (MS. V. 1102) has the most extensive array of text illustrations, in initial-word panels and margins, for almost every Sabbath and every feast or festival day. The first volume of the *Leipzig Maḥzor* opens with a frontispiece representing Samson rending the lion, possibly an allusion to the phrase "Grow strong like a lion to fulfill the will of your Maker," sometimes referring to the *ḥazzan* (Vol. I, fol. 19). At the end of the short introductory prayers, there is a miniature depicting the *ḥazzan* standing covered with his *tallit* ("prayer shawl") in front of a marble pulpit, on which a large open book rests. This probably represents the first volume of the Leipzig manuscript. The second volume is shown in the hands of a young man wearing a Jewish hat, who is standing behind the *ḥazzan* accompanied by a bearded Jew (Vol. I, fol. 27). A man holding a scale is a common illustration for the Sabbath of *Parashat Shekalim* (Ex. 30:11–16), referring to the payment of the annual half-shekel for the Temple sacrifices (pl. 26).

Other common illustrations include the tall tree from which Haman and his ten sons are hanging, illustrating a *piyyut* for Purim.[107] A red heifer illustrates *Parashat Parah;*[108] the sun and the moon illustrate *Parashat ha-Ḥodesh*, (referring to the month of Nisan).[109] A betrothed couple illustrates a *piyyut* for the "Great Sabbath," before Passover, alluding to the Torah as the bride of the people of Israel.[110] In the *Worms Maḥzor*, there is a wedding group being blessed by a rabbi; in the *Leipzig Maḥzor*, the couple are seated as lovers on a bench, while in a *maḥzor* of about 1300 in the Hamburg University Library (MS. Levi 37), the bride is crowned and blindfolded, strangely reflecting the Christian concept of a *synagoga*, the personification of the Jewish people in the form of a blindfolded woman with a falling crown. The bridegroom is wearing a Jewish conical hat.

The illustration for the Passover Eve prayer sometimes represents the Egyptians pursuing the Israelites (e.g., Leipzig, Vol. I, fols. 72v–73). Most German *maḥzorim* have illustrations of the signs of the zodiac for each of the verses of a *piyyut* in the prayer for dew recited on the first day of Passover.[111] The signs of the zodiac are depicted in small medallions in the margin. In the Worms and the Tripartite manuscripts, the labors of the months are depicted in medallions next to the signs of the zodiac. Some specifically Jewish elements have developed in the zodiac illustrations, such as a bucket instead of the Aquarius; in some cases a draw-well is depicted instead of a mere bucket, and in some *maḥzorim* a kid is depicted next to the well to illustrate both Capricorn and Aquarius, which are referred to in one verse of this *piyyut*. In one *maḥzor*, (Oxford, MS. Opp. 161, fol. 84), 11 signs of the zodiac are depicted in one large roundel divided into 12 sections, similar to the arrangements of the signs of the zodiac in floor mosaics of early synagogues (e.g., Bet Alfa). This example may be an indication of a traditional way of depicting the astronomical zodiac *circulus*, which survived into the Middle Ages.

The illustration for Shavuot (The Feast of Weeks) traditionally depicts Moses receiving the Tablets of the Law and giving them to the Israelites, who are standing at the foot of Mount Sinai[112] (pl. 27). In the *Leipzig Maḥzor* (Vol. I, fol. 131) an additional illustration depicts the contemporary custom of initiating children into the study of the Torah. The child is brought to his teacher's lap to lick the honey-covered alphabet tablet in order to sweeten his introduction to the study of the Torah, while the other children, in celebration of his initiation, receive eggs and cakes. The first volume of most of the *maḥzorim* ends with the *kinot* ("dirges") for the Ninth of Av, which are hardly ever illustrated.

The second volume normally starts with the prayers for Rosh ha-Shanah (New Year), illustrated by the sacrifice of Isaac, with the ram caught in a thicket by his horns. The sounding of the ram's horn (*shofar*) on New Year's day is a commemoration of God's covenant with Abraham at the time of the sacrifice.[113] In some *maḥzorim*, a horned and claw-footed devil is depicted next to a *shofar* blower, who sometimes supports his right foot on a three-legged stool in order to ward off the earthly influence of evil. This is in accordance with the common superstition that a three-pointed object wards off evil spirits.

Openings of prayers from Yom Kippur (Day of Atonement) are usually illustrated by initial words and by parts of prayers written within full-page arches resembling doors, an allusion to the Gates of Mercy, now opened to accept the individual prayers of every Jew.[114] The *Leipzig Maḥzor* has an illustration of Abraham saved from the fire of the Chaldeans.

The prayers for Sukkot (Feast of Tabernacles) are sometimes illustrated by a man holding the prescribed "Four Species." In the *Leipzig Maḥzor* there is also a representation of the leviathan and the Behemoth. These two animals look as though they are fighting, an event which is supposed to take place before the end of the world is due. Some *maḥzorim* are merely decorated and contain no illustrations. An example is the *Nuremberg Maḥzor* (pl. 35).

In the 15th century, the illumination of large-sized *maḥzorim* was no longer fashionable. The illuminated *siddur* became more common, one example of which is the *Siddur of the Rabbi of Ruzhin* (pl. 44).

A miscellany in the Hamburg State and University Library, written before 1427 (probably in Mainz), contains a *siddur* and a *Haggadah*. Some of the prayer openings and *piyyutim* have text illustrations in the form of unframed miniatures inserted within the text columns. To illustrate a *piyyut* for Ḥanukkah, the artist chose several scenes of miracles and martyrdom connected with the persecution by the Seleucid king, Antiochus Epiphanes, and the successful rebellion of the Hasmoneans (see pl. 41).

HAGGADOT

The German, like the Spanish *Haggadot*, contain four types of illustrations: textual, ritual, biblical, and eschatological. Unlike the Spanish, however, most of the German *Haggadot* have marginal illustrations and very few full-page ones. The four types of illustrations in the German *Haggadot* can be found in the earliest surviving Ashkenazi manuscript from about 1300, the *Birds' Head Haggadah* (pl. 28).

The most frequent text illustrations in the Ashkenazi *Haggadot* are the traditional *mazzah* and *maror*, usually held by seated people or by isolated hands; the rabbis mentioned in the text; the ten Plagues of Egypt; and the four sons, representing four types of children to each of whom the Exodus story should be recounted in a different way. The wise son is often depicted similarly to the rabbis of the *Haggadah;* the wicked son is usually a soldier, brandishing his sword or lifting his spear; the simple one is usually shown as a jester with cap and bells, while the one who does not know how to ask any questions is most commonly depicted as a prattling child.

In some *Haggadot* the text illustrations are literal. A common example is the portrayal of a man wearing medieval pilgrim's clothes with a satchel and a staff, to illustrate the *Haggadah* passage that begins, "Come out and learn . . ." In illustration of the passage from the *Haggadah*, "In every single generation it is a man's duty to think of himself as one of those who came out of Egypt," some *Haggadot* represent a man looking at himself in a round mirror.[115] The playful custom of a man pointing at his wife on reciting "*maror zeh*" ("this bitter herb") is depicted literally in German, Spanish, and Italian *Haggadot*.

The ritual illustrations of the German *Haggadot* sometimes start with full-page illustrations of the preparations for Passover (e.g., *Second Nuremberg Haggadah*, *Yahuda Haggadah*). These include the baking of the *mazzot*, the cleansing of the house, the search for leaven, and the preparation of the *seder* table. Within the margins of the text pages, the ritual illustrations include the lifting and drinking of the four ritual cups of wine, as in the *Yahuda Haggadah*, (pl. 40); the ritual washing of the hands; the family seated at the Passover meal, as in the *Erna Michael Haggadah* (pl. 38); the hiding and finding of the *afikoman*, as in the *Birds' Head Haggadah* (fols. 6v, 29v); and the opening of the door to the prophet Elijah at the recitation of "Pour out Thy wrath . . ."

The biblical illustrations in most German *Haggadot* pertain essentially to the story of Exodus, although they sometimes portray episodes from other books of the Bible. The *Birds' Head Haggadah* has many detailed episodes from Exodus (see pl. 28). The *Second Nuremberg Haggadah* (and its "Sister," the *Yahuda Haggadah*) contains three sets of biblical illustrations. The first is of Exodus, starting with the story of Moses' birth (fol. 7v) and ending with Miriam and the maidens singing and dancing (fol. 22), this series includes also the Exodus from Egypt (pl. 39). The second set is of Genesis, starting with the story of Adam and Eve (fol. 30v) and ending with Joseph as Pharaoh's viceroy (fol. 37). The third set of pictures is of prophets and leaders of Israel, starting with Moses receiving the Tablets of the Law (fol. 37v), continuing with Joshua and the angel (fol. 38), Samuel and Eli (fol. 38v), Samson and the lion (fol. 39), Samson taking hold of the pillars and bringing down the Philistines' house (fol. 39v), David and Goliath (fol. 40), and Elijah riding his donkey (fol. 41).

Among the biblical illustrations are many legendary episodes from the Midrash, such as Pharaoh's court astrologers prophesying that Moses will destroy Egypt (fol. 7v), Moses taking Pharaoh's crown from his head (fol. 9), Moses's neck being turned into marble at the moment of his supposed execution (fol. 11v), Zipporah feeding Moses during his seven-year imprisonment (fol. 12v), Pharaoh bathing in the blood of Israelite children as a cure for his leprosy (fol. 14), the serpent trying to kill Adam and seduce Eve (fol. 30v), and Abraham being saved from the fire of the Chaldeans into which he was thrown by King Nimrod (fol. 30v). The legendary material of the *Second Nuremberg Haggadah* and the *Yahuda Haggadah* is mostly based on *Sefer ha-Yashar* ("The Book of the Righteous"), an 11th-century legendary re-telling of the Bible story compiled in Spain. The rhymed inscriptions within the floating scrolls are also taken from *Sefer ha-Yashar*.

The last picture in the *Second Nuremberg Haggadah* is of Elijah, the harbinger of the Messiah —one of the best examples of the eschatological illustrations of the Ashkenazi *Haggadot*. It has ever since become traditional to portray Elijah at the foot of a rebuilt Jerusalem, as an illustration to the last verse of the *Haggadah*, "Next year in Jerusalem" (e.g., the *Prague Haggadah* and the *Amsterdam Haggadah*). In fact, as early as 1300, in the *Birds' Head Haggadah*, there is an illustration of a walled city with four people beneath the walls indicating their adoration by stretching one arm toward the city.

Among other eschatological illustrations in Ashkenazi *Haggadot* are the sacrifice of Isaac, an allusion to the Day of Judgment and the fulfillment of God's covenant with Abraham (e.g., *Birds' Head Haggadah* fol. 15v), and the entry of the Righteous into Paradise, illustrating the verse, "This is the gate of the Lord, the righteous may enter it" (Psalms 118:20). In the *Birds' Head Haggadah* (fol. 33), three bearded men, possibly Abraham, Isaac, and Jacob, are depicted being led by an angel through a gate that leads to a three-story building (paradise) in which are the sun, the moon, and four angels.

A whole array of Ashkenazi *Haggadot* of the 15th century that exemplify this type of illustration have survived, some with dated colophons. Not all of them can be discussed in detail, but an outline of the development should be sketched. In the *Erna Michael Haggadah* of about 1400 (pl. 38) besides some marginal illustrations, there are three miniatures depicting families at the *seder* table. This *Haggadah* is stylistically a close relative of two other undated manuscripts, probably of the first quarter of the 15th century: one is in the Preussische Staatsbibliothek; the other is the famous *Darmstadt Haggadah*[116] (pl. 43). Both manuscripts have hardly any text illustrations, and those which exist are painted within the initial-word panels. The *Darmstadt Haggadah* is by far the better manuscript, because of the quality of the illumination, and has become one of the best-known Hebrew illuminated manuscripts since its publication in facsimile in 1927.

The *Darmstadt Haggadah* and *Erna Michael Haggadah* are exceptional in having very few text illustrations. All the other 15th-century *Haggadot* contain textual, ritual, biblical, and eschatological illustrations. This difference cannot be due to a later development in *Haggadah* illustrations, since, as mentioned above, the *Birds' Head Haggadah* of about 1300 already included all of these types of illustrations.

Related to this school from the mid-Rhine area of the first quarter of the 15th century is the *Haggadah* in the *Hamburg Miscellany* (MS. heb. 37), written before 1427. To the second quarter of the 15th century belong the *Rylands Ashkenazi Haggadah* (MS. heb. 7) and the *Paris Haggadah* in the Bibliothèque Nationale (Cod. héb. 1333). To the middle of the century belong the *Second Nuremberg Haggadah* (pl. 39) and the *Yahuda Haggadah* (pl. 40) which, like the *Paris Haggadah*, have rhymed captions written in floating scrolls. There are other *Haggadot* of the mid-15th century, among which are a *Haggadah* in a *maḥzor* written in Ulm, Germany, with later additions made in Udine and Treviso, Italy in 1450–53.

OTHER BOOKS

Apart from Bibles, *maḥzorim*, and *Haggadot*, there are illuminated legal books, the most common of which are copies of Maimonides' *Mishneh Torah*. As in similar manuscripts from Spain, the only illustrations in these manuscripts are plans of the Temple and its implements. The initial-word panels are sometimes elaborately decorated, but hardly ever illustrated. An exception is the *Kaufmann Mishneh Torah*[117] (pl. 30). Other legal manuscripts from Germany: *Sefer Mitzvot Katan*, *Sefer Mitzvot Gadol*, are usually only decorated with initial-word panels.

Secular illuminated Hebrew manuscripts from Germany are very rare. One of the more common is the *Mashal ha-Kadmoni* ("Fable of the Easterner") by the 13th-century Spanish poet Isaac b. Solomon ibn Abi Sahula. This lengthy rhymed collection of exemplary tales dealing with wisdom, repentance, modesty, humility, faith, charity, etc. was usually illustrated with a set of pictures at the opening of each chapter. Since each picture has a rhymed inscription by the author, it is assumed that the manuscript was, from its inception, intended to be illustrated; however, no Spanish example has survived. It must have been a highly popular book in south-west Germany during the 15th century, for several complete copies have survived as well as a few fragments.[118] The book was printed by Gershon Soncino as early as 1490, with wood cut illustrations similar to the hand-drawn illustrations in the manuscripts. During the 16th century the collection was published in illustrated versions in Yiddish, and these in turn made the illustrated Hebrew texts more popular.

ITALIAN SCHOOL

Italian Hebrew illumination may have been one of the earliest schools in Europe, just as the Jewish community in Italy was one of the oldest and culturally most developed in Europe from the early Middle Ages. Hebrew illuminated manuscripts from Italy are most varied in their style and their types. A good number of them were executed by the finest Italian artists. As they originated in various schools from the end of the 13th to the beginning of the 16th century, they vary widely in their mode of illustration, which ranges from marginal illustrations through initial-word panels to full-page decorations and miniatures.

The system of illuminating each type of book differed from school to school, though some elements are common to all, and were influenced by Ashkenazi as well as Sephardi illumination. Most Italian Hebrew manuscripts are decorated with initial-word panels at the openings of sections, sometimes with the entire opening page, or at least the first text column, decoratively framed. This decoration may be a simple foliage scroll surrounding the text (pl. 45), or a stage-like arcade elaborately decorating the frontispiece (e.g., pl. 58). Bibles, *maḥzorim* and *siddurim*, literary texts, books of *halakhah*, and secular works of philosophy, science, and medicine are all usually decorated with framed openings of books, prayers, chapters, or sections. Some manuscripts have text illustrations in the margins and in miniatures within the text or as full pages.[119] The Italian *Haggadot* follow the Ashkenazi system of marginal illustration and initial-word panels.

THIRTEENTH-CENTURY SCHOOLS OF ROME AND CENTRAL ITALY

The *Bishop Bedell Bible* in Emmanuel College, Cambridge (MS. 1. 1. 5–7), dating from 1284, is a typical example of the Roman-Jewish school of illumination at the end of the 13th century (see pl. 46). Similar arcades and painted scrolls are to be found in another Bible, from about 1300,[120] and also in a *Sefer Mitzvot* by Maimonides from 1285. All these manuscripts are Roman, and like the *Bishop Bedell Bible*, were written and decorated by Abraham b. Yom Tov for his patron, Shabbetai b. Mattathias. In central Italy, similar illuminations were used in Bibles. A two-volume Bible in the British Museum (MS. Harl. 5710–11; 54), from about 1300 (and certainly from before 1340, when it was sold) still preserves both techniques of decoration—water-color pen drawings and painted illuminations. The openings of each book of the Bible are headed by painted initial-word panels and surrounded by foliage scrolls—either around the whole page or one text column. The foliage scrolls are wiry and incorporate animals, birds, fish, and grotesques in a style which was common in the province of Emilia and influenced mainly by the Bolognese school. This Bible contains a few text illustrations. Under the initial-word panel of Genesis (fol. 1) there is a painted panel containing seven medallions, five of which represent the creation of heaven and earth, the sun, moon, and stars, water, trees, and beasts. Each medallion shows the hand of God emerging from segments of the sky. At the end of the Pentateuch (fol. 136), there is a full-page drawing of a delicately formed seven-branched *menorah* painted in red, green, ocher and brown. The entire page is framed and filled with painted foliage scrolls combined with grotesques and dragons. Another delicately painted manuscript of Emilian style, from the end of the 13th century, is a psalter in the Biblioteca Palatina in Parma (MS. 1870; De' Rossi 510). Many of the chapter openings have small initial-word panels with grotesques and animals in the margins. Some illustrate the text: weeping people, with their violins hung upon a willow, illustrate Psalm 137, "By the waters of Babylon there we sat down . . . We hung our harps upon the willows in the midst thereof"; a man conducting a choir illustrates Psalm 149, "Hallelujah, sing to the Lord a new song." Another manuscript from the same district is a *Moreh Nevukhim* copied by Solomon of Rome in Viterbo in 1273 (B.M., Add. MS. 14763).

FOURTEENTH CENTURY SCHOOLS

A school illustrating legal books developed in Bologna in the second half of the 14th century, probably under the influence of the Bolognese Latin school, which specialized in papal decrees, urban laws, and other collections of legal documents. A fine example of this school in Hebrew illumination is a manuscript containing the halakhic decisions of R. Isaiah of Trani (13th century) which was copied in Bologna in 1347 (British Museum MS. or. 5024). The text is arranged according to subject matter and has text illustrations attached to the opening panels and margins of most items. Among the most interesting text illustrations are a man lighting a Ḥanukkah lamp (fol. 19), a wood cutter stoned for working on a festival day (fol. 64v), a Tabernacle and a man carrying the symbolic fruits of Sukkot (fol. 79v), carpenters working with stolen wood (184v), a bull attacking a cow (fols. 176–77), a merchant selling a ship (fol. 225v), and a judge (fol. 241). The heavy figure drawing of the text illustration, and the style of the marginal decorations, with their flashy foliage scrolls, flowers and gold dots, resemble the school of Niccolo di Giacomo da Bologna.

Stylistically akin to these illustrated legal books is a manuscript of Maimonides' *Mishneh Torah*, now in the Jewish National and University Library in Jerusalem (MS. Heb. 4° 1193), that was copied in Spain or in Provence in the first half of the 14th century and partially illuminated in Perugia around 1400 in the school of Matteo di Ser Cambio. Apart from border decorations, the *Jerusalem Mishneh Torah* has some text illustrations in initial-word panels and in the margins of the first 40 pages. These are the earliest extant *Mishneh Torah* illustrations. Among the illustrations are a man gossiping about his friend (fol. 18v), a student with his teacher (fol. 20), a worshiper of sun and moon (fol. 22), and a culprit being pushed off a rock (fol. 22v), which was the method of "stoning" an offender according to the Mishnah (*Sanhedrin*, ch. 6).

The beginning of the "Book of Love [of God]" has a man hugging a Torah scroll within the initial-word panel and another reciting morning benedictions in the lower margin (pl. 46). Since it is unlikely that the Christian artist Matteo di Ser Cambio should have invented the system of illustrating a *Mishneh Torah*, we may assume that either there existed an earlier model, which has not survived, or that Matteo di Ser Cambio was instructed by a Jew.

Other schools are known to have existed in central and northern Italy at the end of the 14th century and the beginning of the 15th century. These schools were sometimes initiated by a single patron—a book and art lover who ordered illuminated manuscripts for his private use or as presents for friends and relations. One such school revolved around a physician named Daniel b. Samuel ha-Rofe. Daniel's family badge shows a lion rampant on waves on the shield and a draped lion on the crest.[121] The tinted pen drawings which decorate these manuscripts are typical of Lombard work at the end of the 14th century.

Another group of manuscripts from the end of the 14th and early 15th century was executed for a father and son of the Bet El family, sometimes called Min ha-Keneset ("de Synagoga"). The father, Jehiel b. Mattathias, commissioned manuscripts at the end of the 14th century. A *Sefer Arukh ha-Shalem*, a concordance to the Talmud written by Nathan of Rome, executed in Perugia in 1396 (Parma, De' Rossi, 180) and another, a *siddur* from Pisa of 1397 (MS. Sassoon 1028), were both ordered by Jehiel. Many more manuscripts were ordered by his son, Jekuthiel, between 1415 and 1442.[122] In style, this group of manuscripts is close to that of Daniel ha-Rofe. Although there are a few local elements, on the whole it is influenced by Lombardic tinted drawings.

FIFTEENTH CENTURY SCHOOLS

An elaborately illuminated manuscript (from Mantua) dating from 1436 is the *Arba'ah Turim* in the Vatican Library (see pl. 48). The manuscript is similar in style to Mantuan Latin illumination of the first half of the 15th century. A single page belongs to the Mantuan school of the second half of the 15th century; this is a fragment of another copy of the same treatise, attached now to a different manuscript from 1457 in Vercelli, Seminario Vescovile (pl. 55). Another important manuscript from Lombardy, from either the school of Mantua or Ferrara, is the *Mishneh Torah* manuscript, formerly in the Frankfort Museum Library (see pl. 60).

One of the most elegant and delicately executed of Italian Hebrew illuminations, the *Rothschild Miscellany* MS. 24 is now in the Israel Museum (see pl. 56). The figure drawing in some of its miniatures and border decorations resembles the art of Taddeo Crivelli of Ferrara, one of the artists of the *Bible of Borso d'Este*. However, some of the decorations in the *Rothschild Miscellany* display a Venetian style, which may be due either to the prevailing influence of Venetian illumination at the time or to the collaboration by other artists trained in Venice. Ferrarese style is evident also in a manuscript of *Sefer ha-Ikkarim* by Joseph Albo in the Biblioteca Silverstriana in Rovigo (pl. 57).

The famous medical handbook, the *Canon* of the physician-philosopher Avicenna (988–1037) now in the University Library of Bologna (pl. 54), is also illuminated in the Ferrarese style. Another medical book, a miscellany now in the Cambridge University Library, is decorated by miniatures at the head of each of the various treatises (pl. 51). The style of the figures and of the decoration is very close to that of the Latin school of Padua. Thus, for example, the heavy figures with whitish, drawn faces and heavy outlines are typical of this school. Other Hebrew illuminated manuscripts are known to have been executed in the school of Padua. A *Halakhic Miscellany*, in the State and University Library at Hamburg (Cod. heb. 337) was written and illuminated in Padua in 1477, with later additions in Florentine style. Most of the treatises in it are by Isaac of Düren. Illumination in the earlier Paduan style consists of some initial-word panels (e.g., fols. 44 and 50), one magnificent marginal illustration of an old man slaughtering a doe (fol. 6), and a full-page initial-word panel above a miniature (fol. 75v) illustrating a marriage ceremony within a landscape (pl. 59). The Florentine-style miniatures and initial-word panels illustrating the text at the beginning of the book (fol. 3v), and at the opening of the section by R. Meir of Rothenburg, were added in 1492.

The 1480 *siddur* from Pesaro (pl. 53), in the Sassoon Library (MS. 23), is related in style to the Ferrarese school, rather than to the Florentine.

FLORENTINE SCHOOL

The school of Florence, known to have created dozens of manuscripts, was one of the most important in Hebrew illumination in the 15th century. Most of its products are decorated with delicate filigree work in initial-word panels and border decorations. To these are usually attached pen-drawn masks, profiles, and small animals. The favorite color in these pen decorations is a purple-blue. Painted illumination of the Florentine school is also based on pen drawings. A good example is the *Rothschild Maḥzor*, in the Jewish Theological Seminary in New York (pl. 52). The style of the illustrations in this manuscript closely resembles the Italianate figure style of Joel b. Simeon of Bonn, as in his representation of Elijah riding a donkey in the *Washington Haggadah* (pl. 50). Among other Florentine style manuscripts with painted drawings are two *siddurim*, one in the George Weill collection in Strasbourg, and one in the Jewish National and University Library in Jesusalem. The more "painterly" style of the Florentine school is exemplified in a manuscript comprising the books of Psalms, Job, and Proverbs, now in the Israel Museum (MS. 180/55). Preceding each of these biblical books is a full-page miniature illustrating the text. Psalms (fol. 4v) has David beheading Goliath; Job is shown with his three friends (fol. 134v), and Solomon's judgment (fol. 186v) is depicted before Proverbs (a similar manuscript was sold at Sotheby's on July 20, 1969). A more sumptuous example of the Florentine school is reproduced here from a Portuguese Bible (pl. 58).

The school of Naples was another important center of Hebrew illumination during the 15th century. The best known example of its work is the *Aberdeen Bible* (University of Aberdeen, MS. 23), possibly written in Naples in 1493 by Isaac b. David Balansi (i.e., Valensi) a Spaniard who had probably been expelled from Spain in 1492.[123] While the Spanish influence is evident in the manuscript's masoretic micrography and *parashot* indicators, it does not appear in the fully-decorated pages containing the comparative tables of masorah, initial-word panels, and border illumination; these are purely south Italian and possibly Neapolitan. The heavy borders, decorated with foliage scrolls, animals, birds, and large pearls framing the table of *haftarot*, are typical of the other illuminated pages in this Bible.

With the Renaissance in Italy, Hebrew illumination reached its artistic peak. It developed through the ready patronage of affluent Jewish loan-bankers who supported such fine illuminators as those who produced the *Rothschild Miscellany* (pl. 56) and the Bibliothèque Nationale's *Portuguese Bible* (pl. 58). Unique in the richness of their decoration, these manuscripts were in great demand, but only a few families could afford the single productions. The invention of printing, which enabled the production of books in a large number of copies, was a major cause of the decline of hand-produced books and the art of illumination in Italy and in other European countries.

PLATES

PLATE I

Fragments from the Firkovitch Collection

The two leaves reproduced here are fragments from the Firkovitch Collection in Leningrad. Both served as carpet pages preceding biblical texts before they were stored in the *Genizah* of the Ben Ezra Synagogue of Fostat (Old Cairo). Abraham Firkovitch visited the synagogue in 1865.

PLATE 1A

First Leningrad Bible

Pentateuch with masorah and carpet pages
Egypt, (?) 929

In Hebrew Bibles, the carpet pages are a combination of decorative motifs and masoretic material written in micrography which outlines geometrical or floral shapes. These carpet pages stylistically resemble the decoration on the opening pages of contemporary Korans. Palmette motifs enclosed within roundels and interlacing foliage scrolls are the main element of decoration, colored with gold, blue, green, and red on the parchment ground. The gold is further adorned with colored decorations. In the tenth century, the palmette and foliage motifs were smaller, stylized, and delicate. In the 11th century the motifs are larger, and the artist has paid more attention to details such as decoration on top of the gold fill, as seen in the Bible fragment reproduced here (pl. 1B), or colored ground surrounding the gold motifs, as in the *Second Leningrad Bible* of 1008–1010 (pl. 2). The example reproduced here of a carpet page from the *First Leningrad Bible* contains an exposition of the implements used in the Tabernacle in the desert, or the Temple in Jerusalem. There is another fragmentary page in the *First Leningrad Bible* with a slightly different arrangement of Tabernacle implements and a *menorah* with round branches. Conceivably this has been introduced from another manuscript.

PLATE 1A

A fragment of a carpet page depicting the Tabernacle and its implements, surrounded by a fence with a triple gate. In the court is a rectangular seven-branched *menorah*; above it is the Ark of the Covenant with leaf-like stylized cherubim flanking it. The incense altar is in the top right-hand corner, above the jar of manna. In the left-hand corner is Aaron's flowering rod which looks like a foliage scroll, and other vessels. The two pillars on either side are ambiguous. They may be Jachin and Boaz, the two brass pillars in Solomon's Temple (I Kings 7:21), in which case the artists have combined Tabernacle with Temple imagery.

LENINGRAD PUBLIC LIBRARY, MS. II 17

SPECIFICATIONS: Vellum, 241 leaves, $18\frac{1}{2} \times 15\frac{3}{4}$ ins (47 × 40 cm.). Text space $13\frac{1}{4} \times 11\frac{3}{4}$ ins (33.5 × 30 cm.). Written in square oriental script in three columns, 120 lines to the column.

COLOPHON: States that it was written by Solomon ha-Levi b. Bouya'a. Solomon b. Bouya'a is the scribe of the Pentateuch known as the *Aleppo Codex* (930 C.E.). The Leningrad ms. II 17 was completed on Friday the eighth of Kislev, 1241 of the Selucid calendar (November 929 C.E.), probably in Egypt. It was written for Abraham and Ẓaliḥ, sons of Maimon.

PROVENANCE: The manuscript was taken by Firkovitch to Chufut-Kale in the Crimea (ms. 36) and later sold to the Imperial Library in St. Petersburg.

PLATE 1B

Carpet Page Fragment from a Bible

Egypt, probably Cairo, 11th century

The fragment of carpet page which contained four small and one large central roundel decorated with palmette motifs and framed by rectangular panels of foliage scroll, all outlined in micrography.

LENINGRAD PUBLIC LIBRARY, COD. II 262

SPECIFICATIONS: Parchment, 6 leaves, $12\frac{5}{8} \times 12\frac{5}{8}$ ins (32 × 32 cm.). Six detached fragmentary leaves containing masorah written in decorated carpet pages. Written for Mevorakh b. Ẓedakah, son of Jonah, son of Shelah of the Bagroda family.

PLATE 2

The Second Leningrad Bible

Bible, masorah, masoretic treatises and carpet pages
Egypt, Fostat (Old Cairo), 1008 or 1010

This Bible is textually one of the most important biblical manuscripts, as it contains a very accurate masoretic text based on an earlier manuscript believed to be in the tradition of Moses b. Aaron b. Asher (fol. 479).
The *Second Leningrad Bible* is the earliest extant Bible which is complete and dated. Its completeness offers an excellent example of the rich decoration of oriental illuminated Bibles.
The major decorations in the volume are the carpet pages of various geometrical shapes outlined in micrography with a background of painted gold scrolls and additional green, blue, and brown colors. The manuscript contains at least 16 full carpet pages (fols. 473v–479 and 488v–490). The system of decoration includes criss-cross motifs, roundels, arcades, and stars. The page reproduced here (fol. 476v) is a good example of the arcade type. In some carpet pages, there are inscriptions giving the name of the scribe and the patron of the manuscript (e.g., fols. 474, 479, 489v, and 491). A colophon and dedicatory inscription on fol. 1 states that the biblical *maḥzor* (cycle of readings from the Bible) written for Mevorakh b. Joseph b. Nethanel b. Wazdad ha-Kohen by Samuel b. Jacob was completed in "*medinat Miẓrayim*" (Old Cairo) in the month of Sivan in the year "4470 of the creation" (1010 C.E.), which, according to a different calculation of the scribe, was 1319, according to the Seleucid calendar (1008 C.E.).
Like the *First Leningrad Bible*, it was part of the Abraham Firkovitch Collection. Since the manuscript was dedicated in the 14th century to the Karaite Synagogue of Damascus, one can assume that Firkovitch obtained the Bible from that synagogue at the risk of incurring a curse upon himself (see Provenance, below).

FOLIO 476v
An arcaded carpet page decorated with scrolls and micrography.
LENINGRAD PUBLIC LIBRARY, MS. B. 19a

SPECIFICATIONS: Vellum, 491 leaves, 13 3/8 × 11 3/4 ins (33.8 × 29.8 cm.). Written in square Sephardi script in three columns, 27 lines per column. Masorah magna in two lines on top of each page and three lines at the bottom. Masorah parva between the text columns. Sixteen carpet pages at the end of the manuscript.

COLOPHON: Fols. 1, 474, 479, 489v, 491: Copied, punctuated, and masorated by Samuel b. Jacob for Mevorakh b. Joseph b. Nethanel b. Wazdad ha-Kohen.

PROVENANCE: Signatures and inscriptions, fols. 1 and 491: Maẓli'aḥ ha-Kohen (1134); Manasseh ha-Kohen; Saffar b. Eli; Isaac b. Moses b. 'Abd Algafar of the 14th century dedicated this manuscript to the synagogue in Damascus with "a curse on whomever steals it, sells it, or exchanges it."

PLATE 3

Shelaḥ Lekha

Parashat Shelaḥ Lekha (Num. 13–15)
Egypt, 1106–07

A single *parashah, Shelaḥ Lekha,* is the total content of this small manuscript. Unlike many oriental manuscripts, it is complete and does not originate from a *genizah.* One of its numerous owners, Ehud b. Nethanel b. Abraham, inscribed his name (fol. 2) in a 16th-century oriental script.

It is unclear what purpose this manuscript served. It may have been a gift commemorating an event, such as a wedding or a bar mitzvah, celebrated during the week when this *parashah* was read in the synagogue. Other single *parashah* manuscripts have survived from the Cairo *Genizah.* Most of these are of the first portion of the book of Leviticus, which was traditionally used as a primer for the Jewish child. Indeed, in some, the Hebrew alphabet in decorative script precedes the text of Leviticus. Like other biblical books, both oriental and Spanish, this manuscript contains two carpet pages with side motifs, one at the beginning (fol. 3), the other at the end (fol. 33v). The carpet pages contain golden foliage scrolls on a blue and red ground within geometrical bars and delicate palmette motifs in the same colors. At the opening of the *parashah* there are gold bars above and below the text, open gold flowers, palmettes, and lotus buds in the margins. The masorah magna and parva are written in the borders. Each section is decorated in the outer margin with a large cartouche framing the abbreviation "*parash*[*ah*]." The style of decoration is similar to that of 11th-century Egyptian Korans.

TOP: FOLIOS 3V–4
Decorated opening pages of the *parashah.*
BOTTOM: FOLIOS 33V–34
Closing carpet page of the manuscript and framed colophon.
JERUSALEM, JEWISH NATIONAL AND UNIVERSITY LIBRARY, MS. HEB. 8°2238

SPECIFICATIONS: Parchment, 34 leaves, 5 × 4 ins (12.5 × 10 cm.). Written in square oriental script, 7 lines per page. The masorah magna in smaller script, one line above and two lines below the text. Two full carpet pages (fol. 3, 33v), thin bars, stylized flowers, lotus buds, and cartouches as sectional indicators. The binding is 16th-century, oriental, brown leather (damaged) on wooden boards, blind tooled with geometric interlacings.

COLOPHON: Fol. 34: "Isaac b. Abraham ha-Levi wrote, punctuated, and masorated it in 1418 according to the contract calendar" (1106–07 C.E.).

PROVENANCE: Fol. 2: Ehud b. Nethanel b. Abraham (16th century); Mr. Abraham Tulin of New York, who donated the manuscript to the Jewish National and University Library.

אל משה
שלח לך אנשים
ויתרו את ארץ כנען
אשר אני נתן לבני
ישראל איש אחד
איש אחד למטה
אבתיו תשלחו כל נשיא
בהם וישלח אתם משה
ממדבר פארן על פי
יהוה כלם אנשים ראשי
בני ישראל המה ואלה
שמותם למטה ראובן
שמוע בן זכור למטה
שמעון שפט בן חורי

אני יצחק בן אברהם
הלוי כתבתי ונקדתי
ומסרתי בעירת שדי
שנת אלף ת׳ו׳ח׳
לשטרות

PLATE 4

Yemenite Pentateuch

Pentateuch and the grammatical treatise, *Maḥberet ha-Tigan*
Yemen, Sana'a, 1469

This manuscript is one of the most beautiful examples of a Yemenite Pentateuch. It is illuminated like other oriental biblical manuscripts with carpet pages and decorations at the openings of books and *parashot*, but the motifs are of Yemenite inspiration. Four fully decorated rectangular carpet pages, two at the beginning (fols. 38v, 39) and two at the end (fols. 154v, 155), feature decorated micrography and painted foliage scrolls. The micrography portrays a running circular motif of intertwined fish in the center of which is a rosette. Triangular shapes filled with scale-like formations are centered at the top and bottom of the page. Painted motifs of interwoven foliage scrolls and palmettes of dusky gold mixed with ocher on a blue, red, and green ground fill the remainder of the page. The running fish-motif and the Coptic inscriptions resemble Mamluk metal work of the 15th century, but the foliage scrolls are an archaism. Within the text pages, both "Songs of Moses" are decorated. The first (Ex. 15) is framed with geometric interlacing masorah, while the blessing of Moses (Deut. 32) contains a row of medallions incorporating foliage and geometrical patterns painted in the same color scheme as the carpet pages.
According to the Arabic colophon on the last two carpet pages, written in decorated Coptic script, the manuscript was completed in 1469 C.E. for Ibrahim ibn Yusuf ibn Sa'id ibn Ibrahim al-Israili. The name of the scribe is not given. Most of the numerous Bibles copied and decorated in Sana'a in the second half of the 15th century are dated, making possible a close study of the development of style in this school. One of its major scribes was Banyah b. Saadiah b. Zechariah b. Margaz (d. 1490 C.E.), who executed several illuminated manuscripts. His signed and dated works, especially the Latter Prophets in the British Museum (Or. ms. 2211) copied in 1475, are closely related to the unsigned Pentateuch illustrated here. It is possible that this manuscript was also derived from his workshop.

FOLIO 15V
The prose section of the "Song of Moses" is written in a single column at the top, with two ornamented columns of verse below (Deut. 32:1–43). The masorah is written in the margins and between the columns in micrographic geometric shapes.
LONDON, BRITISH MUSEUM, OR. MS. 2348

SPECIFICATIONS: Paper, 158 leaves, 17 × 11 ins (41.5 × 28 cm.). Written in a square, bold Yemenite script, 25 lines in two columns, except for the "Song of Moses" (Ex. 15), which is in verse form. Four full-page, colored decorations (fols. 38v, 39, 154v, 155), three pages with colored marginal decorations (151v–152v). Masorah magna in geometrical patterns.

COLOPHON: Fols. 154v, 155: In Arabic, "The manuscript was completed on the sixth day of the month of Safar 874 A.H." (1469 C.E.).

PROVENANCE: Fol. 38 (15th–16th-century hand): "Salm b. Joseph b. Ibrahim sold this Pentateuch together with a book of the Former Prophets to the Synagogue of Ibrahim b. Yusuf b. Sa'id on Monday, the sixth of I Adar."

ואעידה בם את השמים ואת הארץ כי ידעתי
אחרי מותי כי השחת תשחתון וסרתם מן
הדרך אשר צויתי אתכם וקראת אתכם הרעה
באחרית הימים כי תעשו את הרע בעיני יהוה
להכעיסו במעשה ידיכם וידבר משה באזני כל
קהל ישראל את דברי השירה הזאת עד תמם

האזינו השמים ואדברה ותשמע הארץ אמרי פי
יערף כמטר לקחי תזל כטל אמרתי
כשעירם עלי דשא וכרביבים עלי עשב
כי שם יהוה אקרא הבו גדל לאלהינו
הצור תמים פעלו כי כל דרכיו משפט
אל אמונה ואין עול צדיק וישר הוא
שחת לו לא בניו מומם דור עקש ופתלתל
הליהוה תגמלו זאת עם נבל ולא חכם
הלוא הוא אביך קנך הוא עשך ויכננך
זכר ימות עולם בינו שנות דר ודר שאל אביך ויגדך זקניך ויאמרו לך
בהנחל עליון גוים בהפרידו בני אדם
יצב גבלת עמים למספר בני ישראל
כי חלק יהוה עמו יעקב חבל נחלתו
ימצאהו בארץ מדבר ובתהו ילל ישמן
יסבבנהו יבוננהו יצרנהו כאישון עינו
כנשר יעיר קנו על גוזליו ירחף יפרש כנפיו יקחהו ישאהו על אברתו
יהוה בדד ינחנו ואין עמו אל נכר
ירכבהו על במותי ארץ ויאכל תנובת שדי

PLATE 5

Damascus Keter

Bible with masoretic notes
Spain, Burgos, 1260

As in many Spanish Bibles, the chief decoration here is the carpet page preceding the main divisions of the Bible — the Pentateuch (fols. 4v–5v), the Prophets (fols. 113v–115v), and the Hagiographa (fols. 309v, 311). There are additional carpet pages before Psalms (fol. 348v) and at the end of the manuscript (fol. 428). The system of carpet pages is derived from the decoration of oriental Bibles and may have been directly influenced by Hebrew illuminated Bibles from Muslim Spain, of which no example survives. The carpet pages—in gold, brown, magenta, purple, and green—are composed of foliage scrolls, geometric motifs, and interlacings, outlined by biblical verses in micrography. Each one of the carpet pages is framed by biblical verses in bold script between lines of smaller script. Decorated gold frames and geometric and floral motifs enrich the small placards which give the number of verses at the end of most of the books. Similar smaller decorated panels indicate the *parashot* and the *sidrot*. Some of them may illustrate the text (e.g., fols. 137, 153—human face, 248—walled city). Though some of the carpet pages preserve an oriental style, the decoration of the manuscript is westernized and shows the influence of Latin illumination in Christian Spain.
According to the colophon (fol. 426v) the manuscript was copied in Burgos by Menahem b. Abraham ibn Malik for R. Isaac b. Abraham Ḥadad in 5020 A.C. (1260 C.E.). This Bible was kept in the synagogue of Hushbasha Al'anabi in Damascus for many years.

FOLIO 310
A carpet page decorated with foliage scrolls painted in gold; the leaves and background are in magenta wash. The scrolls and leaves are outlined by micrographic masorah. The whole carpet is framed by masorah written in large letters and surrounded by smaller script.

JERUSALEM, JEWISH NATIONAL AND UNIVERSITY LIBRARY, MS. HEB. 4°790

SPECIFICATIONS: Parchment, 428 leaves, $11\frac{7}{8} \times 10\frac{5}{8}$ ins (30.2 × 27 cm.). Written in square Sephardi script, 30 lines to the full page, in three columns (Psalms, Proverbs, and Job in two columns); masorah magna in smaller script, three lines above and four below the text. Sixteenth-century binding, oriental, blind-tooled, brown leather (damaged) on wooden boards. Holes indicate metal decorations which stili existed when the manuscript was inspected in Damascus in 1919.
COLOPHON: Fol. 426v was written in smaller script in a fading ink and read with the help of ultra violet light: "Copied by Menahem bar Abraham ibn Malik for Rabbi Isaac ben Rabbi Abraham Ḥadad and completed on Monday, the 17th of Adar 5020 A.C. (Jan. 3, 1260) in Burgos."
PROVENANCE: A sale inscription written in 15th-century oriental script on fol. 427 reads: "R. Abraham bar R. Ma'azia ha-Kohen bought the manuscript from R. Ẓedakah bar R. Abraham." Damascus Synagogue of Hushbasha Al 'anabi. Came to the Jewish National and University Library in 1962.

PLATE 6

Cervera Bible

Bible with masorah and grammatical compendium
Spain, Cervera, 1300

Besides the complete text of the Bible, the Cervera manuscript contains a grammatical compendium, possibly *Sefer Mikhlol* by David Kimḥi. Essentially, the manner of decoration of the *Cervera Bible* resembles that of the Eastern Hebrew Bibles with carpet pages, although instead of a consistent carpet texture, the decoration here frames the grammatical treatise and other masoretic material written in ordinary format (fols. 435–448v). The frames are decorated with geometric interlacings that either shape the text into various geometric forms or enclose it within gabled or round arches. In the frames, mainly in the corners, are depicted animals, birds, grotesques, and animal-life scenes, always on a colored or natural parchment ground. The scribe's colophon (fol. 434) is framed by a thick margin filled with heavy intertwining foliage scrolls. The artist's colophon (fol. 449) is simpler, consisting of five lines of zoomorphic letters, each line framed by a thin, red, interlaced, geometrical band.

Other decorations consist of painted panels at the end of books, used as fillers for the last column of a book, where the text itself does not cover the entire column. Some of these panels frame an inscription of the number of verses in the book; others, such as a seven-branched *menorah* at the end of Exodus (fol. 60) or a full-page picture of the Prophet Zechariah's vision (fol. 316v), illustrate the text. Some openings of books also have a text illustration; one such is Jonah being thrown into the sea and swallowed by a whale (fol. 304). *Parashot* indicators in the Pentateuch, e.g., number titling each Psalm, are also decorated, and some illustrate the text.

French, Spanish, and Italian elements in the style of the decoration may point to Toledo as the place where the book was illuminated. Cervera was a small village where Samuel b. Abraham ibn Nathan resided for one year and wrote the volume while waiting for his broken tibia to heal, "commencing on Thursday, the first of Elul, 5059 [July 18, 1299] and finishing on Thursday, the last day of Iyyar, 5060 [May 19, 1300]." He also states that he wrote the manuscript in 36 quires. The Bible is actually thus bound, each quire containing 12 leaves. The grammatical compendium was written on the pages following the scribe's colophon in the same hand. The artist's colophon terminates the book, stating "I, Joseph ha-Ẓarefati ["the Frenchman"] illustrated this book and completed it" (fol. 449).

The *Cervera Bible* in the National Library in Lisbon is an important example of early Castilian Bibles and influenced the decoration of other manuscripts. One of these was the *Kennicott Bible* of 1476, which was copied in Corunna, the domicile of the owner of the *Cervera Bible*, Don David Mordecai, who, on fol. 415v, recorded the birth of his son Samuel on Friday, the 28th of Tevet, 5136 (Dec. 21, 1375). It is probable that the *Cervera Bible* was still in Corunna 64 years later, when another note, recording the birth of Mordecai b. David ibn Mordecai (perhaps the grandson of Don David Mordecai) was entered in the manuscript on the fifth day of Passover, 1439.

FOLIO 316v

A full-page miniature depicting the *menorah* in Zechariah's vision (ch. 4); two olive trees flank the *menorah* and through two attached spouts pour oil into a bowl from which it is distributed to the *menorah* lamps by seven pipes. The *menorah* symbolizes the restored Jewish state, while the olive trees and their spouts represent the "two anointed ones," Zerubbabel of Davidic descent and Joshua the high priest.

LISBON, NATIONAL LIBRARY, MS. 72

SPECIFICATIONS: Parchment, at least 450 leaves, $11\frac{1}{8} \times 8\frac{1}{2}$ ins (28.2 × 21.7 cms.). Written in square Sephardi script in two columns, 31 lines to the column. Twenty-six carpet-like pages of framed decorations (fols. 435–448v); framed scribe's colophon (fol. 434); full-page artist's colophon (fol. 449); painted panels at end of books and illustrated beginnings of books; decorated *parashot* indicators in Pentateuch; and panels with the numbers of the Psalms.

COLOPHON: Fol. 434: Written by Samuel b. Abraham ibn Nathan, completed on Thursday, the first of Elul, 5059 (July 18, 1299). Fol. 449: Illustrated by Joseph the Frenchman.

PROVENANCE: Fol. 450v: Don David Mordecai, 1375; Mordecai b. David ibn Mordecai, 1439.

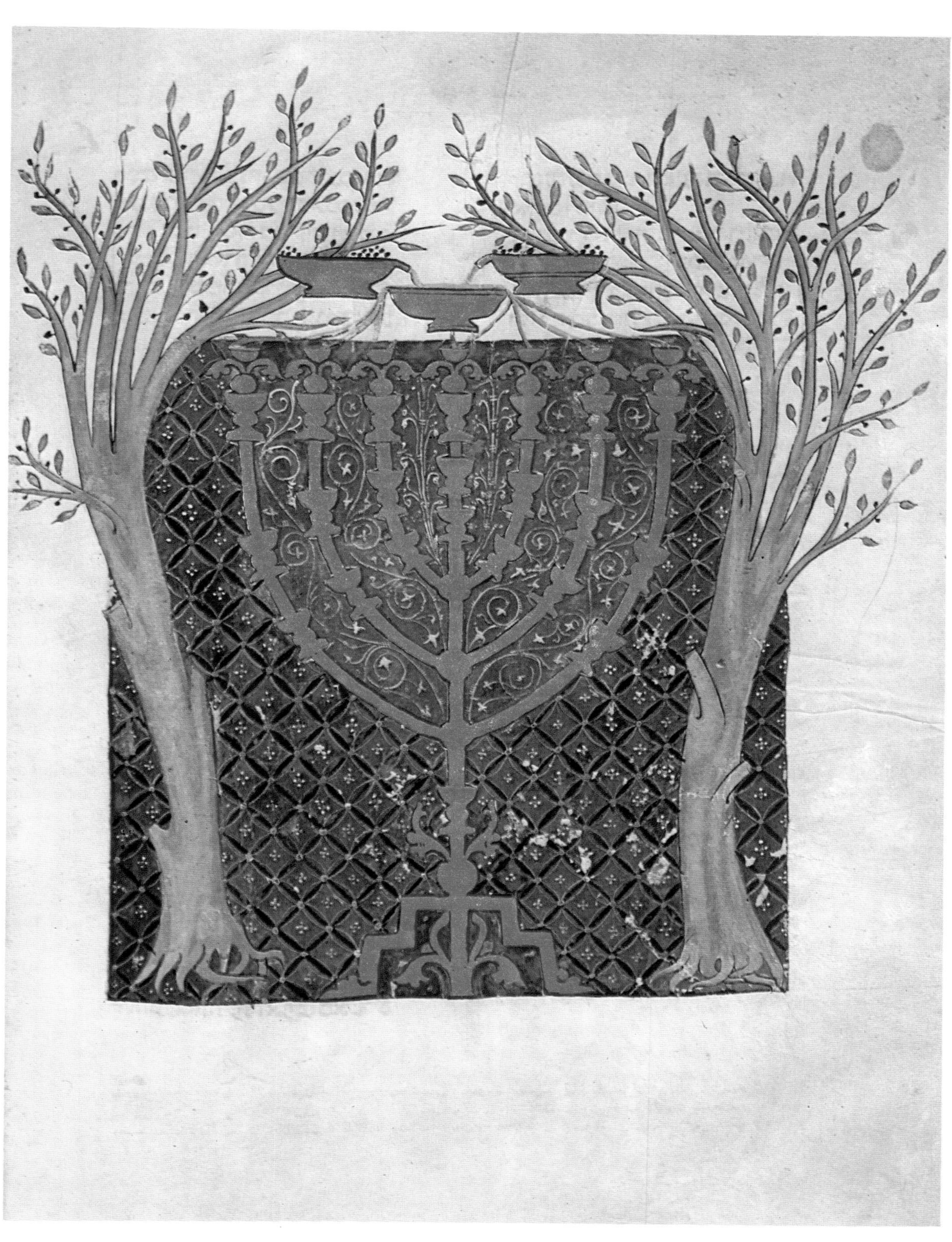

PLATE 7

Hamilton Siddur

Haggadah and *siddur* for the feasts of Passover and Sukkot
Spain, 13th century

Since not many illuminated *siddurim* from Spain have survived, no general system of decorating a Spanish *siddur* is known. The illumination of the present volume consists mainly of marginal foliage patterns and decorated initial words. The most elaborately decorated section is the *Haggadah* (fols. 2v–40v), which, in addition to painted initial words, contains text illustrations such as the *mazzah* and *maror* common to most Spanish *Haggadot*. The initial words are composed of zoo- and anthropomorphic painted letters in bright pastels of yellow, red, purple, and green. The artist has managed to compose decorations in a very ingenious manner, using ascenders and descenders of letters such as *lamed* and final *kaf*. The most interesting are on the page of the poem "*Dayyeinu*," where the combinations of *alef* and *lamed* portray a series of riders on horseback. Grotesque animal and human figures were a common artistic style in most European countries in the 11th and 12th centuries. As zoo- and anthropomorphic letters they were used in Merovingian illumination of the seventh and eighth centuries and also in Armenian initial words. In Hebrew illumination, this method of illustration became ubiquitous, and, although archaic, was still being used by Joseph ibn Ḥayyim, the artist of the 1476 *Kennicott Bible* (pl. 17). The light pen drawing and bright colors were used mainly in Spain during the 13th century, before the frenchified darker colors came into fashion. It is therefore possible that the manuscript was written and illuminated before the end of the 13th century. The manuscript, previously part of the collection of the Duke of Hamilton, was bought by the Prussian State Library. During World War II it was moved for safety to the University Library of Tübingen, where it still is.

FOLIO 34
Hymn of praise to God, part of the *Haggadah* (Ps. 118:27–29). The initial words "*Hodu*" ("thank ye") and "*Yehallelukha*" ("[Thy creatures] shall praise Thee") are composed of painted zoo- and anthropomorphic letters.
BERLIN, PREUSSISCHE STAATSBIBLIOTHEK, MS. HAM. 288

SPECIFICATIONS: Parchment, 106 leaves, $8\frac{1}{4} \times 6\frac{1}{2}$ (21 × 16.4 cm.). Written in square Sephardi script in single column of 11 lines. Decorated initial words of zoo- and anthropomorphic type. Some illustrations to the *Haggadah* (fol. 2v–40v).

PROVENANCE: Collection of William Duke of Hamilton until 1803.

אסרו חג בעבותי׳ סע עד

קרנות המזבח אלי את ה

ואודך אלהי ארומ מך

הודו

ליי כי

טוב כי

לע חסד׳

יהללוך

יי׳ כל מעשיך וחסידיך

וצדיקים עושי רצונך

PLATE 8

Golden Haggadah

Full-page miniatures, *Haggadah*, and *piyyutim*
Spain, probably Barcelona, c.1320

The *Golden Haggadah* is one of the earliest and most sumptuous of the surviving Spanish *Haggadot* of the 14th century. It is composed of three parts: 14 full-page miniatures (fols. 2v–15), a decorated *Haggadah* text (fols. 24v–55v), and a selection of 100 Passover *piyyutim* (fols. 16v–23v, 56v–101v). The miniatures depict episodes from Genesis and Exodus, beginning with Adam naming the animals and ending with the song of Miriam. These are followed by illustrations of the Passover preparations. Each of the miniatures, painted only on the flesh side of the vellum, is divided into four framed panels which read from right to left and from top to bottom. The background of each panel is of burnished gold, decorated with patterned geometrical designs.

The gothic style of the miniatures, directly related to the early 14th-century Catalan school under the patronage of James II (1291–1337), is basically French with Italianate elements. The harmonious composition, pronounced French-gothic figure style, and exaggerated gestures may be compared to the famous manuscript of *Vidal Major* (c. 1280). This manuscript, in its turn, was influenced by the Paris School of Illumination. However, the soft drapery, Italianate architectural style, and coffered ceilings in the miniatures of the *Golden Haggadah* reflect Italian influences which reached Barcelona via Majorca in the early 14th century.

The miniatures were painted by at least two artists, each of whom illuminated one quire of eight folios on one side of the leaf only. Although it may be assumed they belonged to the same workshop, there are some differences in their style. The first artist worked (fols. 2v–9) somewhat crudely, but very expressively. The second artist (fols. 10v–15), one of whose miniatures is reproduced here, is more elegant in style and balanced in color, though the faces in his work are somewhat stereotyped.

In their iconography, both artists follow the common Latin illumination of the mid-13th century in its most developed Parisian version. The first panel in the miniature reproduced here retains the haloed angel of Christian tradition appearing to Moses and the burning bush. In the second panel, the return of Moses and his family to Egypt resembles the common Christian scene of the Holy Family's flight into Egypt. Other miniatures depict specifically Jewish elements. Some contain Jewish legends, such as that of the angel saving Abraham from the fire of the Chaldeans. Such scenes may originally have appeared in earlier Jewish Bible illustrations. The text is decorated with initial-word panels, some of which are zoo- and anthropomorphic, and three text illustrations showing a dragon drinking wine (fol. 27), the *mazzah* (fol. 44v), and the *maror* (fol. 45v). The *piyyutim* have only initial-word panels.

FOLIO 10V
TOP RIGHT: The call to Moses by the angel of the burning bush, Moses hiding his face and removing his shoes (Ex. 3:1–6).
TOP LEFT: Moses, his wife Zipporah, and their two sons meet Aaron while returning to Egypt (Ex. 4:20 and 27).
BOTTOM RIGHT: Aaron's rod turned into a serpent while Moses delivers God's message to the people (Ex. 4:30).
BOTTOM LEFT: Moses and Aaron before Pharaoh (Ex. 5:1–5).
LONDON, BRITISH MUSEUM, ADD. MS. 27210

SPECIFICATIONS: Vellum, 101 leaves, $9\frac{3}{4} \times 7\frac{3}{4}$ ins (24.7 × 19.5 cm.). Written in square Sephardi script, 10 lines per page in the *Haggadah* (fols. 24v–55v) and 26 lines in the *piyyutim* section (fols. 16v–23v, 56v–101v). Fourteen full-page miniatures (fols. 2v–15), initial-word panels in the *Haggadah* and *piyyutim*, some zoo- and anthropomorphic letters, and three text illustrations in the *Haggadah* (fols. 27, 44v, 45). The binding is 17th-century Italian, dark brown sheepskin, decorated with blind-tooled, fan-shaped motifs on front and back covers.

PROVENANCE: The manuscript probably reached Italy with the expulsion of the Jews from Spain in 1492. It was given as a present by a bride, Rosa, daughter of Joab Gallico of Asti, to her bridegroom, Eliah Ravà, in Carpi in 1603. A special title page (fol. 2) and a page with the Gallico family armorial device (fol. 16) were added in honor of the wedding. A mnemonic poem of the laws and customs of Passover was added in the 17th century on the empty pages between the miniatures. FOL. 1: Birth entry of a son in Italy, 1689. FOL. 101V: Censors' signatures of 1599, 1613 and 1629. Acquired by the British Museum in 1865 as part of the collection of Joseph Almanzi of Padua.

ויסתר משה פניו
של נעלך
מלאך הסנה
וירכיבם על החמור
ויפגשהו אהרן

PLATE 9

"Sister" to the Golden Haggadah

Full-page miniatures and *Haggadah*
Spain, probably Barcelona, 14th century

Although apparently illuminated by a relatively unaccomplished artist, both parts of this manuscript belong to the group of rich, Spanish illuminated *Haggadot* of the 14th century. In addition to the full-page miniatures, the decoration consists of initial-word panels and some text illustrations of the *Haggadah*. All but the last two of the full-page miniatures (fols. 1v–18) are divided horizontally into two parts. They depict episodes from Genesis and Exodus, starting with the creation of Adam and ending with Miriam and her maidens dancing and singing after the crossing of the Red Sea. At the end are three miniatures depicting preparations for Passover (fol. 17), a congregation in a synagogue (fol. 17v), and a family around a Passover table (fol. 18). Since the choice of the biblical subjects and their iconographical details are very similar to those in the *Golden Haggadah* (see description to plate 8), it is possible that the artists of both the *Golden Haggadah* and its "Sister" used identical models. In the "*Sister*" *Haggadah*, Italianate elements in the style—such as a greater awareness of perspective or drawing the ground unevenly in nature scenes to indicate depth—are more apparent. In color, also, the "*Sister*" *Haggadah* is more closely related to the Italian style than to the frenchified art of the *Golden Haggadah*.

The "*Sister*" *Haggadah* contains several illustrations in addition to the *mazzah*, *maror*, and initial-word panels, which are common in most *Haggadah* manuscripts. There are pictures of seated rabbis, the four sons mentioned in the *Haggadah*, and, at the beginning of the text, two escutcheons bearing the arms of Aragon and Barcelona (fol. 18v). This may indicate that, like the *Golden Haggadah*, the manuscript was written and decorated in Barcelona, probably in the late 14th century.

FOLIO 17V
Full-page miniature depicting a *ḥazzan* in a Spanish synagogue reading the *Haggadah* to illiterate members of the community who are unable to recite the *Haggadah* in their homes.

LONDON, BRITISH MUSEUM, OR. MS. 2884

SPECIFICATIONS: Parchment, 64 leaves, $9\frac{1}{8} \times 7\frac{1}{2}$ ins (23.3 × 19 cm.). Written in square Sephardi script in one column of 10 lines; 34 full-page miniatures (fols. 1v–18); initial-word panels throughout and text illustrations for the *Haggadah*.

בעל הבית ובנ׳ ביתו שאומרים ההגדה

PLATE 10

Sarajevo Haggadah

Full-page miniatures, *Haggadah*, and *piyyutim*
Spain, Barcelona (?), 14th century

The *Sarajevo Haggadah* is by far the best-known Hebrew illuminated manuscript and has been reproduced in part twice during the last 70 years with scholarly introductions. The full-page miniatures in the manuscript represent the widest range of subjects, starting with the Creation and ending with Moses blessing the Israelites and Joshua before his death. Most of the miniatures are divided horizontally into two framed sections, although there are some with four sections (fols. 1v–2) and some full-page miniatures (fols. 30, 32, 34). They are all painted on the fleshy side of the vellum, with the reverse side left blank. The biblical cycle of pictures is followed by illustrations of the Temple (fol. 32), the preparations for Passover (fol. 33v), and an interior of a Spanish synagogue viewed through an arched door (fol. 34). The iconography is a derivative of Latin Bible illumination of the Franco-Spanish School. Some special Jewish elements can, however, be detected, as in the abstention from divine representation, which results in even the angels being depicted with their wings covering their heads (e.g., Jacob's dream, fol. 10). In the Creation miniatures, rays slanting down from heaven toward a globe represent the Divine Power. The seventh day, which in Latin biblical manuscripts is commonly depicted by a seated, nimbed God the Creator, is represented here in the form of a Jew resting on the Sabbath.

Stylistically, especially in figure and drapery, the miniatures, which are somewhat stiffer than those in the *Golden Haggadah*, are products of the Italian-gothic style prevalent in Catalonia. They are similar to those in the 1343 *Chronicle of James II* (University Library, Barcelona). The inference that the *Sarajevo Haggadah* originates from the Kingdom of Aragon can also be derived from three coats of arms displayed in the manuscript.

Above the decorated opening page of the *Haggadah* (fol. 3*) are the coat of arms of the Kingdom of Aragon, adapted in 1137 from that of the city of Barcelona, with the escutcheon of the family of Sanz and the rose of Margaret of Aragon. The *Sarajevo Haggadah* is akin to the *Kaufmann Haggadah* and the *Haggadah* of the Bologna University Library (ms. 2559) The text of the *Haggadah* and the *piyyutim* are decorated with elaborate, gothic, initial-word panels composed of elongated ascending and descending letters, sometimes extending to the margins of the nine text illustrations in the *Haggadah*. There are depictions of the first born (fol. 20), two towers of the towns of Pithom and Raamses (fol. 13*v), and the usual *mazzah* (fol. 26*) and *maror* (fol. 27*). A full page miniature of Rabban Gamaliel and his students (fol. 25) is extended under the initial-word panel which mentions his name. Many dragons and grotesques are depicted in the initial-word panels and margins.

Only the recent history of the manuscript is known. In 1894 a child of the Sephardi Jewish community of Sarajevo, Bosnia (now Yugoslavia) came to school carrying an ancient Hebrew book. His father had died shortly before, and the destitute family was obliged to sell this heirloom. Thus, the manuscript reached the National Bosnian Museum in Sarajevo. The manuscript was probably brought to Italy when the Jews were expelled from Spain in 1492, and was still in Italy in 1609, when it was censored by Giovanni Dominico Vistorini.

FOLIO 30 (ON THE RIGHT)
Moses holding the Tablets of the Law on top of the flaming Mount Sinai, which is surrounded by the Israelites. Joshua appears above them with another pair of Tablets. In the sky, a trumpet appears. The background is a diapered pattern in magenta.

FOLIO 32 (ON THE LEFT)
A stylized façade of the Temple with three gates. The middle gate has a conched arch which contains the Ark of the Covenant, covered by the wings of the cherubim, and the Tablets of the Law, with the opening words of the Ten Commandments.

YUGOSLAVIA, SARAJEVO NATIONAL MUSEUM

SPECIFICATIONS: Vellum, 165 leaves, $8\frac{1}{8} \times 6\frac{1}{4}$ ins (22 × 16 cm.). Written in square Sephardi script, 10 lines per page; 34 full-page miniatures (fols. 1v–34). Initial-word panels to almost every page of the *Haggadah* (fols. 1*–50*) (the miniatures and the text have separate pagination and the star indicates the text folios) and to many of the *piyyutim* (fols. 53v*–81*). Nine text illustrations in the *Haggadah* (fols. 13v*, 20*, 25*, 26*, 27*, 31*, 31v*, 36v*, 47v*).

PROVENANCE: Sold in Italy, 1510. Censor's signature, 1609. Sarajevo Museum since 1894. In 1941, the Nazis endeavored to lay hands on the *Haggadah*, but it was hidden away by the director of the museum.

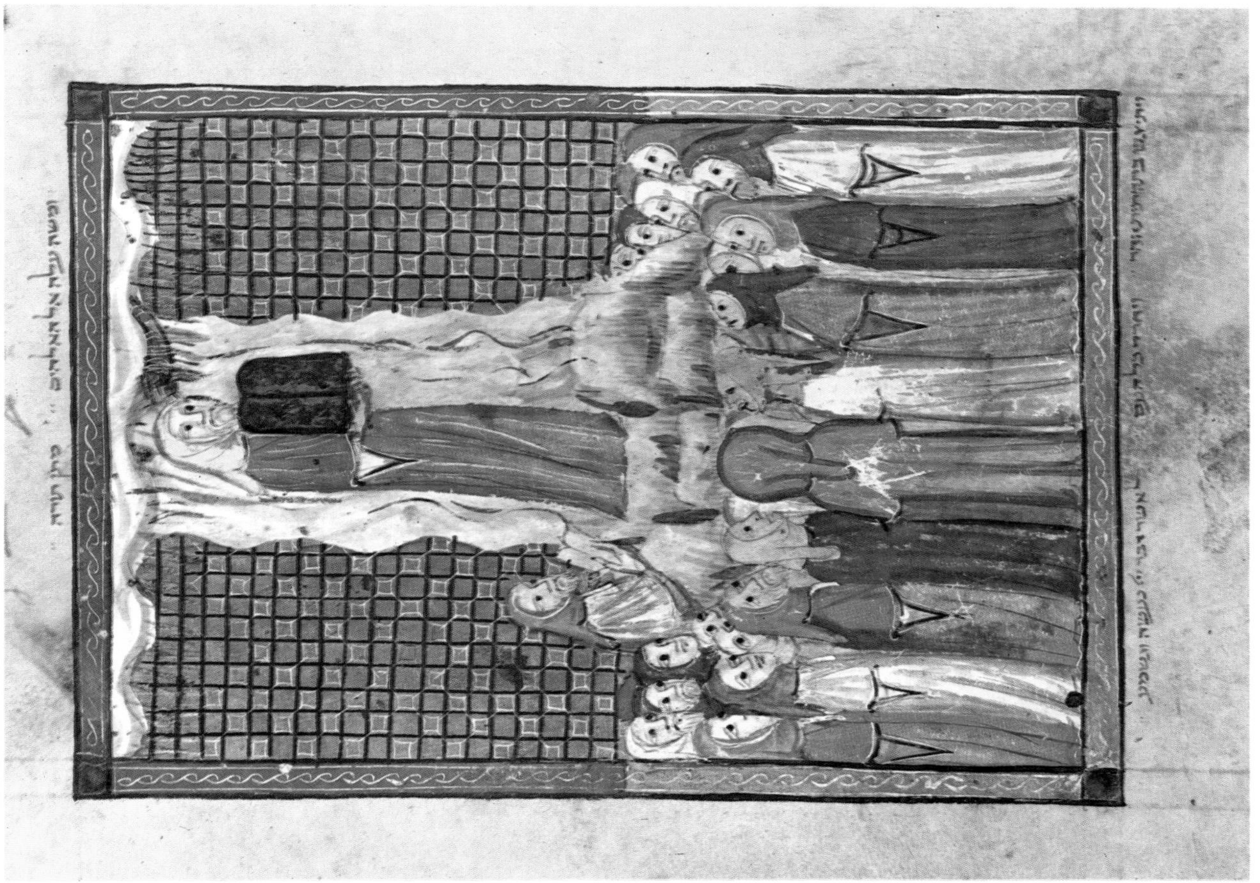

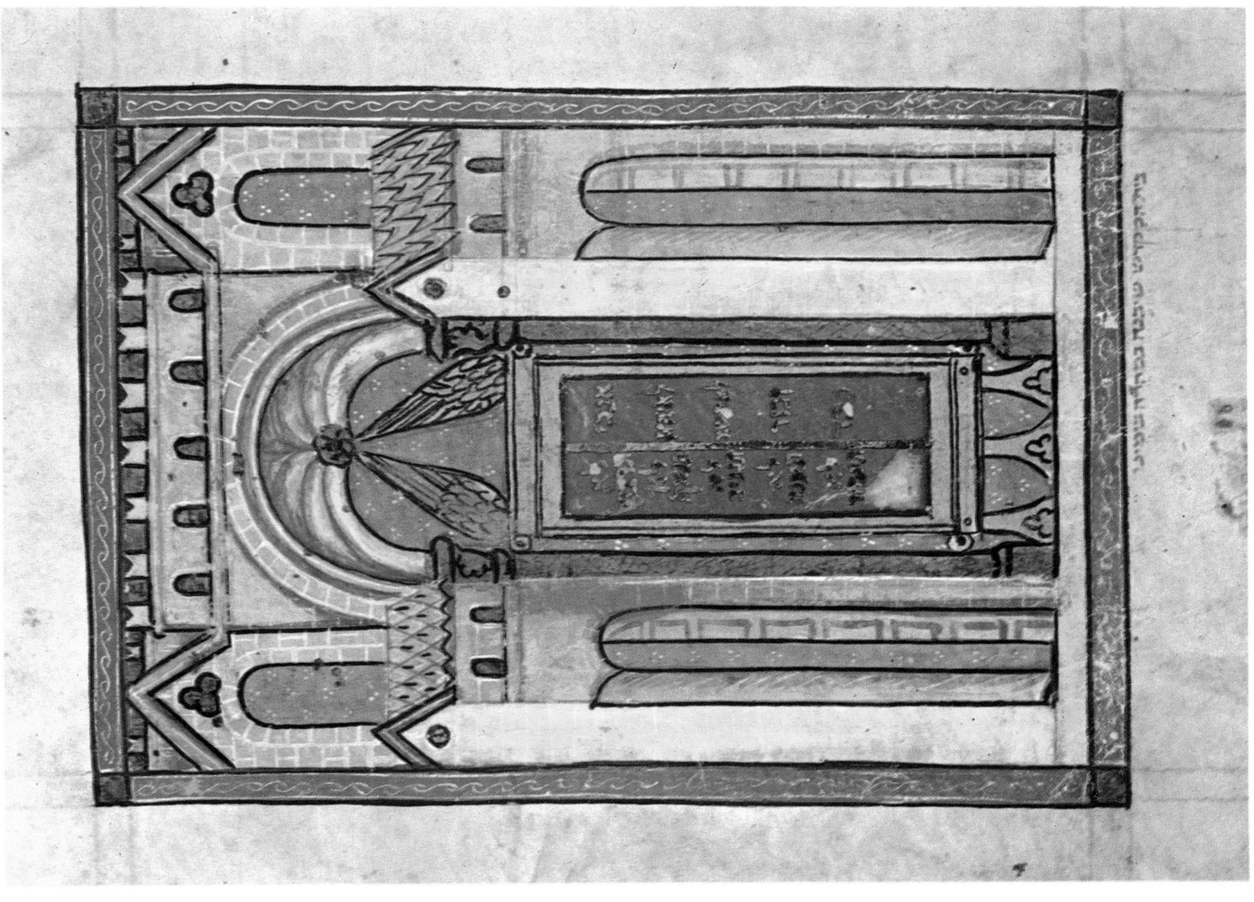

PLATE 11

Sassoon Spanish Haggadah

Laws for Passover, *piyyutim* for Sabbath before Passover, *Haggadah*, *parashot* for Passover and Shavuot, *piyyutim* for Shavuot
Franco-Spanish, 14th century

This manuscript—combining the *Haggadah* with other ritual material connected with Passover, as well as Shavuot—seems to have been the more common type of illuminated *Haggadah*. In contrast to the more sumptuous *Haggadot*, it does not contain full-page biblical miniatures, but rather biblical scenes in the form of text illustrations. Human figures, animals, and edifices illustrating the text are incorporated in most initial-word panels or in the margins. Some are more elaborate and spread across the entire page, leaving room for only a few lines of text; on other pages, as in the Passover Laws (pp. 2–41), the text is framed into two arched columns. Standing or seated people illustrate the text on many of the pages of the *Haggadah*. These illustrations vary from biblical to ritual or even literal character, such as a man descending a ladder in an illustration to the text, "And he went down to Egypt" (p. 70). Some legendary midrashic episodes are also depicted among the text illustrations. The pages of the *Haggadah*, with large initial-word panels and scrolls framing the text and the commentaries, as well as the arcades in the beginning of the manuscript, are rather crudely executed; at the same time, however, they are expressive. The style as well as the script is Spanish, though some elongated figures (e.g., p. 119) and the grotesques (e.g., p. 2) show French origin. The thin foliage scrolls on most pages give evidence of Byzantine-Bolognese influence in Spain in the first half of the 14th century, which can be seen by comparing this manuscript with the *Decretum Gratiani* in the Vienna National Library (cod. Series Nova 4444). The manuscript's place of origin might have been the eastern Pyrenees, Majorca, or southern France (in the first half of the 14th century), for in all of these there was a mingling of Spanish, French, and Italian styles. The end of the manuscript (pp. 253–336) is written in a 15th-century avignonese hand. On page 26, in the first part of the manuscript, there is a man on a horse whose housing is striped in a pattern resembling the arms of Aragon.

PAGES 138–9
Two people in prayer, each within an initial-word panel, are depicted on the first page. A man leaving prison holding his chains, illustrating the text "I called upon the Lord in distress. The Lord answered me" (Ps. 118:3–7), is found on the second page.

LETCHWORTH, SASSOON COLLECTION, MS. 514

SPECIFICATIONS: Vellum, 336 pages, $8\frac{1}{8} \times 6\frac{1}{2}$ ins (21 × 16.5 cm.). Pages 1–51 are written in square Sephardi script, 18 lines in two columns in the arcaded pages (pp. 2–34) and eight lines per page in the *Haggadah*, surrounded by a commentary. Pages 253–336 are written in cursive, avignonese script, 19 lines per page. Thirty double-arcaded pages (pp. 2–31), many initial-word panels, with text illustrations sometimes expanding to full-page size (e.g., pp. 22, 94, 109, 112, 114), foliage scrolls surrounding the text of the *Haggadah* as well as other parts of the text (pp. 42–251).

PROVENANCE: Solomon b. Joseph Karmi [Crémieu], censor's signature of 1687 on page 332. D. S. Sassoon; S. D. Sassoon.

יאמרו
נא בית אהרן כי לע
חסדו
יאמרו
נא יראי יי כי
לעלם
חסדו
138
מן המצר
קראתי יה ענני במ
במרחב יה יי לי לא
אירא מה יעשה לי
אדם יי לי בעוזרי
139

PLATE 12

Barcelona Haggadah

Piyyutim for the Sabbath before Passover, *Haggadah, piyyutim,* and *parashot* for the week of Passover
Spain, Barcelona, 14th century

The *Barcelona Haggadah* is of the type of Spanish *Haggadah* which contains only illustrations within the text and no full-page miniatures. Most of the illustrations are initial-word panels on almost every page of the *Haggadah*. Some text illustrations and many grotesques are to be found in the margins, interspersed with intricate foliage scrolls. The illustrations are lively in presentation, unlike the more stereotyped illustrations in the *Sassoon Spanish Haggadah* (see description to pl. 11).

The text illustrations may be divided into three types, all relating to the text: biblical, ritual, and textual. Among the biblical illustrations are many of midrashic origin, such as Abraham being saved from the fire into which he was thrown by the order of Nimrod. Of special interest in the ritual group is the illustration accompanying the mnemonic "signs" for the order of the ritual of Passover eve: two panels depict a sequence of nine people, each performing his particular rite (fol. 27v–28). Another ritual picture portraying people praying in a Spanish synagogue (fol. 65v) illustrates Psalm 113, "Hallelujah." The textual illustrations include the four sons (fols. 34–35v), many seated rabbis, and a full-page depiction of a large *mazzah* (fol. 61).

The Italianate style of this Spanish *Haggadah* is evident in the soft drapery, expressive facial features, and occasional attempts at perspective. The elaborate foliage scrolls interspersed with grotesques, the more naturalistic animals, birds, butterflies, snails, and small gold dots also indicate Italian influence. The obvious Franco-Spanish style and composition, however, indicate that the volume is an aragonese work of the middle of the 14th century; but since, like all Spanish *Haggadot*, it lacks a colophon, there is no definite proof of its origin. The coat of arms of Barcelona, which appears in many places throughout the *Haggadah*, as in the four shields decorating the *mazzah* (fol. 61), indicates that this was the manuscript's city of origin. The manuscript seems to have reached Italy before the expulsion of the Jews from Spain, since there is a note of sale on fol. 161v dated Bologna, 1459.

FOLIO 61

The round wafer in the middle of the panel illustrates the passage "This *mazzah*." It is decorated with four identical shields of the Barcelona coat of arms alternating with four blank shields. The *mazzah* seems to represent the roundel of the world, with the four naked winds blowing trumpets in the corners. The five musicians within the five arcades under the panel probably allude to the harmony of the universe. Above the panel, between the two initial words, is a seated man holding two decorated *mazzah* wafers.

LONDON, BRITISH MUSEUM, ADD. MS. 14761

SPECIFICATIONS: Vellum, 161 leaves, $10\frac{7}{8} \times 7\frac{1}{4}$ ins (27.5 × 18.2 cm.). Written in square Sephardi script, eight lines to the full page in the *Haggadah* (fols. 17v–99) and 26 lines in the *piyyutim* and *parashot* (fols. 1–16). Three full-page initial-word panels (fols. 22 and 61), one full-page decorative panel (fol. 88), many large and small initial-word panels, some with text illustrations and painted foliage scrolls surrounding the text. Calf binding on wooden boards.

PROVENANCE: Fol. 161v: Note of sale in Bologna, 1459. Fol. 160: Censor's signature, 1599. Owner's signatures: Fol. 1: Jehiel Naḥman Foà; fol. 151v: Mordecai Ottolenghi, Raphael Ḥayyim Ottolenghi.

ויקד העם וישתחוו
מצה
זו

PLATE 13

Rylands Spanish Haggadah

Piyyutim for the Sabbath before Passover, full-page miniatures, *Haggadah* with commentary, *piyyutim* for Passover week
Spain, mid-14th century

The *Rylands Spanish Haggadah* is one of the Spanish *Haggadot* which contain full-page miniatures in addition to text illustrations. The full-page miniatures depict episodes from Exodus onward, starting with the call to Moses (fol. 13v) and ending with the crossing of the Red Sea (fol. 19). The latter is succeeded by a miniature depicting preparations for Passover (fol. 19v). Most of the miniatures are divided horizontally, sometimes with more than one episode in a panel. Of all the known Spanish *Haggadot*, the inconography of the biblical miniatures in this manuscript is by far the closest to the biblical narration and depicts almost no legendary episodes.

The text of the *Haggadah* (fols. 20–36v) is illustrated only by ritual and textual figures in the margins or alongside the numerous initial-word panels, which sometimes have delicate scrolls extending from their corners, interspersed with animals and grotesques. Among the text illustrations are many rabbis, the four sons (fol. 23), the *mazzah* (fol. 31) and *maror* (fol. 31v), and three decorated pages of the poem "*Dayyeinu*" ("It would have sufficed") (fols. 29–30).

The decoration of the *piyyutim* (fol. 2–12v, 37v–53v) consists of initial-word panels in delicate filigree work, sometimes with additional vertical panels of interlacing scrolls outlined with micrography in the outer margins. The last page of the manuscript (fol. 54) contains grace after the meal decorated with 15th-century initial-word panels and, in the margin, a seated man lifting a cup.

The style of the full-page miniatures is the same as that of the text illustrations, revealing Italo-Byzantine expressive gestures, facial features, and techniques, coupled with Franco-Spanish composition and background. The decoration of the initial words and scrolls in the *Haggadah* text is in a different, soft style of French origin, somewhat earlier in date, and with very few Italianate motifs. The style variation may indicate that each part of the manuscript was executed in a different workshop, perhaps at different times, and only later bound into the manuscript. The script of the two *piyyut* sections differs from that of the *Haggadah*. The double page of "*Dayyeinu*" reproduced here is in the smoother French style.

Like many other Hebrew illuminated manuscripts in the John Rylands Library in Manchester, this manuscript originates from the earlier collection of the Earl of Crawford.

FOLIOS 29V–30
The initial-word panels of each verse of the poem "*Dayyeinu*" are written one below the other, in an architectural form, within horizontal panels on both sides of the text. Among the many grotesques surrounding the page is a hare hunt.
MANCHESTER, JOHN RYLANDS LIBRARY, MS. 6

SPECIFICATIONS: Vellum, I + 57 + II, 11 × 9⅛ ins (28 × 23 cm.). Written in square Sephardi script, 14 lines to the full page in the *Haggadah* and 30 in the *piyyutim*. Commentary on the *Haggadah* in two lines at the top and three at the bottom of the page. Thirteen full-page miniatures of the Exodus story (fol. 13v–19v), initial-word panels and text illustrations in the *Haggadah* (fol. 5v–10v, 37v–53v). Fifteenth-century decorations and illustrations to grace after the meal (fol. 54).

PROVENANCE: Biblioteca Lindesiana of the 25th Earl of Crawford, acquired for the Rylands Library in 1901 by Mrs. Rylands.

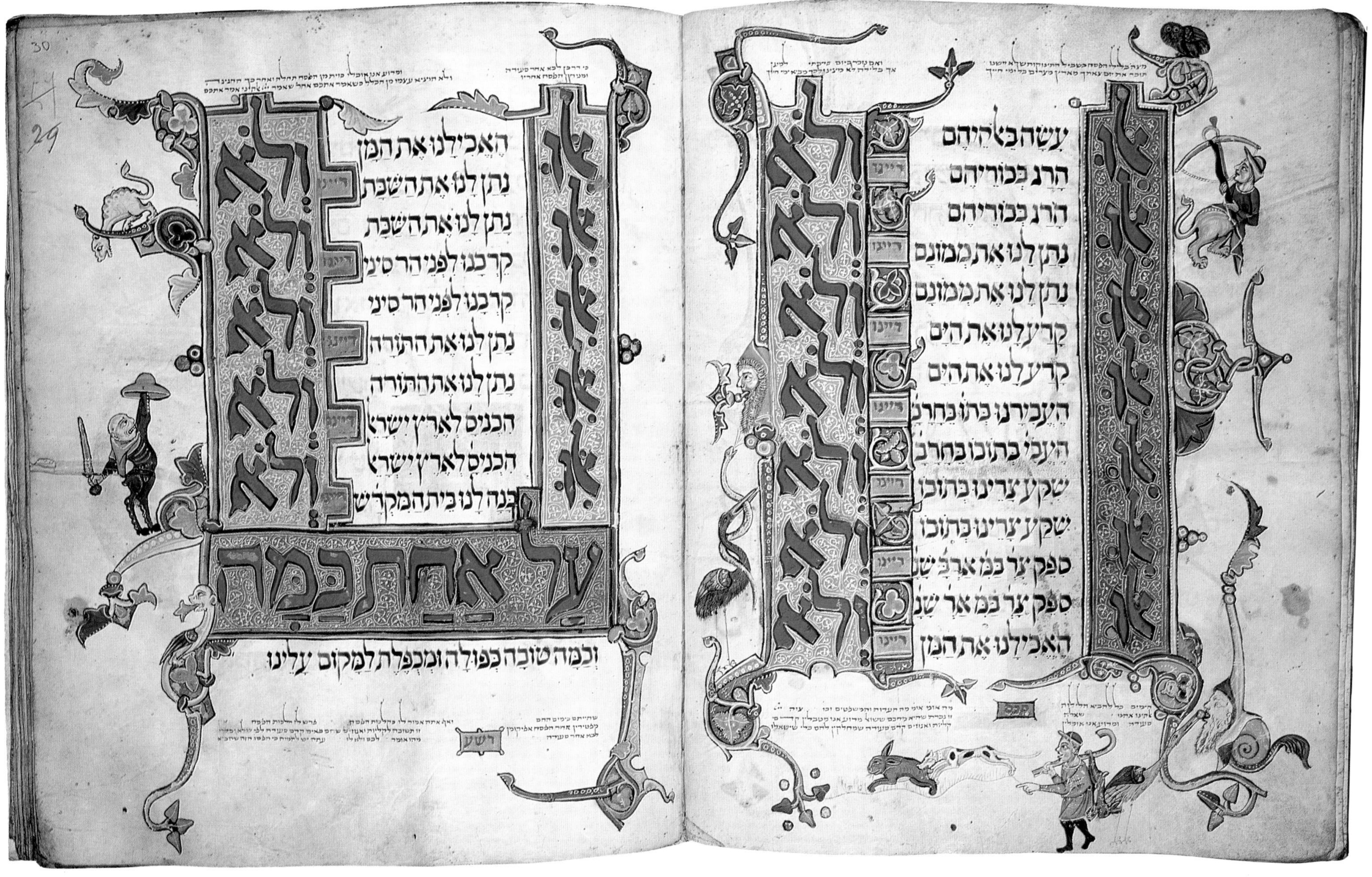
עשה באלהיהם
הרג בכוריהם
הרג בכוריהם
נתן לנו את ממונם
נתן לנו את ממונם
קרע לנו את הים
קרע לנו את הים
העבירנו בתוכו בחרבה
העבירנו בתוכו בחרבה
שקע צרינו בתוכו
שקע צרינו בתוכו
ספק צר' במ' ארב' ש'
ספק צר' במ' אר' שנ'
האכילנו את המן
האכילנו את המן
נתן לנו את השבת
נתן לנו את השבת
קרבנו לפני הר סיני
קרבנו לפני הר סיני
נתן לנו את התורה
נתן לנו את התורה
הכניס לארץ ישראל
הכניס לארץ ישר'
בנה לנו בית המקדש
על אחת כמה
וכמה טובה כפולה ומכפלת למקום עלינו

PLATE 14

"Brother" to the Rylands Spanish Haggadah

Full-page miniatures, *Haggadah* with commentary and *piyyutim* for Passover week
Spain, 14th century

The manuscript of this *Haggadah* in the British Museum is so similar to the *Rylands Spanish Haggadah* in scope, system of decoration, subject matter, iconography, and style that it may be regarded as originating in the same workshop, or at least as having been based on the same model. In this manuscript, too, the text illustrations of the *Haggadah* are in an italianized Spanish style; they are probably by the same artist who painted the full-page miniatures (fol. 1v–7v). The inital-word panels and some of the grotesques, both in the *Rylands Haggadah* and in this manuscript, are of frenchified style, although in the present instance they were done by the same artist who executed other more Italianate illuminations. The illumination of this manuscript is definitely not by the artist of the *Rylands Haggadah,* since his personal style is markedly different from that of the "Brother" manuscript. The human figures in the "Brother" *Haggadah* fill the entire miniature space and are much larger and more expressive than those in the *Rylands Haggadah,* where they are better proportioned against the landscape or background. There is evidence that the manuscript was sold in Spain in 1402. Among the owners was a member of the Shaltiel family who signed his name in an Italian script.

FOLIO 18
"*Maror zeh*" ("this bitter herb"). In the center panel is a large artichoke held by two men, illustrating the text. The man in the lower panel is pointing at his wife while reciting "*maror zeh,*" a playful custom common in many European Jewish communities during the Middle Ages.
LONDON, BRITISH MUSEUM, OR. MS. 1404

SPECIFICATIONS: Vellum, 50 leaves, $10\frac{7}{8} \times 9\frac{1}{4}$ ins (27.5 × 23.5 cm.). Written in square Sephardi script, 15 lines per page in the *Haggadah* (fol. 8–22) and 26 lines to the full page in the *piyyutim* (fols. 23v–50v). Commentary on the *Haggadah* in two lines at the head and three at the bottom of the page. Thirteen full-page miniatures (fols. 1v–7v) depicting episodes from Exodus. Initial-word panels and text illustrations in the *Haggadah* and delicate initial-word panels in the *piyyutim*.

PROVENANCE: Fol. 1: Meir b. Malchiel Ashkenazi sold the *Haggadah* to his brother-in-law, Moses ibn Kavash in the month of Sivan 5162 A.C. (1402 C.E.). Fol. 50: Signature of Abraham Ḥen b. Judah b. Immanuel Ḥen, the physician, of the house of Shaltiel.

מרור זה
שאנו אוכ על שום מה
על שום שמררו
המצרים את חיי
אבותינו במצרים
שנאמר וימררו את חייהם
בעבודה קשה בחמר
ובלבנים ובכל עבודה
בשדה את כל עבודתם
בכל דור
אשר עבדו בהם בפרך
ודור חייב אדם לראות
את עצמו כאילו הוא יצא
ממצרים שנאמר והגדת לבנך ביום ההוא לאמר בעבור

PLATE 15

Kaufmann Haggadah

Full-page miniatures and *Haggadah*
Spain, late 14th century

The *Kaufmann Haggadah* has an incomplete miniature cycle of Exodus. The manuscript is incorrectly bound, as the entire group of full-page miniatures is dispersed, with some attached to the beginning of the manuscript (fols. 1v–10) and others to the end (fols 57v–60). The facsimile edition of the manuscript, which was published by the Hungarian Academy of Sciences in 1954 with an introduction by A. Scheiber, did even more to prevent the understanding of the miniature cycle by printing the miniatures on both sides of the pages and omitting alternate blank pages, and thus preventing a correct reconstruction of the sequence. The episodes represented in the extant miniatures begin with the discovery of the infant Moses and end with Miriam's song and dance after the crossing of the Red Sea, with one miniature of the preparations for Passover eve (fol. 2).

Among the biblical illustrations are many midrashic ones such as Moses removing Pharaoh's crown from his head, or the Test of Moses, in which he is offered the choice between gold and a burning coal (fol.9v). In the text of the *Haggadah* there are some illustrations of either ritual, biblical, or textual nature. In most cases these illustrations are within the large, painted, initial-word panels, but sometimes they appear in the margins between the extended foliage scrolls. The *Haggadah* also contains some red, green, and purple filigree-work panels. The text illustrations are elaborate and contain, besides the usual rabbis, four sons, *mazzah* and *maror*, some repetitions of the biblical episodes depicted in the full-page miniatures, such as the labor of the Israelites (fol. 15v), the throwing of the male children into the river (fol. 27v), and the Israelites coming out of Egypt (fol. 43).

The Italianate style of the illumination is pronounced, both in the full-page miniatures and in the text. In describing this *Haggadah* in the introductory volume of *Die Haggadah von Sarajevo*, J. von Schlosser attributed the style to northern Italy. In fact, the style is Castilian of the late 14th century, characterized by many Italian stylistic elements. The Byzantine-Bolognese figure style and the very colorful, fleshy leaves support this assumption, as does the triple-towered castle—the emblem of the Kingdom of Castile—which is depicted in the center of the round decorated *mazzah* surrounded by four naked personifications of the winds blowing trumpets.

FOLIO 43
An initial-word panel of Psalm 114 depicts the exodus from Egypt in which Moses is leading the Israelites, while the Egyptians watch from their tower. On the right, a mounted Pharaoh is in pursuit. A tongueless dog stands in the foreground, illustrating the verse "But not a dog shall snarl at any of the Israelites," (Ex. 11:7).

BUDAPEST, LIBRARY OF THE HUNGARIAN ACADEMY OF SCIENCES, KAUFMANN COLLECTION, MS. A422

SPECIFICATIONS: Thick vellum, 60 leaves, $8\frac{3}{4} \times 7\frac{1}{2}$ ins (22 × 19 cm.). Written in square Sephardi script, mostly 9 lines to the full page (directions in smaller script, 17 lines to the full page). Fourteen full-page miniatures (fols. 1v–10, 57v–60) depicting Exodus episodes. Initial-word panels and text illustrations in the *Haggadah* (fols. 11v–56). Two of the panels extend to a full page (fols. 11v, 39).

PROVENANCE: Owners' signatures on fols. 1, 2, 3, and 60v barely legible

עקרת הבית אם הבנים
שמחה הללויה

בצאת
ישראל ממצרים
בית יעקב מעם לועז היתה
יהודה לקדשו ישראל

PLATE 16

Farḥi Bible

Carpet pages, Bible with masorah and several masoretic, grammatical, and chronological treatises
Hispano-Provençal, 1366–82

The *Farḥi Bible* is one of the richest illuminated Bibles of the Spanish School. The text and illuminations are the work of Elisha b. Abraham b. Benveniste b. Elisha called Crescas, which, as he states in his colophon (p. 2), "[he] completed for himself." It took him 17 years, from 1366 to 1382, to write and illuminate it.

Before the actual Bible text, Elisha Crescas illuminated 192 fully decorated pages, 29 of which were painted carpet pages of geometrical interlacings, in which none of the patterns was repeated (pp. 42–71). The carpet pages and preliminary texts to the Bible are all framed by wide or thin painted bars with foliage motifs adorning the outer corners. Within the framing bars are biblical verses in gold, monumental script, one line at the top and one at the bottom of the text and carpet area. Additional grammatical texts are written in smaller script around the framing bars. The largest of these texts is the Hebrew lexicon, *Sefer ha-Shorashim* by David Kimḥi (pp. 42–165). The initial-words of each entry in the lexicon and in the other grammatical treatises are written within a small panel of filigree. The Catalan (or Provençal) translation of the Hebrew entries is given in the lexicon.

A few illustrations, mostly full-page miniatures, are found in these preliminary pages. Among them are a labyrinth representing the seven-walled city of Jericho (p. 22); the tents of Jacob, his wives, and concubines (p. 23); the cluster of grapes carried back by the spies from the Land of Canaan (p. 149); the *menorah* of Zechariah's vision (p. 150); the plans of the Tabernacle and of Noah's ark (p. 154); the Temple *menorah* (p. 182) and other implements of the Temple (p. 183); the *urim* and *thummim* (high priest's breastplate) (p. 184); the Holy Ark (p. 185); musical instruments of the Temple (p. 186); and the Tablets of the Law and implements (p. 197). Preceding each book a title and a descriptive name are written within a panel of delicate filigree work which is sometimes placed alone on the page (e.g., p. 193, Genesis). In the outer margins, the masorah magna is written in micrography in geometric forms or surrounding painted, stylized trees.

Elisha Crescas displayed his talent in the gothic style common to the second half of the 14th century in northern Spain and southern France. The main carpet page decoration, however, is derived from Muslim arabesque motifs which had been traditionally used in Spain for carpet pages in Korans and Hebrew Bibles. The stylized carpet pages illustrating the implements of the Temple also belong to an older oriental tradition. The assumption that the manuscript comes from Provence (Catalonia area) is strengthened by the use of dialect in the Hebrew lexicon.

Pages 182–3

Two full-page miniatures with implements of the Temple. The page on the right shows the *menorah*, the tongs, and the fire pans. It also depicts the table of showbread and the laver; above it is the altar of burnt offering. On top left are basins, flesh hooks, and fire pans. In the margins is the text of *Midrash Alpha Beta* and a comparison between the Jerusalem and Palestinian Targum with explanations in Arabic.

LETCHWORTH, SASSOON COLLECTION, MS. 368

SPECIFICATIONS: Vellum, 1,056 pages, $10\frac{1}{4} \times 8\frac{1}{4}$ ins (26×21 cm.). Written in square Sephardi script, 31 lines of two columns in the Bible (pp. 194–1056) and 31–33 lines per page in the additional material on pages 5–192. Of the 192 fully-decorated pages, 29 are carpet pages (pp. 42–71) and 9 are full-page miniatures (pp. 22, 23, 150, 154, 182, 187). Marginal decoration of the masorah in micrography, initial-word panels to all books. Eighteenth-century, red Morocco binding with gold tooling.

COLOPHON: PP. 1–2: Elisha b. Abraham b. Benveniste b. Elisha Crescas completed the Bible called *Mikdashiyah* on Wednesday, the 13th of Kislev 5143 (Nov. 19, 1382) for himself, having started to write it when he was 41, in the year 1366.

PROVENANCE: In the 19th century, the manuscript belonged to the Farḥi family of Damascus and Aleppo and was in British custody in Aleppo on April 15, 1908, pending inquiries as to its ownership. Its present owner is S. D. Sassoon.

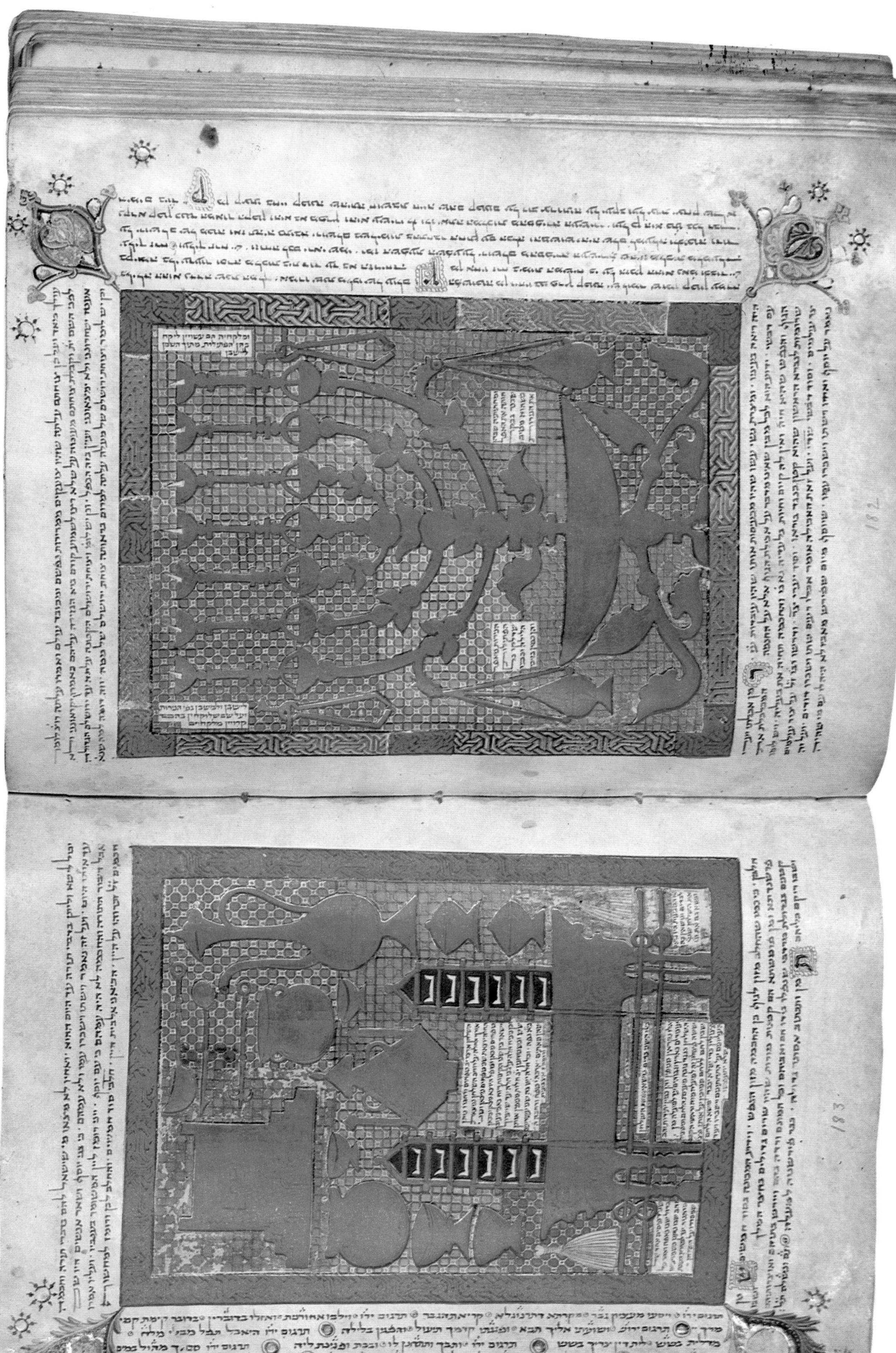

PLATE 17

Kennicott Bible

Bible with masorah and David Kimḥi's grammatical compendium, *Sefer Mikhlol*
Spain, Corunna (La Coruña), 1476

A masterpiece of medieval Spanish-Jewish art, the *Kennicott Bible* was copied, punctuated, and masorated by Moses b. Jacob ibn Zabara and completed, according to his colophon (fol. 438), on Wednesday, the third of Av, 5236 A.C. (July 24, 1476) in La Coruña for Isaac b. Don Solomon de Braga. The manuscript was planned and fashioned in scope and decoration according to the *Cervera Bible* of 1300 (see description of plate 6). The illumination, according to the artist's colophon (fol. 447), was done by Joseph ibn Ḥayyim, who fashioned his colophon in zoo- and anthropomorphic letters, similar to those of Joseph ha-Ẓarefati, the artist of the *Cervera Bible*.

The illumination of the *Kennicott Bible* consists of 14 fully decorated pages, including 10 ornamented carpet pages of which two are stuck to the original inner covers of the manuscript. There are 27 pages with decorated arcades surrounding Kimḥi's compendium, some with pictorial borders (fols. 1v, 8v, and 433v–444). In the top part of the arches, there are many animals, birds, grotesques, and some animal-life scenes on a colored or natural parchment ground. Some of the scenes resemble those of the *Cervera Bible*, such as chickens in a barn-yard (fol. 7v), while others are more original, such as the army of hares besieging a wolf in his castle (fol. 443). Two pages with highly stylized implements of the Temple (fols. 120v and 121) are placed at the end of the Pentateuch.

The *Kennicott Bible* repeats some of the text illustrations of the *Cervera Bible* as well. For example, Jonah being thrown into the sea from a sailing boat and swallowed by a whale (fol. 305). The Kennicott artist also included original paintings, such as one of old King David enthroned at the beginning of the second book of Samuel (fol. 185). *Parashot* indicators are also more profusely decorated than those in the *Cervera Bible*, with animals, grotesques, and some text illustrations, such as two bound captives confronting each other to illustrate the *parashah* dealing with the treatment of slaves (Ex. 21:1, fol. 47), a red heifer illustrating Numbers 19 (fol. 88v), or Balaam the sorcerer holding an astrolabe to illustrate Numbers 22 (fol. 90). The masorah magna, on the top and bottom of the text pages, is sometimes also written in decorative shapes or in micrography.

The style of Joseph ibn Ḥayyim is somewhat archaic. His human figures and animals are highly stylized and decorative with hardly any facial expressions. Single colors are outlined in dark ink. Other archaisms are the arabesque interlaced carpet pages and the zoo- and anthropomorphic letters, dragons, and grotesque figures. The contemporary 15th-century, late-gothic stylistic elements are the colored foliage scrolls and the heavy intricate filigree work used as a background in the full page miniatures, and as feather scrolls in the borders.

FOLIO 443
An arcaded page of David Kimḥi's *Sefer Mikhlol* showing an army of hares besieging a wolf in his castle.
OXFORD, BODLEIAN LIBRARY, MS. KENNICOTT 1

SPECIFICATIONS: Vellum, 447 numbered + 9 unnumbered blank leaves, $11\frac{5}{8} \times 9\frac{1}{8}$ ins (29.5 × 23 cm.). Written in square Sephardi script, 30 lines in two columns. In *Sefer Mikhlol*, 22 lines in two columns. Forty fully decorated pages, including 27 decorated and illustrated borders (fols. 1v–8v, 433v–444), two pages with implements of the Temple (fols. 120–121), 10 carpet pages (fols. 120, 122, 123, 317v, 318, 352, 438) and inner covers (fols. Av and B), and the illuminator's colophon (fol. 447). Many text illustrations, mostly as *parashot* indicators in the Pentateuch. Blind-tooled, 15th-century, box-like brown leather binding on wooden boards.

COLOPHON: Scribe, Fol. 438: Moses b. Jacob ibn Zabara copied, punctuated, and masorated the manuscript in La Coruña in 1476 for Isaac b. Don Solomon de Braga. Artist, Fol. 447: "I, Joseph ibn Ḥayyim, illustrated and completed this book."

PROVENANCE: The manuscript was bought in 1771 by the Radcliffe Trustees at Oxford University at the suggestion of their librarian, Dr. B. Kennicott. It was transferred to the Bodleian Library with the Radcliffe Library non-scientific collection in 1872.

PLATE 18

Copenhagen Moreh Nevukhim

Moses Maimonides' "Guide of the Perplexed" and Samuel b. Judah ibn Tibbon's accompanying glossary
Barcelona, 1348

Maimonides wrote his philosophical treatise *Moreh Nevukhim* ("Guide of the Perplexed") in Arabic. The most popular translation into Hebrew was done by Samuel b. Judah ibn Tibbon, who added an introduction explaining the difficulties of translating the book and a glossary of the esoteric words within the text (fols. 317–351). Since then, these additions have become an integral part of Maimonides' text. Not many illuminated copies of the "Guide" have survived. Those extant have elaborate decorations at the beginning of each of the three parts of the text and minor decorations at the beginning of each chapter. The manuscript reproduced here is unique in its having not only decoration, but actual illustrations. The opening of the first part (fol. 3v) has two faded miniatures, one depicting the scribe presenting the complete work to the patron and the other portraying a teacher in front of a group of pupils. The second part of the manuscript begins with an illustration of scientists discussing the laws of nature (fol. 114). At the beginning of the third part, the four beasts of Ezekiel's heavenly chariot illustrate the text dealing with mystic philosophy. The four beasts are similar to the four symbols of the Evangelists in Christian art: winged man, lion, bull, and eagle. The illumination is closely related in both iconography and style to a group of Hebrew and Latin manuscripts from Catalonia, dating from the middle of the 14th century. One of these is another copy of Maimonides' "Guide" in Hebrew, which is stylistically similar to the *Copenhagen Moreh Nevukhim* in its foliage scrolls that weave around a straight bar on which birds are perched, strong colors, and heavy use of gold, as well as in the use of cursive script. The Copenhagen manuscript is the only one of this Catalonian group which mentions its date and place of origin. Its close similarity to the others in the group has directed Millard Meiss in dating and placing the entire school and attributing it to the artist he has called the "Master of St. Mark," after a triptych depicting St. Mark which is now in the J. Pierpont Morgan Library in New York. Rafael Edelmann has conjectured that the scribe of the Copenhagen manuscript, Levi b. Isaac Hijo Caro (i.e., of the family of Caro from Salamanca) was the artist for the entire group.

The manuscript was brought from Spain to Italy, probably at the time of the expulsion of the Jews from Spain in 1492. It was censored by Dominico Hierosolomitano and Alessandro Scipione in Mantua in 1597 and Giovanni Dominico Carretto in 1619. At the end of the 17th century it was acquired in Amsterdam (?) by the Danish theologian Johannes Bartholin, who gave it as a gift to Frederik Rostgaard. It then passed into the possession of the great Danish book collector Count Christian Danneskiold-Samsoe, upon whose death it was purchased by the Royal Library in 1732.

FOLIO 114
An astronomer holding an astrolabe and discussing the laws of nature and the attributes of God with his fellow philosophers as an illustration to the second part of Maimonides' "Guide of the Perplexed."
COPENHAGEN, DET KONGELIGE BIBLIOTEK, COD. HEB. 37

SPECIFICATIONS: Vellum, 352 leaves, $7\frac{3}{4} \times 5\frac{3}{8}$ ins (19.5 × 13.5 cm.). Written in cursive Sephardi script. One text illustration to each of the three divisions of the book (fols. 3v, 114), surrounded by foliage scrolls, many initial-word panels, and decorated pages in many of the chapters.

COLOPHON: Fol. 316: Levi b. Isaac Hijo Caro of Salamanca has written (and illuminated?) the manuscript for the learned physician Menahem Bezalel in Barcelona, 5108 A.C. (1347–8 C.E.).

PROVENANCE: Johannes Bartholin (1665–1731) acquired the manuscript in Amsterdam (?) and later presented it to Frederik Rostgaard (1671–1745). Possessed by Count Christian Danneskiold-Samsoe. It was purchased by the Royal Library in 1732 after his death.

PLATE 19

British Museum Mishneh Torah

Moses Maimonides' *Mishneh Torah*
Portugal, 1472

The *Mishneh Torah* by Maimonides is a collection of the Jewish precepts and customs arranged systematically and divided into 14 books according to subject matter. It is usually decorated only in the various introductions to the entire treatise, on the opening pages of each of the 14 books, and on the colophon. There are very few illustrated *Mishneh Torah* manuscripts, and those that are illustrated were not written in Spain. The decoration of the *British Museum Mishneh Torah* is stylistically typical of late 15th-century Portuguese illumination. Wide painted borders surround the entire text and contain different types of foliage scrolls interspersed with animals, birds, dragons, and grotesques. The initial words and sentences of the opening verses of each book are written on the top part of the two text columns in gold on a background of delicate purple and red filigree work of different shapes. The other Portuguese manuscripts illuminated in the same style are mainly Bibles. The style of decoration is best compared with that of the *Lisbon Bible* of 1483 (see description of pl. 20).

The most impressive border decorations have fleshy, multicolored leaves with spread peacocks; rampant lions; long-necked dragons, with scrolled leaves shooting from their open mouths; flower pots; and vases. On the bottom border of the opening page of Book Ten (Vol. 2, fol. 189v) there are two crouching beasts with human heads—one bearded and one shaven. The colophon (Vol. 2, fol. 424v) is similarly framed, while the opening page (Vol. 1, fol. 2) is framed with interlacing, geometrical forms outlined in micrography. According to the colophon, the manuscript was written in 1472, but no place is indicated. On the basis of the style of the decoration alone, it may be presumed that the manuscript was both written and illuminated in Portugal, possibly in Lisbon.

The manuscript was in Italy during the late 16th and early 17th centuries, when many censors put their signatures to it. It was owned by Bernard Mould in Smyrna in 1724. From him it passed on to the Robert Harley Collection, which was purchased by the British Museum in 1753 from the Countess of Oxford and Mortimer and the Duchess of Portland. This two-volume *Mishneh Torah* was without question the finest and most beautiful of the Hebrew manuscripts among the 130 Hebrew items in the Harley Collection.

FOLIO 12
A decorated opening page of the general introduction to the *Mishneh Torah.*
LONDON, BRITISH MUSEUM, HARLEY MS. 5698 (and 5699)

SPECIFICATIONS: Vellum, 2 volumes, 301 and 435 leaves, $13\frac{1}{4} \times 9\frac{3}{4}$ ins (33.5 × 24.7 cm.). Written in square Sephardi script, 36 lines in two columns. Nineteen fully decorated pages at the openings of books (Vol. 1, fols. 31v, 63v, 106v, 197v, 252; Vol. 2, fols. 2v, 34v, 94v, 161v, 189v, 277v, 313v, 355v, 397v) and introductions (fols. 11v, 12, 13v), title page (fol. 2), and colophon (Vol. 2, fol. 434v).

COLOPHON: Vol. 2, fol. 434v: Written by Solomon ibn Alzuk for Joseph b. David b. Solomon b. R. David Gedaliah ha-Zaken ibn Yaḥya in the year 5232 (1472).

PROVENANCE: Censors' signatures from 1574, 1601, 1613, 1625, 1640. Bernard Mould, Smyrna, 1724. Harley Collection. Acquired by the British Museum in 1753.

בינו עמי עשו

אז לא אבוש בהביטי אל כל מצותיך

כל המצות שנתנו לו למשה בסיני בפירושן נתנו שנא ואתנה לך את לוחות האבן והתורה והמצוה תורה זו תורה שבכתב ומצוה זו פירושה וצונו לעשות התורה על פי המצוה ומצוה זו היא הנקראת תורה שבעל פה כל התורה כתבה משה רבנו קודם שימות בכתב ידו ונתן ספר לכל שבט ושבט וספר אחד נתנהו בארון לעד שנא לקוח את ספר התורה וגו׳ והמצוה שהיא פירוש התורה לא כתבה אלא צוה בה לזקנים וליהושע ולשאר כל ישראל שנא את כל הדבר אשר אנכי מצוה אתכם אותו תשמרו לעשות וגו׳ ומפני זה נקראת תורה שבעל פה ואע״פ שלא נכתבה תורה שבעל פה למדה משה רבנו כלה בבית דינו לשבעים זקנים ואלעזר ופינחס ויהושע שלשתם קבלו ממשה וליהושע שהוא תלמידו של משה רבנו מסר לו תורה שבעל פה וצוהו עליה וכן יהושע למד כל ימי חייו על פה וזקנים רבים קבלו מיהושע וקבל עלי מן הזקנים ומפינחס ושמואל קבל מעלי

ובית דינו ודוד קבל משמואל ובית דינו ואחיה השילני מיוצאי מצרים היה ולוי היה ושמע ממשה רבנו והיה קטן בימי משה והוא קבל מדוד ובית דינו אליהו קבל מאחיה השילני ובית דינו ואלישע קבל מאליהו ובית דינו ויהוידע הכהן קבל מאלישע ובית דינו וזכריה קבל מיהוידע ובית דינו והושע קבל מזכריה ובית דינו ועמוס קבל מהושע ובית דינו וישעיה קבל מעמוס ובית דינו ומיכה קבל מישעיה ובית דינו ויואל קבל ממיכה ובית דינו ונחום קבל מיואל ובית דינו וחבקוק קבל מנחום ובית דינו וצפניה קבל מחבקוק ובית דינו וירמיה קבל מצפניה ובית דינו וברוך בן נריה קבל מירמיה ובית דינו ועזרא ובית דינו קבלו מברוך ובית דינו. בית דינו של עזרא הם הנקראים אנשי כנסת הגדולה והם חגי זכריה מלאכי ודניאל וחנניה ומישאל ועזריה ונחמיה בן חכליה ומרדכי בלשן וזרבבל והרבה חכמים עמהם תשלום מאה ועשרים זקנים האחרון מהם הוא

PLATE 20

Lisbon Bible

Bible with masorah magna and parva and Ben Asher's grammatical treatise, *Dikdukei ha-Te 'amim*; masoretic tables; lists of precepts according to the *parashot* in the Pentateuch; and an allegorical poem on the conflict between the Bible and the Talmud
Portugal, Lisbon, 1483

This three-volume Bible was completed in Lisbon in 1483 by Samuel ha-Sofer ("the scribe"). It took him at least three years to write and is one of the most elaborately decorated manuscripts of its school, although it has no illustrations. There are three decorated pages at the beginning and end of each volume and sometimes within the books. The decorations are either carpet pages or additional texts surrounded by wide concentric borders—usually an inner border of monumental script on a ground of red and purple filigree work, a middle border of thinner script on a plain ground, and a thick outer border of varied, painted scrolls. Within the outer border, the scrolls vary from multicolored, fleshy ones, twining around central poles and interspersed with animals, birds, peacocks, owls, dragons, and vases to delicate feathery scrolls, sometimes in brushed gold on a plain or colored ground, intersected by small colored flowers and gold dots. This type of border decoration is typical of the Portuguese school toward the end of the 15th century, and can be found in many other Portuguese manuscripts. The page reproduced here is a typical carpet page, decorated with a rosette within a circle on a ground of pen-work scrolls and filigree work and outlined in micrography with the three characteristic concentric frames which, in this case, are in reverse order.

The initial-word panels of each book are written in gold on a filigree ground and framed by gold fillet with painted scrolls extending on both sides. Some of the opening pages of books are entirely framed by wide, decorated bands, similar to those of the additional texts. Each of the 54 *parashot* of the Pentateuch are indicated by the abbreviation, "*parash*[*ah*]," written and framed in burnished gold and surrounded by elongated, feathery pen scrolls in different shapes with small flowers in colors and in gold.

VOLUME II, FOLIO 185
A carpet page outlined in micrography, containing part of the allegorical poem on the conflict between the Bible and the Talmud, and framed by a wide, decorated border.
LONDON, BRITISH MUSEUM, OR. MS. 2628 (also 2626 and 2627)

SPECIFICATIONS: Vellum, three volumes of 184, 273, and 286 leaves, 12 × 9½ ins (30.5 × 24 cm.). Written in square Sephardi script, 26 lines in two columns. Eighty-two decorated pages with wide painted borders framing the additional treatises (Vol. I, fols. 1v-22v, 179-184v; Vol. II, fols. 134-135v, 178-185). The opening of each book and the colophon (Vol. III, fol. 186) are framed in a similar way. The oriental bindings in which the three volumes reached the British Museum were replaced by modern green, gold-tooled, Moroccan bindings.

COLOPHON: Vol. II, fol. 185v: Samuel ha-Sofer ("the scribe") b. Samuel ibn Musa wrote the Bible for R. Joseph b. Judah, surnamed Al-Ḥakim, completed on a Friday in the month of Kislev 5243 (Nov. 12–Dec. 10, 1482) in Lisbon. Vol. II, fol. 50v (end of Chronicles) within a rosette in micrographic script: "The book of Chronicles was finished on the fourth day of the month of Kislev 5243" (Nov. 1482).

PROVENANCE: Acquired by the British Museum from Benjamin Cohen of Bukhara, Nov. 17, 1882.

PLATE 21

Hispanic Society Bible

Bible with masorah magna and parva, comparative masoretic tables, and other grammatical treatises
Portugal, Lisbon (?), late 15th century.

This manuscript is one of the most sumptuous Bibles of the Portuguese school. The decoration consists of wide bands framing the text of the additional material as well as the opening and closing pages of each of the books of the Bible. Most of the framing decoration is typical of the late 15th century Portuguese school of illumination. The framing decoration ranges from multicolored foliage scrolls interspersed with birds, animals, and grotesques to delicate, feathery scrolls on plain or colored ground. The typical spread peacock, the gray owls, long-tailed colored birds, and the winged dragons with foliage scrolls protruding from their mouths can be seen in both pages reproduced here.

We must rely on the style of decoration alone for the identification of this manuscript since it lacks a colophon or any other clues to its origin. In addition to the many coats of arms displayed in the manuscript, there is a combined escutcheon carrying the rampant lion of Leon, the three-towered castle of Castile, and the gold and red bands of Aragon (p. 288). Such a combined coat of arms could have existed only after the marriage of Ferdinand of Aragon and Isabelle of Castile in 1469. It is possible that the decoration of the manuscript began in Spain before the expulsion in 1492 and was completed in Portugal immediately after the expulsion. It is safe to assume that it was completed before 1497, when the Jews were expelled from Portugal. The numerous other coats of arms used in the manuscript do not seem to relate to any kingdom or particular family. Most of them display the sun, moon, stars, a double-headed eagle, rampant lions.

PAGES 288–9

Double page showing the end of II Kings and the opening chapter of Isaiah. The shield at the bottom of the right-hand page is the combined coat of arms of Leon, Castile, and Aragon. At the top right-hand corner of the same page is a shield displaying a face of a fool with a jester's cap.

NEW YORK, THE HISPANIC SOCIETY OF AMERICA, MS. B. 241

SPECIFICATIONS: Vellum, 585 pages, 11 × 8$\frac{3}{8}$ ins (28 × 22 cm.). Written in square Sephardi script, 26 lines in two columns. Decorated, framed pages of additional treatises (seven in all) and at openings and closing of books of the Bible. One full-page illustration of the *menorah* (p. 7); initial-word panels to all the books and *parashot* indicators.

PROVENANCE: Jacob Curiel (formerly Duarte Nuñez da Costa) had the manuscript in Pisa in 1618. The manuscript was in the library of David Henriques de Castro and was acquired in 1899 after his death by the Marquis de Jerez de los Caballeros. The Hispanic Society of America acquired it in 1910.

PLATE 22

Dragon Haggadah

Haggadah and prayers for Passover and Sukkot
France, 13th century

Originally this small manuscript was probably part of a prayer book, since some fragments of prayers for Passover and Sukkot are still part of the manuscript and are written in the same script. Illuminated *Haggadot* of the 13th century are very rare, even as part of a *siddur*. This French manuscript displays a system of illumination which became common in Ashkenazi manuscripts of the 14th and 15th centuries. Since the art here is somewhat crude, one can assume that the artist did not design the system, but rather based himself on a system already in use in the 13th century. The decoration of this *Haggadah*, painted in the margins, is composed mainly of grotesques and dragons. However, there are some other illustrations of textual, ritual, and biblical subjects.
Among the text illustrations are pictures of some of the rabbis mentioned in the *Haggadah*, such as R. Yose (fol. 31v) and R. Akiva (fol. 34v); hands holding *mazzah* (fol. 39) and *maror* (fol. 40); and the paschal lamb, portrayed as a ram caught in a thicket (fol. 39v). The ritual illustrations mainly portray people reading the *Haggadah* while partaking of the Passover feast (fols. 4, 4v, 6, 6v, 8, 9v, 10, 44). Among the biblical illustrations are depictions of the labor of the Israelites in Egypt (fols. 25v, 26), some of the ten plagues in Egypt (fols. 27v, 28), and the miraculous multiplication of the Israelites, symbolized by a woman giving birth to six children at once (fol. 23v). The latter is an illustration to a midrashic interpretation of Exodus 1:7 :"And the children of Israel were fruitful, and increased abundantly, and multiplied, and waxed exceedingly mighty; and the land was filled with them," according to which the six main verbs and modifiers were interpreted to mean that every woman gave birth to six children.
The crudely executed stylized figures and objects were drawn in a black outline and then filled in with faint wash colors without shading. The simple facial expressions, e.g., squinting eyes, indicate an artistic style prevalent in Hebrew illumination of the 13th century. It would be difficult to suggest a date or place of origin only from the style of illumination. However, the style of the script and the version of the text do serve as corroborating evidence that the manuscript is of 13th-century French origin.

FOLIOS 23V–24
Marginal text illustrations to the *Haggadah*. On the right-hand page is a woman giving birth to six children, illustrating a midrashic interpretation to Exodus 1:7. On the left-hand page, an Egyptian taskmaster is striking an Israelite who is lying on the ground. *Arur* ("cursed") is inscribed next to the Egyptian, whereas the word *barukh* ("blessed") is written on the Israelite.
HAMBURG, STAATS- UND UNIVERSITAETSBIBLIOTHEK, COD. HEB. 155

SPECIFICATIONS: Vellum, 116 + 1 leaves, $7\frac{1}{4} \times 5\frac{1}{4}$ ins (18.7 × 13.8 cm.). Written in square French script, 7 lines per page. Colored decorations in the margins of many pages, some illustrating the text, others decorative with many grotesques and dragons.

ויעצמו במאד מאד
ותמלא הארץ אותם:
ורב כמה שנ' רבבה
כצמח השדה
נתתיך ותרבי ותגדלי
ותבואי בעדי עדיים
שדיים נכונו ושערך

צמח ואת ערום ועריה:
וירעו אותנו
המצרים
כמה שנ' הבה נתחכמה
לו פן ירבה והיה כי
תקראנה מלחמה ונוסף
גם הוא על שונאינו /

PLATE 23

British Museum Miscellany

Miscellany of biblical, ritual, legal, grammatical, astronomical, historical, mystical, calendric, and other treatises
Eastern France, Troyes (?), c. 1280

One of the richest 13th-century Hebrew illuminated manuscripts of Franco-German provenance, this small-sized but thick volume of almost 750 leaves covers a large variety of subjects both in text and illumination. The most important part of the illumination consists of four series of full-page miniatures, dealing mainly with biblical, though also some eschatological, subjects. Most of the miniatures are divided into two horizontal sections, and one is divided vertically (fol. 119). Two of the miniatures of the second series (fols. 259, 260) are surrounded by a marginal text, which may indicate that they were originally intended as part of the manuscript. Many of the miniatures in the third and fourth series are circular, and are framed by a solid gold band. Most of the miniatures have Hebrew captions, some of which were added at a later date.

In the absence of a regular colophon, the date of the manuscript may be determined from the chronological tables (fols. 444, birth of the new moon for the years 1280–96; 536v, general calendar for 1267–1370; 543–545v, specific calendar for 1278–1311) written by the principal scribe of the text. Folios 534v–535 contain a poem composed by the scribe about a certain Samson, martyred in Metz in 1276. The inclusion of *Sefer Mitzvot Katan*, which was composed by R. Isaac of Corbeil around 1278 (fols. 546v–640), sets the date of the manuscript nearer to 1280. The scribe mentions (fol. 252) as his contemporary (and still alive) R. Jehiel of Paris (the father-in-law of R. Isaac of Corbeil), who died in Acre in 1286. The manuscript, therefore, must have been written before 1286. The mention (fol. 242) of R. Hezekiah of Troyes (possibly b. Menoah), author of *Ḥezkuni*, the kabbalistic commentary on the Pentateuch, as an acquaintance of the scribe, suggests a Burgundian provenance, possibly Troyes. A formula of a 12th century ruling mentioning the three Burgundian communities of Troyes, Auxerre, and Sens is a further indication of the area of origin.

The style of the full-page miniatures indicates that they were executed by several hands and may have been added to at a later date, up to the first quarter of the 14th century. The technique, style, and colors of the miniatures are similar to that of the text decorations. These are all painted mainly in deep grayish-blue, magenta, pink, some vermilion, a small amount of green, and gold, applied to non-figurative details, with a background of checkered and diapered magenta, blue, and burnished gold.

FOLIOS 518 AND 114

Two full-page miniatures: On top: "This is Solomon the King who passes judgment on the two women" (fol. 518). On the bottom: "This is the *menorah* and Aaron who pours oil into the lamps" (fol. 114).

LONDON, BRITISH MUSEUM, ADD. MS. 11639

SPECIFICATIONS: Vellum, 747 leaves (fols. 515 bis., 739 bis., not numbered; 1 folio between fols. 175 and 176, 2 after fol. 515 bis., and 3 after fol. 716 are cut out), $6\frac{1}{4} \times 4\frac{3}{4}$ins (15.7 × 12 cm.). The main text written in a square French script, 27–32 lines in one or two columns, with other treatises in smaller script in the inner, outer, and lower margins. Forty-one full-page miniatures in four series, illustrating biblical, eschatological, and symbolic scenes (fols. 114–122, 259v–260v, 516v–527v, 740v–743v). Seven marginal text illustrations (fols. 205–208, 309v–354), the first five of which are in the *Haggadah*. Many initial-word panels and marginal decorations in colors and gold (fols. 1–452 only). North Italian, 16th-century, brown Morocco binding on wooden boards, gilt-tooled fillets and corner flowers. Gilt-stamped center ornament on front and back covers depicting Jacob's dream. Gold edges, goffered.

COLOPHON: Benjamin the Scribe signed on fols. 142v, 306v, 514. Fol. 535: A dirge for Samson martyred in Metz in the year 5036 A.C. (1276 C.E.). Fol. 242: "And I, the scribe, heard from R. Hezekiah of Troyes . . . " Fol. 252: "And I, the scribe, have heard from R. Jehiel of Paris . . . "

PROVENANCE: Fol. 745, in Ashkenazi script: "The manuscript was given on loan on the first of Nisan 5186" (March 9, 1426). "Sold by R. Samuel b. Ḥayyim to R. Abraham b. Moses of Coburg on the 25th of Tevet, 5191" (Jan. 10, 1431). Fol. 744v: Obituary notes—Venice, 5239 (1479), Padua, 5240 (1480). Fol. 746v: M. Reina Collection, Milan. Sold in Paris, 1838. Purchased by the British Museum on July 13, 1839.

זה שלמה המלך העשה משפט משתי נשים״

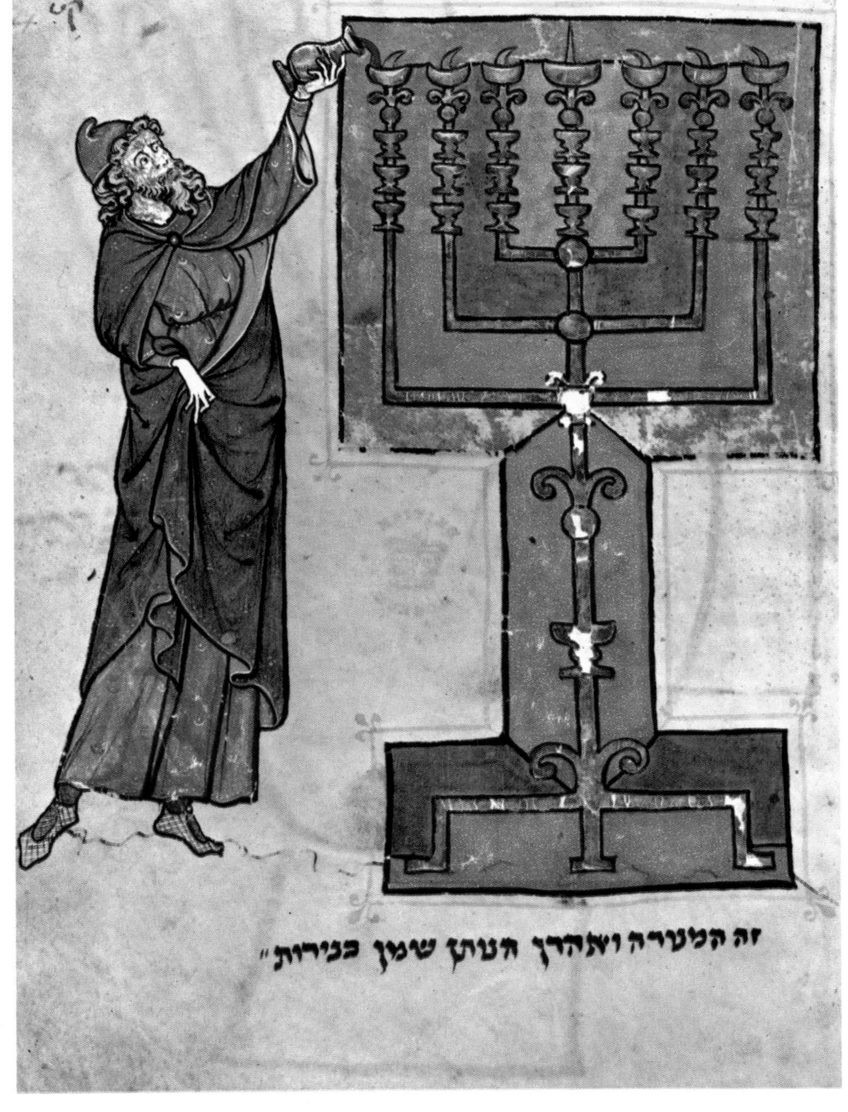
זה המנרה ואהרן הנתן שמן בנירות״

PLATE 24

Bibliothèque Nationale Pentateuch

Pentateuch with Targum, five *Megillot*, *haftarot*, and Job
Eastern France, Poligny, 1300

In addition to the five books of the Torah, an Ashkenazi Pentateuch manuscript usually contains the five *Megillot* (Song of Songs, Ruth, Lamentations, Ecclesiastes, Esther), and the *haftarot*. The book of Job, and the "passages of doom" from Jeremiah are sometimes added to such a Pentateuch as biblical excerpts to be read on the Ninth of Av. The system of decorating a Pentateuch was so similar on both sides of the Rhine (in Germany and in France) that it is sometimes difficult to define a specific manuscript's origin. Poligny, in the Jura region (now on the Swiss border), where the manuscript was copied, had a Jewish community and was within the French domain in 1300. The typical Ashkenazi script is more frenchified because the scribe, Joseph ha-Sofer, was of Pontarlier, France.

Either a small or large initial-word panel decorates the beginning of each book and each section of a typical Ashkenazi Pentateuch manuscript. One illustration, usually a *menorah*, is sometimes added to the end of the Pentateuch or to one of the other books included in the manuscript. The illustration reproduced here was added to the end of the Pentateuch (fol. 283v).

The initial-word panels are written in ink in large script over one to three columns on a ground of alternating red and purple filigree. For the most part they are framed on two or three sides by blue bars filled with thick yellow scrolls that are interspersed with multicolored dragons, dogs, hare, deer hunts, and rams. The *Megillot* are decorated with smaller panels, and the *haftarot* have none.

The style of the full-page miniatures and the panels is that of the southeastern French school, which is characterized by bright single colors with very little modeling. The white faces, rather flat at times, resemble the manuscripts of Rashi's commentary on the Bible from Würzburg, 1233, which are now in the Munich State and University Library (Cod. Heb. 5). It is obvious that the decoration was done at the same time as the copying (in 1300) since there are signs that the scribe had to copy the last part of the Pentateuch again after it had become illegible on fol. 283, when the *menorah* was being painted on the *verso* of his first copy (fol. 283v). The manuscript reached the Bibliothèque Nationale through the Library of the Sorbonne, to which it had been donated by Cardinal Richelieu, whose coat of arms is tooled in gold on the red Morocco binding.

FOLIO 283V

The illustration portrays a large, full-page *menorah* of decorated rectangular branches with Aaron standing on one side lighting the candles. Between the branches of the *menorah* are grotesques and hunting scenes on a painted blue ground. Below the branches of the *menorah*, on the same blue ground, are two illustrations presented vertically. On the right the judgment of Solomon (I Kings 3:16–28) is depicted with the two women flanking Solomon and the soldier, who is holding the naked infant. On the left is the sacrifice of Isaac, who is tied, naked, to the top of the altar. A spread-winged angel is holding Abraham back with one hand while pointing with other hand to a ram caught vertically in a thicket. Behind Abraham are two youths who stayed behind with the ass (Gen. 22). A lion and a dragon are drawn between the legs of the *menorah*.

PARIS, BIBLIOTHEQUE NATIONALE, MS. HEB. 36

SPECIFICATIONS: Vellum, 1 + 364 + 1 leaves, 20¼ × 14 ins (51.4 × 35.5 cm.). Written in square Ashkenazi script, 35 lines in three columns. One full-page miniature of the *menorah* at the end of the Pentateuch (fol. 283v), many initial-word panels to the openings of books. Seventeenth-century, red Morocco binding with the coat of arms of Cardinal Richelieu.

COLOPHON: Fol. 364: "Completed on Thursday, 12th of Tammuz, 5060 A.C. [June 30, 1300 C.E.] according to the reckoning of our date, here in Poligny by Joseph ha-Sofer, for the respected Rabbi Aaron, son of ha-Nadiv ["the benefactor"]."

PROVENANCE: Fol. 365: A list of books written in an Ashkenazi hand in 1449. Owned by Hezekiah and Obadiah, sons of Jacob b. David, in 1528. Cardinal Richelieu owned and bound the manuscript and gave it to the Library of the Sorbonne, from where it passed to the Bibliothèque Nationale.

PLATE 25

Ambrosian Bible

Bible with masorah magna and parva in the margins
Germany, Ulm (?), 1236–1238

This giant, three-volume Bible is one of the few examples of a complete, large-size Bible of south German origin. The illumination consists mainly of decorated and illustrated initial-word panels, with some miniatures attached to the end of books, and two full-page miniatures at the end of the entire manuscript. Most of the initial words are written in gold on painted panels, decorated with grotesques, animals, and birds, as running motifs. Some of the panels have text illustrations which do not always apply to the immediate text.

The closing miniature of the book (fol. 136), depicts the feast of the Righteous in Paradise. They are seated, all wearing gold crowns and feasting from a table covered with food and drink. Two musicians, one playing a viol and the other a flute, are stationed at either end of the table. At the top of the miniature are the leviathan and wild ox, the legendary food of the Righteous in Paradise, and the dragon-like mythical bird, *ziz*, symbolizing the last days of Judgment. This is a unique eschatological picture, in that it combines the Righteous repast with the mythical food, unlike other representations which only have the leviathan, wild ox, and the mythical bird (see *British Museum Miscellany*, Add. MS. 11639, fols. 518v, 519; also description of pl. 23).

The Righteous have animal heads: deer, lion, eagle, bear, and donkey; the musicians have heads of lion cubs. In fact, the faces of all the human figures in the manuscript are distorted in some way. Besides animal and bird heads, the Righteous are also portrayed with blank faces, are seen from the back, or with their faces covered. This style was chosen to overcome the aversion to representing the complete human form that probably developed in southern Germany through the ascetic influence of R. Judah and R. Samuel, "the Pious," of the late 12th century. The artist borrowed the animal heads from Christian and Muslim art, where such images symbolized righteous and holy people, evangelists, and the saints in heaven. Once this motif was adopted by Jewish illumination, it became a specific Jewish characteristic used in southern Germany throughout the 13th and up to the beginning of the 14th centuries. Four other manuscripts reproduced here (pl. 26–29) have the same characteristic element.

The style of the *Ambrosian Bible* can be compared to that of south German Latin illumination of the same period, and they probably influenced each other. The bright, non-shaded colors, outlined in clear, dark lines, resemble the stained-glass technique typical of this south German school.

VOLUME III, FOLIO 136
Feast of the Righteous in Paradise.
MILAN, AMBROSIAN LIBRARY, MS. B. 32, INF. (also MS. B. 30–31 INF.)

SPECIFICATIONS: Vellum, three volumes of 222, 208 and 136 leaves, 18 × 13⅝ins (45.3 × 34.3 cm.). Written in square German script in three columns (text space 12 × 9 ms: 30.5 × 23 cm.). Masorah magna in smaller script, one line in the top and three in the bottom margin. Twenty-five illuminated initial-word panels to the openings of each book and seven panels at the end of some books, some of which illustrate the text. Two full-page miniatures at the end of the third volume (fols. 135v and 136).

COLOPHON: Vol. 1, fol. 222v: "I, Jacob b. Samuel ha-Sofer ["the scribe"] wrote this book for R. Joseph b. Moses of Ulmna [Ulm] and completed it on the first of Shevat in the year 996 A.C." (Jan. 10, 1236 C.E.). Under this, in smaller script: "And I, Joseph b. Kalonymus, masorated and punctuated the manuscript, completed in the year 998 in the month of Shevat" (1238 C.E.).

PROVENANCE: Fol. 1: Joseph b. Abun b. Judah's signature, written in 15th-century Ashkenazi script. The manuscript was pawned in Italy for ten dinars and redeemed on Monday, Jan. 28, 1499, by Judah b. Solomon of Monreale. Censor's signature of 1601 in Italy.

PLATE 26

Worms Mahzor

Maḥzor of German rite for special Sabbaths, Passover, Shavuot, and the Ninth of Av.
Germany, Middle Rhine (Mainz?), 1272

The *Worms Maḥzor* consists of two unrelated volumes which were kept together in the Worms Synagogue. Neither of the volumes was intended for the use of the Worms community, since they contain *piyyutim* and parts of prayers which are not included in the Worms rite, while one *piyyut* is characteristic of the Mainz rite. Both volumes contain, in addition to the conventional prayers, *Megillot* and biblical passages recited during the different feasts. The fact that the book of Ecclesiastes is repeated in both volumes, and that the page size, text space, and style of script are different in each volume, is further proof that they were executed independently.
The first volume of the *Maḥzor* is one of the earliest dated, illuminated *maḥzorim* from southern Germany. Associated with the colored initial words and panels are many text illustrations for the special Sabbaths, Passover, and Shavuot (fols. 39v, 57, 59, 69v, 72v, 86v, 95v–97v, 131, 133, 151, 169, 170v). The volume is not bound correctly, and some of the illustrations are out of order.
Although it is crude, the illumination of the *Worms Maḥzor* resembles south German Latin miniatures of the second half of the 13th century in style, motifs, and colors. Another link with the south German school is the animals, birds, and distorted heads of human figures—a motif common in other Hebrew illuminated manuscripts of the same provenance, such as the *Ambrosian Bible* of 1236 (see description to pl. 25). A pen drawing, depicting the story of Ruth, was added in the 15th century as an initial-word panel for the second day of Shavuot (fol. 35). The first volume contains a colophon (fol. 34v), which is placed at the end of the biblical passages for the Ninth of Av (Job; Jer. up to 33:6, and Isa. 34–35), probably originally at the end of the manuscript. The colophon states that the scribe, Simḥah b. Judah, wrote the *maḥzor* for his uncle R. Baruch b. Isaac and completed it on January 1, 1272, and that it was specifically written for the use of a *ḥazzan*. Most of the text of the manuscript is written by the same hand, and there are two other colophons mentioning the scribe's name—one at the end of the prayer for Passover (fol. 146v) and one at the end of Shavuot (fol. 197). On fol. 133, next to the word *ve-soferai* ("and my scribes"), there is the picture of a man lifting a book on which three names are inscribed: "Simḥah ha-Sofer" (the scribe of the manuscript), "Judah, the scribe of *Nurnbrk* [i.e., Nuremberg]" (the scribe's father), and "Shemaiah ha-Ẓarefati" ("the Frenchman"), who may have been the artist.

VOLUME I, FOLIO 39V

The illustration for *Parashat Shekalim* (Ex. 30:11–16), or the first of the four special Sabbaths preceding the Passover festival, depicts a man holding a balance—weighing the shekels for the payment in the Temple—and two savage beasts. The scales are symbolic of the weighing of the souls on the last day of Judgment, and the wild beasts stand for Satan attempting to tip the scales in his favor. Within the large ligature *El* ("God"), the owner has inscribed his name: "Mine, Baruch bar Isaac."

JERUSALEM, JEWISH NATIONAL AND UNIVERSITY LIBRARY, MS. HEB. 4°781/1 (Also HEB. 4°781/2)

SPECIFICATIONS: Vellum, 1 + 226 + 1 leaves, $15\frac{3}{8} \times 12\frac{1}{4}$ ins (39 × 31 cm.).

COLOPHON: Vol. 1, fol. 34v: "I, Simḥah bar Judah ha-Sofer, wrote [it] in 1272 for my uncle, Rabbi Baruch bar Isaac, in 44 weeks, from the beginning to the end of the *ḥazzan's* prayer, and completed it with the help of God, on the 28th of Tevet, 5032" (Jan. 1, 1272). Other colophons (fols. 146v and 197). Fol. 133: Scribe and Artist's colophon—"Simḥah ha-Sofer, Judah ha-Sofer of *Nurnbrk*, Shemaiah ha-Ẓarefati."

PROVENANCE: In the Jewish community of Worms, from 1578. On several pages (especially on fols. 38v–39, 226v) are inscriptions and signatures of cantors who used the *maḥzor* in Worms.
During the "Kristallnacht" (Nov. 9, 1938), when the Nazis burned the Worms Synagogue, the manuscript was transferred, together with the community's archives, to the Princes' Castle in Darmstadt. It was brought to the Worms Cathedral tower in 1943 by the Director of the Cultural Institute of Worms, Dr. F. M. Illert.
In November 1956, after a series of legal claims, the State of Israel was awarded ownership. Both volumes of the *Worms Maḥzor* reached the Jewish National and University Library in Jerusalem in March 1957.

מתנשא
לכל לראש בחר באום דלת ראש׳ כביכורה כתאינה בראש׳ כיטוה
אותה דרוש מכל אום לפרוש׳ לנשאה על כל ראש׳ גועלה תשית
למנוד ראש׳ והיא תרים ראש׳ בכסא כבוד מראש״

PLATE 27

Laud Maḥzor

Maḥzor of German rite for the entire year
Southern Germany, c. 1290

This is another of the large-format *maḥzorim* from southern Germany, characterized by bird and animal heads or blank faces attached to human figures. In place of the more common two volumes, this *maḥzor* is bound in only one, with some pages in the wrong order. The system of decoration is the usual one, with initial-word panels sometimes surrounding an entire page and in other cases attached to text illustrations. In the *Laud Maḥzor* there are 19 text illustrations, most of which illustrate the traditional scenes at the openings of the prayers for the important feasts. In this category are the tree on which the 10 sons of Haman are hanging (fol. 51), the red heifer (Num. 19, fol. 53), the 12 signs of the zodiac in the prayer for dew (fols. 89–91), the sacrifice of Isaac for the prayer on the second day of the New Year (fol. 184), and the circumcision of Isaac as an illustration for the last prayer of the Day of Atonement (fol. 303). Of the more unusual illustrations are King Ahasuerus extending his scepter to Esther (fol. 48v), a second set of the signs of the zodiac for the prayer for rain (fols. 324–326v), and the large panel for Shavuot illustrating a *piyyut* concerning the Torah (fol. 127v), which is reproduced here. On this page, the transmission of the Tablets of the Law by an angel is depicted without Moses. The Israelites kneeling on the right are receiving a scroll of the Torah, rather than the conventional two tablets. Within the arch, next to a stone altar on which a sacrificial ram lies, Moses is seen carrying two bowls, from one of which he is sprinkling blood onto the Israelites (Ex. 24:8). In the lower margin the baking of *maẓẓah* for sacrificial use is depicted (Lev. 2:5,7; 6:7–10; 7:9).

The distortion of human faces in the *Laud Maḥzor* is accomplished mainly by the application of dragon or dog-like heads which are similar to the heads of the dragons on both sides of the text reproduced here. Other types of distortion, however, are also used in the manuscript, such as the blank-faced angel on the left, the bird- and fox-like heads on the right, or the sharp-beaked nose of Moses and the *maẓẓah* baker. The human faces of the Israelites, on whom the blood is being sprinkled, were probably added later by a different artist and in a darker ink. All these types of distortion occur in the other illustrations throughout the manuscript.

The soft, light drapery and the gothic sway of the human figures is typical of southwest German illumination at the end of the 13th century. The dark green used by the artist, like the other colors, was very common in south German ateliers in the last decade of the 13th century.

FOLIO 127V

A full-page panel for Shavuot illustrating—in the top portion of an arched page—the giving of the Torah to the Israelites in the form of a Scroll of the Law. Within the arch Moses is sprinkling the Israelites with the blood of the Covenant (Ex. 24:8), and below it the baking of the *maẓẓah* is depicted.

OXFORD, BODLEIAN LIBRARY, MS. LAUD OR. 321

SPECIFICATIONS: Thick vellum, 362 leaves (seven folios missing—new foliation of August 4, 1962, different from that of Neubauer), 17½ × 12¼ ins (44½ × 31 cm.). Written in a square Ashkenazi hand. The biblical parts—30 lines in 3 columns; the *maḥzor*—29 lines per page (excluding fols. 62–71v, 80, 80v, 164–165, 360–362, all of which were added in a later Ashkenazi hand with 30–40 lines per page). Four fully-arcaded and illustrated pages (fols. 38v, 127v, 248v, 308). Twenty-two colored initial-word panels, 15 of which have illustrations alongside. Some marginal illustrations, including the hanging of Haman (fol 51), a lamb (fol. 128), two sets of the signs of the zodiac (fols. 89–91, 324–326v), and some musical notes for the blowing of the *shofar* (fols. 194v, 196v, 199v).

PROVENANCE: Notes in many additional text pages written in various Ashkenazi hands of the 14th and 15th centuries. Fol. 1v: The signature of Archbishop Laud (1636), who presented the manuscript to the Bodleian Library in November 1641.

אמנני
איגלו שבנני
ארם הקנני
יי׳ קנני
בגנז בערכי
כי עץ ינרכי
בשעשועי ברכי
ראשית דרכי

PLATE 28

Birds' Head Haggadah

Haggadah of German rite
Southern Germany, c. 1300

The earliest surviving illuminated German *Haggadah*, the *Birds' Head Haggadah*, displays the characteristics which now serve to identify the entire system of illustration of Ashkenazi *Haggadot*. It contains biblical, ritual, and eschatological, illustrations. Most illustrations are painted in the margins, there are only two full-page miniatures, one in the beginning and one at the end of the manuscript (fols. 1v and 47). The illustrations are not arranged in chronological order, but rather according to the text of the *Haggadah*. The illustrations of the biblical story start with seven persons entering Egypt, symbolizing the 70 souls who came down to Egypt (Ex. 1:5) (fol. 12); and continue with the labor of the Israelites (fol. 15); their cry unto the Lord (fol. 15v); the slaughter of the paschal lamb (fol. 21); the carrying of the dough for the *mazzah* (fol. 25); the crossing of the Red Sea (fol. 21v); the pursuing Egyptians (fol. 24v); Moses receiving and handing down the Tablets of the Law (fol. 23); and the manna and quails falling from heaven (fol. 22v).

The ritual illustrations begin with a damaged full-page miniature (fol. 1v) depicting a family seated at a Passover table. Other ritual illustrations accompany the various benedictions for wine (fols. 2v, 26v, 28, 30, 34, 39v, 46v), light (fol. 5v), the washing of hands (fols. 6, 28, 29v), and the eating of the different herbs (fols. 6v, 29); a man reclining (fol. 8); a man eating a *mazzah* (fol. 28v); the hiding of the *afikoman* (fol. 6v); a child giving the *afikoman* back to his father (fol. 29v); and a *ḥazzan* reading from a pulpit (fols. 32v, 33v, 38v, 40). Part of the ritual illustrations are the preparations for Passover, such as the pounding of *ḥaroset*, and the making, pricking, and baking of *mazzah* (fols. 25v, 26).

The eschatological illustrations include the sacrifice of Isaac, referring to the covenant between God and the Patriarchs (fol. 15v). An illustration of the Righteous entering Paradise (fol. 33) refers to the personal hope for life after death. The most important eschatological illustration is the last full-page miniature, depicting the heavenly Jerusalem adored by four Jews (fol. 47), illustrating the last passage of the *Haggadah*: "Next year in Jerusalem."

Most of the human figures have pronounced birds' heads, although other methods of distorting human heads are used, such as blank faces, heads covered by helmets, and a servant with a bulbous nose.

The scribe, Menahem, decorated the letters of his name in the textual word *MuNaḤiM* (fol. 11), by dotting the consonants which spell his name. The same scribe wrote and indicated his name similarly in the same word in the *Leipzig Maḥzor* (Leipzig Univ. Library, MS. V. 1102, fols. 113 and 137). In the absence of any colophon here, this may indicate that the *Birds' Head Haggadah* was written around 1300, the time at which the *Leipzig Maḥzor* was written.

FOLIOS 22V–23

A double page illustrating the hymn "*Dayyeinu.*" On the right, the manna and quails are falling from heaven. On the left, Moses is receiving two Tablets of the Law while passing on five (an allusion to the five books of the Pentateuch).

JERUSALEM, ISRAEL MUSEUM, MS. 180/57.

SPECIFICATIONS: Vellum, 47 leaves (two leaves missing after fols. 27v and 31v), $10\frac{5}{8} \times 7\frac{1}{8}$ins (27 × 18.5 cm.). Written in square Ashkenazi script, generally 12 lines per page. Two full-page miniatures (fols. 1v and 47); initial-word panels to main sections of the manuscript, many marginal text illustrations.

PROVENANCE: Fol. 11: The name Menahem is indicated by marking the consonants which constitute the Hebrew word *MuNaḤiM* in the text. Owners' signatures were found on folio 1 before it was pasted on the modern parchment binding: "This book of redemption belongs to Samson Bibatz," and "1864/13/6 von Wb Hern Maiern das abgekauft Bendet Benedikt." The manuscript belonged to the Benedikt family in the 19th century, until Dr. Ludwig Marum of Karlsruhe acquired it when he married Johanna Benedikt. After his death in the Kisslau concentration camp in 1934, the *Haggadah* came into the possession of Mr. Herman Kahn, who sold it to the Bezalel National Museum in 1946.

ולא שקע צרינו
בתוכו דיינו
אילו שקע צרינו
בתוכו
ולא ספק צרכינו במדבר
ארבעים שנה דיינו
אילו ספק צרכינו במדבר
ארבעים שנה
ולא האכילנו
את המן דיינו
אילו האכילנו
את המן

ולא נתן לנו
את השבת דיינו
אילו נתן לנו
את השבת
ולא קרבנו לפני
הר סיני דיינו
אילו קרבנו לפני
הר סיני
ולא נתן לנו
את התורה דיינו
אילו נתן לנו
את התורה

PLATE 29

Regensburg Pentateuch

Pentateuch, five *Megillot* and *haftarot*, also containing Job, and the "passages of doom" in Jeremiah (2:29–8:12; 9:24–10:16)
Germany, Bavaria (Regensburg?), c. 1300

Although the text of the manuscript is to be found in any ordinary Ashkenazi Pentateuch containing *Megillot* and *haftarot*, the illustrations of this manuscript are uncommon. The six full-page miniatures of the manuscript are divided into several sections and depict biblical and midrashic scenes. Among them are the circumcision and sacrifice of Isaac, together with the midrashic scene of the temptation of Sarah by the devil (fol. 18v); Moses receiving the Tablets of the Law (fol. 154v); an array of the implements of the Tabernacle, influenced by the full-page arrangements of the Spanish Bibles with the addition of the figure of Aaron kindling the *menorah* (fols. 155v–156); Esther in front of Ahasuerus; the hanging of Haman and his ten sons, and Mordecai on horseback (fol. 157); and Job on the dung heap confronted by his friends (fol. 225v). Only the last miniature is part of a full-page initial-word panel. Other decorations in the manuscript contain small initial-word panels in gold and colors, which head all Pentateuch *parashot*, *Megillot*, and *haftarot*. There is one large panel at the beginning of the book of Esther (fol. 158). The masorah magna is sometimes written in geometric and floral forms in micrography. The catch-words of quires have animals and dragons.

The style of the illumination is influenced by northern French manuscripts of the 13th century in composition, gestures, and stocky figures; but the lively colors point to its southern German origin. The feature of animal-headed people, which was common in southern German Hebrew illumination of the period, hardly appears here. The long noses of some of the figures seem to result from the fact that most of the human figures are painted in profile. Only one angel, in the sacrifice of Isaac, appears to have a bird's head, probably to illustrate the idea that animal heads should be applied to the heavenly creatures.

There is no colophon in the manuscript, but it is inferred that the name David b. Shabbetai, which appears in the acrostic of a poem following the end of Deuteronomy (fol. 152), indicates the scribe. According to an inscription at the end of the manuscript (fol. 245), the masorete and punctuator was Jacob b. Meir who executed it for his teacher, R. Gad b. Peter ha-Levi of Regensburg, the *parnas* ("head of the community"). On folio 158, before the book of Esther, there is a short masoretic treatise in which is mentioned a R. Elijah the Elder, who was the great grandfather of the scribe's mother. Ernst Roth suggests that, if the scribe is referring to R. Elijah b. Judah of Paris of the 12th century, the manuscript was written around 1300. The style of the miniatures confirms this date. A certain Gadel of Regensburg is mentioned in a document, along with two other Jews, as having made a loan to the Bishop of Regensburg.

FOLIO 154V

A full-page miniature showing Moses receiving the Tablets of the Law inscribed with the initial words of the Ten Commandments and passing them on to the Israelites, who are standing enclosed in the fiery mountain. The scene may allude to a midrashic exposition of this episode which states that God enclosed the Israelites within Mount Sinai, as under an overturned tub, until they agreed to accept the Law.

JERUSALEM, ISRAEL MUSEUM, MS. 180/52

SPECIFICATIONS: Vellum, 246 leaves, $9\frac{3}{4} \times 7\frac{3}{8}$ ins (24.5×18.5 cm.). Written in square and cursive Ashkenazi script, 30 lines per page (book of Esther in 20 lines). Masora magna in smaller script two lines at top and three at the bottom of the page. Six full-page miniatures, on fols. 18v, 154v, 155v, 156, 157, 225v. Small initial-word panels to all books and *parashot* headings. Eighteenth-century brown leather binding on wooden boards, blind-tooled in geometric interlacings, with two leather straps and metal clasps. Binding renewed in 1925.

PROVENANCE: Fol. 245: 15th-century signature of "Uri Shraga Feibush bar Israel." Fol. 156v: Mention of a loan given to David, the father-in-law of the widow Zichelnof Nikolsburg, for which the book was used as collateral (16th-century script). Fol. 167: a list of births from the years 1546 to 1562. Fol. IV: Notation of two different owners—Aaron b. Israel of Dresnitz (16th century) and a member of the community of Cracow (1601). Transferred to the Bezalel National Art Museum, 1963.

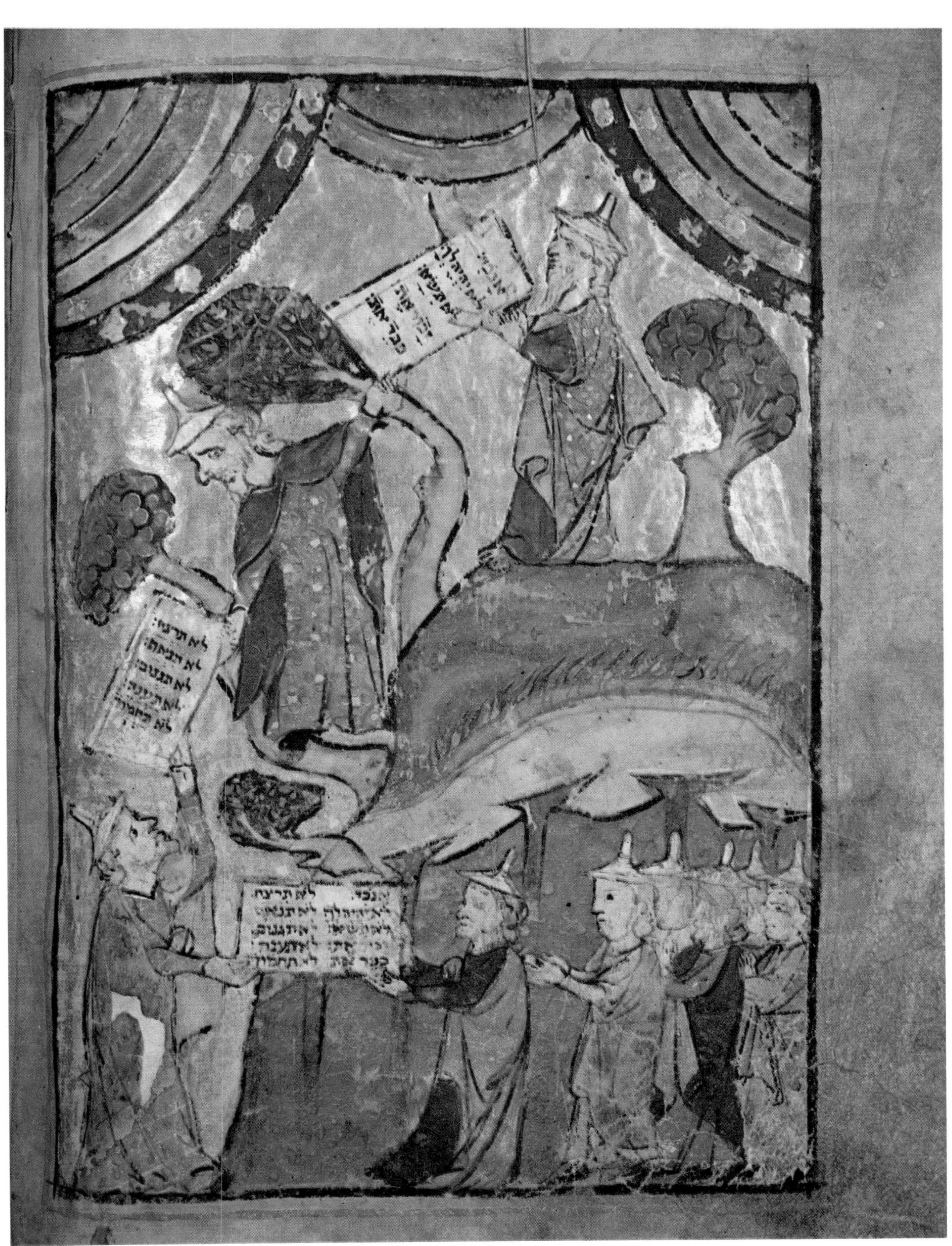

אנכי לא תרצח
לא תנאף
לא תשא לא תגנב
לא תענה
כבד את לא תחמוד

PLATE 30

Kaufmann Mishneh Torah

Maimonides' *Mishneh Torah*
Cologne, 1295–96

This four-volume, giant manuscript is one of the most beautiful manuscripts of its kind. Both in script and illumination, it represents the zenith of Hebrew illumination in Germany at the end of the 13th century. The opening pages of each of the 14 books into which the treatise is divided and its general introduction are delicately framed by foliage scrolls and headed by a large, painted initial-word panel. At the bottom of some of the pages are marginal illustrations; some of them are biblical, though none illustrates the text. The most significant biblical illustrations are: Samson rending the lion (Book VI, vol. 2, fol. 90); David and Goliath (Book VII, vol. 2, fol. 118); David playing the harp (Book VIII, vol. 3, fol. 1); the sacrifice of Isaac (Book X, vol. 3, fol. 81); Moses passing the Tablets of the Law to the Israelites, who are enclosed within a mountain (Book XII, vol. 4, fol. 32); and Adam and Eve flanking the tree of knowledge (Book XIII, vol. 4, fol. 70). Most of the nonbiblical illustrations are of jousting and hunting scenes (e.g., vol. 1, fols. 2, 16v, 46v, 83; vol. II, fol. 1).

The most delicate German-gothic illumination of the Middle Rhine is displayed in the style of this manuscript. The thin scrolls—with grotesques, dragons, animals, and birds—the elegant gothic sway of the figures, the soft drapery, and the delicate facial features are but a few characteristics of this style. It is closely related to the French-gothic illumination of that period, though it has a peculiary German element in it.

According to the colophon (vol. 4, fol. 153), the manuscript was written by Nathan b. Simeon ha-Levi for his brother-in-law R. Abraham b. Berechiah. It was begun in 1295 and completed 16 months later, in 1296. On folio 169v of vol. IV, there is an inscription of 1413 by Ephraim b. Uri ha-Levi Gumprecht ha-Levi on "Sunday, 2nd of Nisan," when the corrections and explanations were completed in Cologne. According to this evidence and the style, it is possible that the manuscript was written and illuminated in Cologne.

VOLUME I, FOLIO 118

Opening page of Book VII of the *Mishneh Torah*. A title panel with foliage scrolls surrounds the table of contents of this book. In the lower margin is an illustration of the battle between David and Goliath.

BUDAPEST, LIBRARY OF THE HUNGARIAN ACADEMY OF SCIENCES, KAUFMANN COLLECTION, MS. A77/I–VI

SPECIFICATIONS: Vellum, four volumes, 320, 338, 308, and 338 leaves, $19\frac{3}{4} \times 13\frac{3}{4}$ ins (50 × 35 cm.). Written in square and cursive Ashkenazi script, 21–30 lines to the page. Fifteen fully decorated opening pages to the 14 books and the introduction: vol. 1, fols. 2, 16v, 46v, 83; vol. 2, fols. 1, 48, 90, 118; vol. 3, fols. 1, 57, 81; vol. 4, fols. 1, 32, 70, 108.

COLOPHON: Vol. 4, fol. 143: "I, Nathan bar Simeon ha-Levi, wrote this book for Rabbi Abraham ben Rabbi Berechiah, my brother-in-law, and started in 5055 on Thursday 9th of Iyyar [April 26, 1295] and completed it on the 8th Elul 5056" (August 8, 1296).

PROVENANCE: Vol. 4, fol. 169v: "The corrections and explanations . . . completed here in Cologne by Ephraim bar Uri ha-Levi Gumprecht ha-Levi on Sunday, 2nd of Nisan, 173 A.C." (March 5, 1413).

Vol. 1, fol. 1: Sale contracts from Italy of 1482–1520. The manuscript was acquired by David Kaufmann from the Trieste Collection at Padua and after Kaufmann's death passed to the Hungarian Academy of Sciences in Budapest.

בשם יי׳ א׳ עולם

תהי נא ידך לעזרני כי פקודיך בחרתי

ספר זרעים

והוא ספר זרעים
הלכותיו שבע וזהו סדורן
הלכות כלאים
הלכות מתנות עניים
הלכות תרומות
הלכות מעשרות
הלכות מעשר שני ונטע רבעי
הלכות בכורים ושאר מתנות כהונה
הלכות שמטה ויובל

הלכות כלאים

יש
בכללן חמש מצות לא תעשה
וזהו פרטן
א שלא לזרוע כלאי זרעים
ב שלא לזרוע תבואה או ירק בכרם
ג שלא להרביע בהמה כלאים
ד שלא לעשות מלאכה בכלאי בהמה
ה שלא ללבוש כלאים

הלכות מתנות עניים

יש בכללן שלש עשרה מצות ש׳
שבע מצות עשה ושש מצות
לא תעשה וזהו פרטן
א להניח פאה
ב שלא יכלה את הפאה
ג להניח לקט
ד שלא ילקט לקט
ה לעזוב עוללות בכרם
ו שלא יעולל הכרם
ז לעזוב פרט הכרם
ח שלא ילקט פרט הכרם
ט להניח השכחה
י שלא ישוב לקחת השכחה
יא להפריש מעשר לעניים
יב ליתן צדקה כמסת יד
יג שלא יאמץ לבבו על העני

הלכות תרומות

יש
בכללן שמנה מצות שתים מצות
עשה ושש מצות לא תעשה
וזהו פרטן
א להפריש תרומה גדולה
ב להפריש תרומת מעשר
ג שלא יקדים תרומות ומעשרות
זה לזה אלא יפריש על הסדר
ד שלא יאכל זר תרומה
ה שלא יאכל אפילו תושב כהן או
שכירו תרומה
ו שלא יאכל ערל תרומה
ז שלא יאכל כהן טמא תרומה
ח שלא תאכל חללה תרומה ולא מורם
מן הקדשים

הלכות מעשרות

מצות
עשה אחת והיא להפריש מ׳
מעשר ראשון בכל שנה ושנה מן
משני הזריעה ולתנו ללוים

הלכות מעשר שני ונטע רבעי

יש
בכללן תשע מצות שלש מצות עש׳
ושש מצות לא תעשה וזהו פרטן
א להפריש מעשר שני
ב שלא להוציא דמיו בשאר צרכי
אדם חוץ מאוכלה ושתיה וסיכה

PLATE 31

Schocken Bible

Bible with masorah magna and parva
Southern Germany, c. 1300

This Bible is small and thin compared with the large German Bibles such as the *Ambrosian Bible* (see plate 25). It was written by a scribe called Ḥayyim ("life") who decorated his name whenever it appeared in the biblical text, and sometimes attached the phrase *Ḥayyim Ḥazak* "Ḥayyim, be strong" at the end of books of the Bible. The manuscripts of plates 32, 33, and 34 were produced in his workshop and signed by him.

The illumination of the *Schocken Bible* consists of 35 initial-word panels, one at the opening of each book of the Bible; the opening to Genesis is a full-page illumination (fol. 1v–reproduced here).

This page serves as a frontispiece to the manuscript and is composed of 46 medallions arranged symmetrically around the initial-word panel. Within the roundels are biblical illustrations, the subjects of which are arranged chronologically from right to left and top to bottom, covering the entire Pentateuch—beginning with Adam and Eve and ending with Balaam and the angel. These roundels resemble arrangements in stained glass church windows of the 13th century. There is evidence that such stained glass also existed in synagogues in the southern part of Germany. The iconography of the pictures, however, could be either Jewish or Christian. The style of the figures is that of southwestern Germany, and the decoration in the background of the panels—dragons, grotesques intertwined with foliage scrolls and open composite flowers seen from above—is typical of German illumination around Lake Constance, c. 1300.

The bright elementary colors of blue, white, and red are also characteristic of southern Germany, though the styling and coloring considered together are definitely influenced by the east French school of illumination.

FOLIO 1V

The 46 roundels should be read from right to left, top to bottom. First row: Adam and Eve and the serpent; expulsion from Paradise; Cain kills Abel; Noah's ark resting on Mount Ararat; Noah pruning his vine; the tower of Babel. Second row: the destruction of Sodom and Gomorrah; sacrifice of Isaac; Isaac blesses Jacob; Esau returns from his hunt; Jacob's dream; Jacob wrestles with the angel. Third row: Joseph's first dream; Joseph's second dream; Joseph meets an angel; Joseph's brothers tending their flocks; Joseph stripped of his coat; the caravan of Ishmaelites who bought Joseph. Fourth row: Joseph and Potiphar's wife; the baker's and the butler's dream. Fifth row: Joseph interpreting the baker's and the butler's dream; Pharaoh's dream of seven cows. Sixth row: Joseph interprets Pharaoh's dream; Joseph as Pharaoh's viceroy; Joseph and his brothers; Joseph's brothers return to Canaan; Benjamin departs from Jacob; Benjamin and his brothers before Joseph. Seventh row: Judah and Benjamin before Joseph; Joseph reveals himself to his brothers; Jacob and Joseph before Pharaoh; the Israelites receive the land of Goshen; the labor of the Israelites; Pharaoh's daughter stretches her arm to the infant Moses among the reeds. Eighth row: Pharaoh's daughter gives Moses to his mother Jocheved; an angel appears in the burning bush; Moses approaches the burning bush with his flocks; Moses and Aaron before Pharaoh; the Israelites leave Egypt; Moses parts the Red Sea. Ninth row: the Egyptians drown; Miriam and the women of Israel play, sing, and dance; Moses receives the Torah; the spies carry the bunch of grapes; Korah and his company are swallowed by the mouth of hell; Balaam, the angel, and the she-ass.

JERUSALEM, SCHOCKEN LIBRARY, MS. 14840

SPECIFICATIONS: Fine uterine vellum, 4 + 274 + 4 leaves, $8\frac{3}{8} \times 6$ ins (22×15 cm.). Written in square Ashkenazi script, 50 lines in two columns. One full-page miniature (fol. 1v) and 34 initial-word panels.

בראשית

PLATE 32

Duke of Sussex Pentateuch

Pentateuch, with Targum, *Megillot*, *haftarot*, masorah magna and parva
Southern Germany, c. 1300

This Pentateuch is one of the fine-vellum manuscripts derived from the south German workshop of a scribe named Ḥayyim. At the beginning of each of the five books of the Pentateuch is a large initial-word panel surrounded by a full-page decoration. Most of the panels are merely decorated with grotesques and dragons, and only two are text illustrations. The opening of the book of Numbers has a picture of the four leading tribes of Israel as they camped around the Tabernacle (fol. 179v), and the book of Ecclesiastes portrays David playing the harp (fol. 302). Masorah magna written in varied-shaped micrography sometimes illustrates the text, as, e.g., a ram caught in a thicket next to the text of the sacrifice of Isaac (fol. 28).
The pronounced south German style resembles the manner of the artists of the *Aich Bible* of 1310 (Kremsmünster, Stiftsbibliothek, Cod. 351–354) in its strongly contrasted colors and exaggerated grotesque dragons and gestures. Although the faces of the human figures are somewhat strange, they are not as distorted as those drawn in the south German school. The manuscript was sold in 1469 in Italy and belonged to the Royal Hebraist, the Duke of Sussex (1773–1843), on whose death it was acquired by the British Museum.

FOLIO 179V
A full-page initial-word panel to the book of Numbers illustrates four knights holding the emblematic banners of the four leading tribes of Israel as they camped around the Tabernacle (Num. 2). The emblems are: a lion for the tribe of Judah (Gen. 49:9); an eagle for the tribe of Reuben (a Midrash on Gen. 49:3); a bull for Ephraim (Deut. 33:17); and a serpent for Dan (Gen. 49:17). The surrounding grotesque dragons are merely decorative.
LONDON, BRITISH MUSEUM, ADD. MS. 15282.

SPECIFICATIONS: Fine vellum, 360 leaves, 9 × 6⅜ ins (22.8 × 16.2 cm.). Written in square Ashkenazi script; 30 lines in 3 columns. Illuminated initial-word panels to the different books and some of the *haftarot*. Five full-page openings to the books of the Pentateuch (fols. 1v, 75v, 137, 179v, 238). Some micrographic masorah illustrations. Sixteenth-century gold-tooled Venetian leather binding.

COLOPHON: The name of the scribe, Ḥayyim, written at the end of the book of Esther (fol. 313v) and the end of *haftarot* (fol. 358).

PROVENANCE: Fol. 358v: Sale inscription, "The Pentateuch was sold to Rabbi Jeḥiel bar Uri by Jacob bar Mordecai on Wednesday, 28th of Iyyar, 5229" (May 10, 1469). The Duke of Sussex Collection. Purchased from his estate by the British Museum in 1844.

וידבר

PLATE 33

Tripartite Maḥzor (Vol. I)

Maḥzor of German rite, for special Sabbaths, Purim, Passover, with Song of Songs and commentary.
South Germany, c. 1320

The decoration of this *maḥzor* comprises 14 initial-word panels for the beginning of prayers, and five pages with roundels containing the signs of the zodiac and the occupations of the month, illustrating the prayer for dew at the feast of Tabernacles. Some of the initial-word panels contain text illustrations, although most of them are only decorative, with grotesques, dragons, and scrolls. Among the illustrative panels are a stag hunt, probably symbolizing the persecuted Jewish nation, in a panel for Ḥanukkah (fol. 18); two jousting knights with the coats of arms of Austria and Bavaria on their horses' housing (fol. 103v); and the judgment of Solomon, illustrating the Song of Songs (fol. 183). The jousting knights may allude to the battle between Ludwig of Bavaria and Frederick the Fair of Austria, at Muhldorf on Sept. 28, 1322, in southern Germany. The style of the manuscript also points to the south of Germany around the first quarter of the 14th century. The bright, strong colors, the large trees, the gesturing dragons are close to the illumination in the *Aich Bible* of 1310 (see description to pl. 32). The soft modeling of the drapery and the facial expressions are closer to the illumination of the *Gradual of St. Katharinental* (1312), in the Zurich Landesmuseum.

The prayers for the feasts of Shavuot, Sukkot, the New Year, and Day of Atonement are lacking. Two other manuscripts supply the missing parts of the text and have similar illumination. One is in the British Museum (Add. ms. 22413), and the other in the Bodleian Library, Oxford (ms. Mich. 619). All three manuscripts once formed a complete *maḥzor*. It seems that the *Tripartite Maḥzor* may have started with the prayers for New Year, and ended with the feast of Shavuot.

Although the three volumes of the *Tripartite Maḥzor* are not exactly the same size (Budapest ms. A384 measures 31 × 21.5 cm.; BM Add. ms. 22413 measures 31.5 × 22 cm.; and the Bodl. ms. Mich. 619 measures 34 × 24.5 cm.), all of the text areas, including the prayers and the commentary, measure 20 × 15.5 cm.

The fact that R. Meir of Rothenburg (d. 1293) is mentioned in all three manuscripts as the teacher of the original scribe, who included his teacher's personal *piyyutim*, gives a *terminus a quo*.

The decoration in all three manuscripts is the same, with large initial-word panels framed by narrow bands and decorated with similar grotesques or with large flowering trees in the middle of the panel, and all are related to the south German school of illumination. Another element common to all three manuscripts is the manner in which the distortion of human faces is accomplished. All women in the manuscripts have bird and animal heads, while men usually have normal heads, although in some cases, they too are painted with distortions. For instance, King Solomon reproduced here (pl. 33) is given a human head, although the facial features are faint, while the two pleading women next to the initial word have dogs' heads. In the page reproduced from the British Museum volume (pl. 34), Moses, Aaron, and their companions have human heads, while the women behind them are painted with animal heads.

FOLIO 183
An initial-word panel for the Song of Songs, depicting the judgment of Solomon. On the right is King Solomon on his legendary throne with the animals and birds which carried him up to the throne.

BUDAPEST, LIBRARY OF THE HUNGARIAN ACADEMY OF SCIENCES, KAUFMANN COLLECTION, MS. A384

SPECIFICATIONS: Vellum, 251 leaves, $12\frac{1}{4} \times 8\frac{1}{2}$ ins (31 × 21.5 cm.). Written in square Ashkenazi script, 26 lines to the page for the main text, and smaller cursive script in many more lines in the three outer borders. Large initial-word panels to the main divisions (fols. 18, 34, 49, 61v, 63, 68, 73, 75v, 103v, 115v, 120, 154, 174, 183, 197, 228), and medallions of the signs of the zodiac and occupations of the month in the prayer for dew (fols. 142v, 145v), sometimes illustrate the text. The commentary, written horizontally, is sometimes in geometrical, floral, or animal forms.

PROVENANCE: The owners' signatures on fol. 1 are hardly legible, with one exception; that of David Kaufmann, who bought the manuscript from N. Rabinowitz on Nov. 14, 1883.

השירים אשר לשלמה׃
ישקני מנשיקות פיהו
כי טובים דדיך מיין׃
לריח שמניך טובים
שמן תורק שמך על כן
עלמות אהבוך׃ משכני
אחריך נרוצה הביאני
המלך חדריו נגילה ונ׳
ונשמחה בך נזכירה דדיך
מיין מישרים אהבוך׃
שחורה אני ונאוה בנות
ירושלם כאהלי קדר
כיריעות שלמה׃ אל

PLATE 34

Tripartite Maḥzor (Vol. II)

Maḥzor of German rite for Shavuot and Sukkot, with commentary
Southern Germany, c. 1320

This is the second volume of the *Tripartite Maḥzor*, the first of which is described in plate 33. In this volume the scribe's name, Ḥayyim, appears after the book of Ruth (fol. 80v), relating the manuscript to others signed by the same scribe, such as the *Schocken Bible* (plate 31), the *Duke of Sussex Pentateuch* (plate 32), etc. This part of the *maḥzor* has seven illustrations, while the volume in the Bodleian Library (Mich. 619) has none, and that at Budapest (MS. A384) has four. The illustrations depict the giving of the Law, reproduced here (fol. 3); a deer hunt (fol. 49); the story of Ruth (fol. 71); a man carrying an *etrog*, *lulav*, etc. at the beginning of Sukkot; and a man carrying a water jug (fol. 148). The prayer for rain on the feast of Sukkot has medallions with signs of the zodiac incorporated within the marginal commentary (fols. 138–142v).
The manuscript is not as large as the fashionable *maḥzorim* of the 13th and 14th centuries. The fact that there are both human and animal heads together in one panel may mean that the original purpose of distorting the human figure was no longer understood by the artists of the 14th century, who saw it only as a decorative motif. The bright colors and the modeling of the garments and faces are of the upper-Rhenish school, as is the large tree and open flowers decorating the panel.

FOLIO 3
An initial-word panel for a *piyyut* of Shavuot, referring to the Torah, depicts Moses receiving the Tablets of the Law. The beardless Moses is kneeling on a hillside receiving the Tablets which are inscribed with the opening words of the Ten Commandments. Behind Moses stands the mitered Aaron, and the men and women of Israel.

BRITISH MUSEUM, ADD. MS. 22413

SPECIFICATIONS: Vellum, 167 leaves, $12\frac{1}{2} \times 8\frac{3}{8}$ ins (31.5 × 22 cm.). Written in square Ashkenazi script, 26 lines to the page for the main text and smaller cursive script in many more lines in the three outer borders. Large initial-word panels to the main divisions, sometimes illustrating the text (fols. 3, 49, 71, 85, 106, 131, 148), and medallions with the signs of the zodiac in the prayer for rain (fols. 138–142v). The commentary written horizontally, sometimes in geometrical, floral, and animal forms.

COLOPHON: Fol. 80v: "Ḥayyim *Ḥazak*," Fol. 103v: The word "Ḥayyim" is decorated.

PROVENANCE: Fol. 1: Owner's signature in Italian script, Jacob Daniel bar Abraham Ulmo. Fol. 167v: An obituary entry of 1572.

3

א מנני · א יצרו שכנני ·
א רם הקנני · יי קנני ·
ב נין בערכי · ב יעין ערכי ·
ב שעשועי ברכי · ראשית דרכי ·
ג שתי לרגליו · ג חתי בגליו ·
ג עטועי עליו · קדם מפעליו ·
ד תותי עולם · ד דרי להועלם ·
ד עת הנעלם · מאז מעולם ·
ה גיגי לארוש · ה מוקק לפרוש ·
ה נפלא לדרוש · נסכתי מראש ·
ו אחיה בעדין · ו שעשועי עדן ·
ו קדמוני במעדין · מקדמי ארץ ·

PLATE 35

Nuremberg Maḥzor

Maḥzor of German rite for the entire year, including the five *Megillot*, Pentateuch, *parashot*, and *haftarot*
Southern Germany, 1331

This manuscript falls within the tradition of the large-format illuminated *maḥzorim* that were fashionable in rich Jewish communities during the 13th and 14th centuries. All the different prayer openings are decorated by large initial-word panels—some within full-page, architectural frames— in which the main embellishments are medallions filled with grotesque animals. The decoration of this *maḥzor* does not include any text illustrations. There are red, green, and blue initial-words decorated with outline drawings for all of the prayers. The style of the decoration is very refined and points to the Upper or Middle Rhine as the place of origin. The foliage scrolls and architectural details are influenced by northern French illumination of the end of the 13th century. According to the colophon (fol. 528v), the manuscript was written in 1311. Although no place is given, it is known that the manuscript belonged to the Jewish community of Nuremberg up to the expulsion of the Jews from that city in 1499, at which time it was taken from the synagogue and transferred to the municipal library of Nuremberg (MS. Cent. IV 100). In 1804, soldiers of Napoleon's army cut 11 pages out of the manuscript, but their absence was discovered only in 1882. At the beginning of the 20th century, five loose pages came into the possession of Mayer Selig Goldschmidt of Frankfort, whose library is now at the Hechal Shelomo in Jerusalem. These five pages were transferred to Mr. Heinrich Eisemann of Frankfort (later London) when he married Alice Goldschmidt in 1918. In 1937, one page was given to S.Z. Schocken as a gift on his 60th birthday and in 1938 he acquired three more pages. The fifth page is now in the collection of Mr. Eisemann's son-in-law, Mr. Ernst Bodenheimer of New York. In 1951, the entire *maḥzor* (less the seven missing pages) was transferred to the Schocken Library in Jerusalem.

FOLIO 78
A large, decorated initial-word panel for a *piyyut* of the first day of Passover.
JERUSALEM, SCHOCKEN LIBRARY, MS. 24 100

SPECIFICATIONS: Vellum, 521 leaves (the following 11 of the original 528 leaves were cut out of the manuscript: 37, 78, 80, 120, 154, 155, 364, 371, 422, 439, 447. Of these, five were found, and the following four are in the Schocken Library: 78, 120, 154, 364), $19\frac{3}{4} \times 14\frac{5}{8}$ ins (50 × 37 cm.). Written in square Ashkenazi script, 30 lines to the page, with the commentary in small cursive script, up to 105 lines in the upper, outer, and lower margins. 15th-century brown leather binding on wooden boards, blind-tooled with geometric interlacing.

COLOPHON: Fol. 528v: "I wrote this *maḥzor* for Rabbi Joshua bar Isaac and completed it on Thursday, the fourth of *Elul* in 5091 A.C." (August 8, 1331). Fol. 298: The name Mattaniah, which may be the scribe's name, is decorated within a *piyyut*. Fols. 139v and 143v: The name Matan is decorated on the folios.

PROVENANCE: In the Jewish community of Nuremberg until 1499. Fol. 1v. Stadtbibliothek, Nürnberg, MS. Cent. IV. Nr. 100. In 1880, 11 pages were cut out by soldiers of Napoleon's army. Mayer Selig Goldschmidt Collection, Frankfort (five detached leaves). In 1918, Heinrich Eisemann Collection (five detached leaves). In 1937, one page given to S. Z. Schocken. In 1938, S. Z. Schocken acquired three more pages. Ernst Bodenheimer, New York (one detached leaf). In 1951, the entire *maḥzor* was transferred to the Schocken Library, Jerusalem.

א דר ורשע מאושרים · ש ימוזר זה מוזבשרים ·
א הורנו ביררך בשרים · שיר השירים ·
א יילת איורי השוקות · ל יהלוה עיזה שוקורת ·
א סמיי שבע להשקות · ישקני מנשיקות ·
ב רוכי מעלמות משמנך · מ ושלי גנזבי מבמנך ·
ב יסמתב תמרוק כממנך · לריח שמניך ·
ב ני ביתר והוריך · ה נס חור סחריך ·
ב ית מריץ צחריך · משכני אחריך ·
ג אה ורב עניה · ה ורי מבנות נירה ·
ג ס בי רוה · שחורה אני ונאוה ·
ג חל בי מהוררת · ק רב רתו סחרחרת ·
ג הן קרורנית בחרת · אל תראוני שאני שחרחרת ·

PLATE 36

Parma Bible

Incomplete Bible, with masorah magna and parva
Franco-German, early 14th century

This two-volume manuscript is an example of the large Ashkenazi Bibles of the 13th and 14th centuries. The Bible is incomplete, beginning with Exodus, and has pages missing throughout. Its decoration consists of large, initial-word panels in the opening of most of the books of the Bible, sometimes extending to a full page. No text illustrations are attached to these panels, and the most common ornaments are foliage scrolls on different colored backgrounds supplemented by hunting scenes and grotesques. The initial-words of the *parashot* and *haftarot* are written in blue, black, and green ink. Some blue and red filigree work surrounds the initial-word panel, and sometimes the whole panel. The masorah magna is sometimes written in different grotesque shapes in micrography.

The style of the illumination, which is of Franco-German origin, was common in the Upper Rhine area in the first quarter of the 14th century. The artist shows a free, expressive hand in the very few, thinly-outlined drawings, colored in light wash colors.

The manuscript was written by Joseph the Scribe (fol. 161v), and punctuated by Meir ha-Nakdan ("the punctuator") (fols. 158–161). Whether or not these two scribes collaborated on the writing and punctuating of another manuscript, a Pentateuch (Parma MS. 3289) with *Megillot* and *haftarot*, of the same place and date, as has been suggested by Louisa Mortara Ottolenghi, is not clear, though in this manuscript too a certain Meir ha-Nakdan wrote his name in micrography, one character to a page (fols. 358–369).

VOLUME TWO, FOLIO 92V

An initial-word panel for the opening chapter of Isaiah, with a geometrical, checkered background to the initial word, and three arcades framing the three text columns. The entire page is framed in red and blue filigree work with masorah magna in micrography. A unicorn hunt is painted on the top of the page.

PARMA, BIBLIOTECA PALATINA, MS. 3287 (and MS. 3286)

SPECIFICATIONS: Vellum, one + 202 + 1 leaves, $19\frac{1}{2} \times 14\frac{3}{8}$ ins (49.6 × 36.5 cm.). Written in square Ashkenazi script, 26 lines in three columns. Four initial-word panels in the openings of some of the books (fols. 1, 46v, 92v, 131). Colored initial words in the *haftarot*. Masorah magna in the form of different human, animal, and floral motifs, with some in the shape of letters.

COLOPHON: Fol. 161v: Joseph the Scribe mentioned under the text, with no date or place. Fols. 158–161: The name Meir is written in micrography, one character to a page.

PROVENANCE: The manuscript was part of the De' Rossi Collection and passed to the Palatine Library along with the rest of this collection.

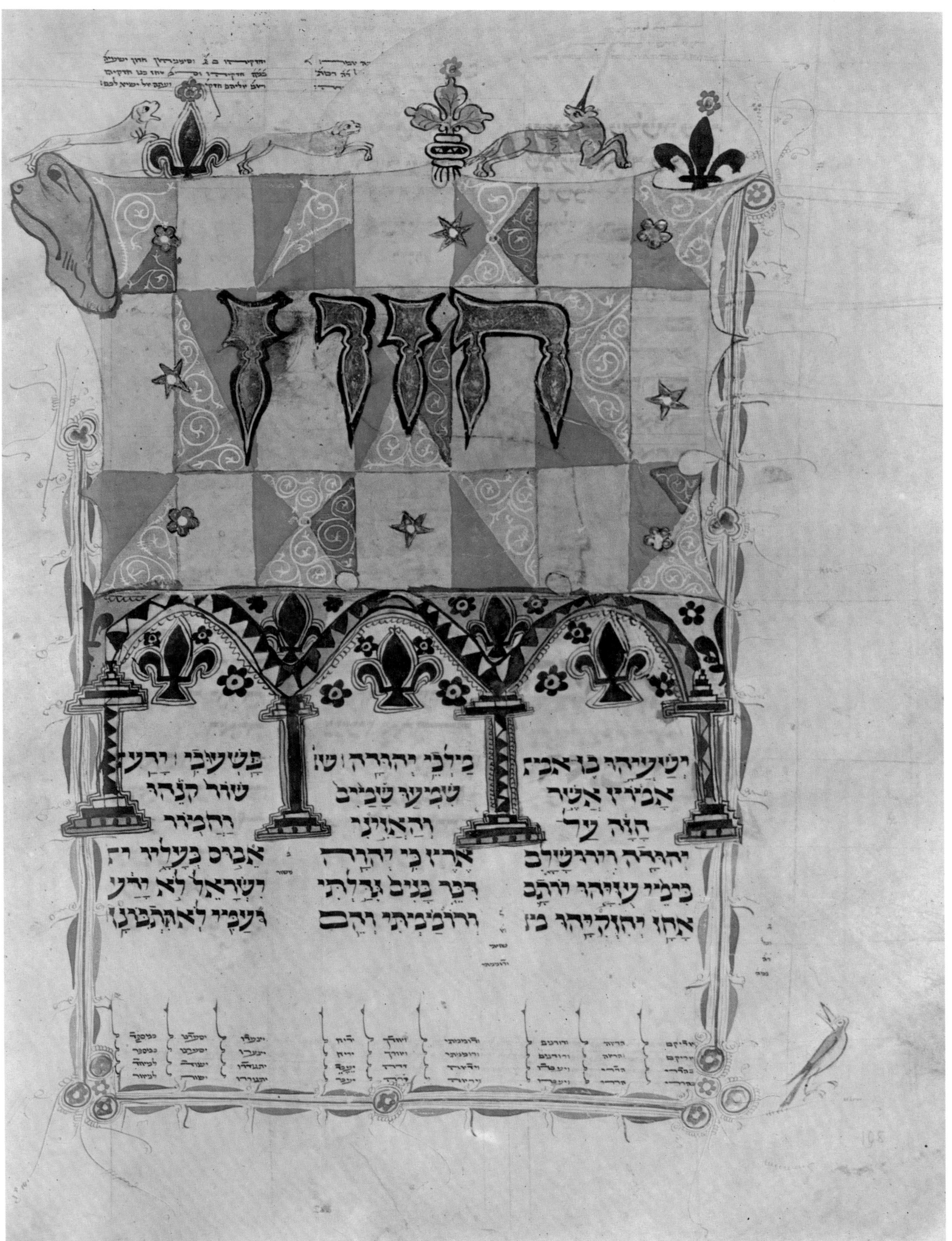

PLATE 37

Coburg Pentateuch

Pentateuch, *Megillot*, *haftarot*, and grammatical treatises by Jekuthiel b. Isaac Kohen ha-Nakdan, including *Ein ha-Kore*
Germany, Coburg, 1396

The grammatical material added to this manuscript makes it somewhat unusual, compared with other Ashkenazi Pentateuchs, which normally have only the *Megillot* and *haftarot* as additions. However, from the script and the colophons, it is clear that the entire manuscript was written by the same scribe, Simḥah b. Samuel ha-Levi in Coburg, between 1390 and 1396, although two *nakdanim* punctuated the manuscript. Samuel b. Abraham of Molerstadt punctuated the Pentateuch in Bamberg while Gershom b. Judah punctuated the *Megillot*, *haftarot* and grammatical treatises. From the inscription at the end of the manuscript (fol. 252), it appears that it was written for a certain Meir b. Obadiah called Leibertrot, who composed a poem incorporating his name and those of the three scribes in an acrostic.

The opening of each book and section in the manuscript has a decorated initial-word panel. Most of the decorations are floral, and there are some fluffy-feathered animals, dragons, and grotesques. Two of the initial-word panels are pen-drawn in brown ink. An entire panel (fol. 170) is covered in a ground of brown ink, in which a pattern of delicate scrolls has been left uncovered so that the impression is of brown and vellum-colored lace work, around a gold initial word. The panel is surrounded by a wide frame executed in the same technique, depicting hunting scenes in which some additional wash colors, mainly green and red, have been added to the figures. For the treatise on the masoretic annotations by Jekuthiel (fol. 190), the initial word, *Bereshit*, is decorated in the same technique, although of an earlier type, with dragons, angels, and grotesques. At the end of three of the books in the Pentateuch, there are illuminated panels illustrating teachers and a *ḥazzan*, incorporating mnemonic verses for the number of verses in each book. At the end of Exodus (fol. 54v), a man is shown sitting on a bench with a small chained dog holding a foliage scroll in his mouth, a dragon, and a lion at his feet. At the end of Leviticus (fol. 72v), a teacher and his pupil are shown (see below). At the end of Numbers (fol. 96), a *ḥazzan* is seen reading from an open scroll on a pulpit, on which is written the name of the punctuator.

Dragon and scroll illumination of this sort was prevalent in Germany at this time in both Latin and Hebrew manuscripts. The delicate colors and modeling are also characteristic of this area. The manuscript may have been illuminated in or near Coburg when it was copied (c. 1395). The technique of the sketchy brushwork decoration, with no apparent outline drawing, as can be seen in one panel (fol. 170), is somewhat unusual. The panel is reminiscent of the work of Joel b. Simeon in the second quarter of the 15th century. It may have been added to the manuscript at a later date.

FOLIO 72V

A miniature at the end of Leviticus showing a teacher admonishing his pupil with a whip. Hillel's maxim is written in the pupil's book: "Whatever is hateful unto thee, do it not unto thy fellow. [This is the whole Torah]; the rest is explanation." Behind the pupil hangs an hourglass.

LONDON, BRITISH MUSEUM, ADD. MS. 19776

SPECIFICATIONS: Vellum, 252 leaves, $11\frac{1}{2} \times 8\frac{1}{2}$ ins (29×21.5 cm.). Written in square Ashkenazi script, 32 lines in two columns. Three colored illustrative panels at the end of three books of the Pentateuch. Eight painted initial-word panels with floral and animal decoration, one with figurated frame. Four of the initial words of the *Megillot* are in ink, outlined with pen work, with space left around the word for the decoration.

COLOPHON: Fol. 252: Written for Meir b. Obadiah called Liebertrot by Simḥah b. Samuel ha-Levi, completed at Coburg in 5156 (1395). Fols. 96, 112v: Samuel b. Abraham of Molerstadt punctuated the Pentateuch. Fol. 252: Gershom b. Judah punctuated the *Megillot* and *haftarot* as well as the grammatical treatise.

PROVENANCE: Fol. 117: First owner, Meir, 1396. Fol. 252: Entries of the deaths of an owner's parents, 1535, 1538. Fol. 1: Owner's inscription: Alexander b. Solomon Zalman Kohen, 1750 (Metz?). Purchased in April 1854 by the British Museum from M. Aschkenazi (through D. Nutt).

ובהמה ומשדה אחזתו לא ימכר ולא יגאל כל חרם קדש קדשים הוא ליהוה׃ כל חרם אשר
יחרם מן האדם לא יפדה מות יומת׃ וכל מעשר הארץ מזרע הארץ מפרי העץ ליהוה
הוא קדש ליהוה׃ ואם גאל יגאל איש ממעשרו חמישתו יסף עליו׃ וכל מעשר בקר
וצאן כל אשר יעבר תחת השבט העשירי יהיה קדש ליהוה׃ לא יבקר בין טוב לרע ולא
ימירנו ואם המר ימירנו והיה הוא ותמורתו יהיה קדש לא יגאל׃ אלה המצות אשר
צוה יהוה את משה אל בני ישראל בהר סיני

חזק

סימן סכום פסוקי דסיפרא גנ״ט

PLATE 38

Erna Michael Haggadah

Haggadah of German rite, Passover rules with commentary on the text and rules
German, Middle Rhine, c. 1400

The *Erna Michael Haggadah* is the earliest of the 15th-century illuminated *Haggadot* of the south German school. Its decoration is a mixture of the old south German tradition intermingled with Italianate elements in drawing perspective and decorative motifs. The script and the style of the illumination point to a west German provenance. Typical of the illumination of the Rhineland area are the large, stylized, open flowers seen from above, floral scrolls, and dragons, as well as the architectural structures in the full-page illuminations. The human figures are executed in a primitive style. The use of well-drawn Hebrew script within the illustration (fol. 9v) implies that the artist was a Jew.

There are two full-page miniatures (fols. 40, 45) and one half-page miniature (fol. 10) illustrating the different stages of the Passover eve service, and many initial-word panels, including two initial-letter panels (fols. 40v, 65v). In several outer margins (fols. 6v, 7v, 8v, 11, 32v, 33, 34v), and in one wide border decoration (fol. 9v), there are text illustrations of people performing the Passover eve ritual. One person is shown holding a *mazzah* (fol. 32v) and another *maror* (fol. 33). In one margin (fol. 14) there is a sepia line-drawing of the "wise son" that was probably executed when the manuscript was copied, since the commentary is written around it. Many initial words, and some of the text, are written alternately in red, brown, and green ink. The initial-word panels are richly decorated with floral, geometrical, and foliage motifs, at times incorporating animals and grotesques. Four of the initial-word panels have extended foliage scrolls that frame the entire text of the page (fols. 10v, 11, 40v, 45v).

According to the script of the owners' inscriptions, the manuscript was in Ashkenazi hands during the 16th and 17th centuries, either in Germany or in Italy. It was seen in the house of Mme. Garsin (in Marseilles), in 1950, by the late Mordecai Narkiss. It was presented to the Israel Museum in 1966 by Mr. Jakob Michael of New York in memory of his wife, Erna.

FOLIO 40
The Passover eve table with seated men reading the *Haggadah*. A full-page miniature framed by architectural structure. A gold Sabbath oil-lamp hangs in the middle of the room.
JERUSALEM, ISRAEL MUSEUM, MS 180/58

SPECIFICATIONS: Vellum, 1 + 75 + 1 leaves, $13\frac{3}{4} \times 10\frac{1}{8}$ ins (35 × 25.5 cm.). Written in square Ashkenazi script, the main text in ten lines to the page. In smaller cursive script: Passover rules (fols. 1v-3), 35 lines in 2 columns; the commentary in the outer margins; and 38 lines on a separate page (fol. 39). Three full-page miniatures and gold-colored initial-word panels to the main divisions of the *Haggadah*. Ritual text illustrations in the margins of nine pages (fols. 6v, 7v, 8v, 9v, 11, 14, 32v, 33, 34). Eighteenth-century, brown leather binding in a poor state of repair.

PROVENANCE: On fol. 1: Birth of a daughter in 1570, and two owners—Moses bar Ephraim (1691) and Jacob bar Abraham Meshulam. Nissim—burned into the top cover. Mme. Garsin, Marseille, at least up to 1950. Presented to the Bezalel National Art Museum in 1966 by Mr. Jakob Michael, New York, in memory of his wife, Erna.

PLATE 39

Hamburg Miscellany

A miscellany of synagogal prayers for the whole year, *haftarot*, *Haggadah*, dirges, and prayers for such ceremonies as circumcision and marriage, and a calendar
Germany (Mainz?), about 1427

The *Hamburg Miscellany* is more than an ordinary *siddur*. This collection of liturgy, customs, and lamentations is a more personal selection that was probably made for a man of knowledge and taste. The illustrations in the manuscript were no doubt planned by the scribe, Isaac b. Simḥah Gansmann, who signed his name at the beginning of the calendar, which started with the year 1428. The scribe made room for the illustrations by leaving spaces within the text column wherever he deemed it appropriate. The illustrations in the manuscript appear both in the initial-word panels and as random, unframed miniatures. Even the conventional initial-word panels are miniatures with landscapes, and the initial-words are dwarfed by the illustrations. There are, however, more conventional initial-word panels and some initial-letter panels.

The book begins with an eschatological illustration of the Day of Judgment (fol. 1). In the left-hand corner a Jew is standing in prayer behind an angel who is guarding the gates of paradise. On the opposite side is an angel appearing from heaven holding the scales of judgment, which are being tipped by a hairy black devil. In the middle, occupying the main part of the miniature, is the sacrifice of Isaac—serving as a reminder to God of His covenant with the nation and His promise for their salvation..

All of the other illustrations are arranged in groups, but since the manuscript is incorrectly bound they seem to be scattered at random. The *Haggadah* (fols. 22v–40v) has many text illustrations depicting biblical, ritual, and eschatological subjects. Some of them are legendary, some literary. Another group of illustrations is related to the *piyyutim* of Ḥanukkah (fols. 78v–81). These illustrations are mainly apocryphal, concerning the events of miraculous salvation throughout Jewish history. The illustration reproduced here is derived from this group (fol. 79v). A section of various *kinot* ("dirges") for different historical events, beginning on folio 133, comprises another group of text illustrations. Not all of the miniatures and marginal illustrations were executed by the same artist. The first and last groups are closely related, though not necessarily done by the same hand. The group related to Ḥanukkah is the least sophisticated, though quite expressive. The soft figure and drapery style is evident in the page reproduced here. The free compositional feeling, an element which developed through Italian influence, is common in southwest German illumination. The stage-like landscape is likewise Italianate.

Although other cities of the Rhine, such as Cologne, Würzburg, Rothenburg, and Nuremberg, are mentioned as places where martyrdom occurred, the fact that the customs of Mainz are emphasized may seem to imply that the manuscript originated there.

FOLIO 79V

Two miniatures illustrating a *piyyut* for Ḥanukkah. In the top one, Hannah is lamenting her sons who were killed for refusing to obey the king's order to bow to his idols. Her youngest son is standing bound in ropes next to the king, who is holding a ring. According to legend, the king threw the ring in front of the idol and asked the child to pick it up which would have simulated bowing in front of the idol. In the bottom miniature, a Jewess is immersing herself in a *mikveh* before going to her husband, who is awaiting her in bed. According to the midrashic legend, the Syrian king forbade the use of *mikva'ot*, and in order to keep Jewish women from sin, God supplied them with secluded ritual baths.

HAMBURG, STAATS- UND UNIVERSITAETSBIBLIOTHEK, COD. HEB. 37

SPECIFICATIONS: Vellum, 205 leaves, $11\frac{7}{8} \times 9$ ins (30×22 cm.). Written in square Ashkenazi script, 22 lines to the full page. Many miniatures and initial-word panels illustrating the text. Some decorative initial words and initial letters in pen drawing and colors.

COLOPHON: Folio 122: Isaac b. Simḥah Gansmann, at the beginning of a calendar starting with the year 1428.

PLATE 40

The Second Nuremberg Haggadah

Haggadah of German rite for Passover eve
Southern Germany, mid-15th century

The *Second Nuremberg Haggadah* is a typical 15th-century Ashkenazi *Haggadah*. The manuscript begins with three full-page paintings depicting preparations for Passover, mainly the baking of the *mazzot* and the cleansing of the house (fols. 1v–2v). Text illustrations containing a cycle of biblical and legendary episodes, as well as ritual and eschatological ones, are in the outer and lower margins of all pages. The illustrations are followed by explanatory rhyming captions, which are written somewhat comically in popular Hebrew mixed with Yiddish within flying banners. Two examples are: (fol. 12) "Moses had much pleasure and fun, with the seven daughters of Midian;" (fol. 18v) "Daughters of Israel, lovely to behold, carry in their pockets pieces of gold."

The biblical and midrashic illustrations are in three consecutive cycles. The first one depicts the story of Exodus, starting with the birth of Moses and ending with Miriam and the women singing and dancing (fols. 7v–22). The second, illustrating Genesis (fols. 30v–37), starts with Adam and Eve and ends with Joseph as Pharaoh's viceroy. The third illustrates episodes from the rest of the Bible (fols. 37v–41), starting with Moses receiving the Tablets of the Law, and depicting events from the lives of Joshua, Samuel, Samson, David, Solomon, and Job. Within the biblical illustrations are dozens of midrashic ones based mainly on the medieval legendary compilation of Bible stories, *Sefer ha-Yashar*. Some of the captions use the wording of this biblical paraphrase. On almost every page, illustrations of the different customs and rituals of the *Haggadah* appear between these biblical illustrations.

The eschatological illustrations mainly depict the relationship between the redemption of the nation and its traditional harbinger, the prophet Elijah. One illustration (fol. 29v) shows a child opening the door for the prophet while reciting "Pour out Thy wrath." At the end of the manuscript (fol. 41v), Elijah is depicted in the traditional manner—riding a donkey with the Israelites following him.

The style, decorations, and colors of the illustrations prove to be of mid-15th century south German provenance. The shape of the script and its arrangement and the choice of illustrations and their style are very close to the *Yahuda Haggadah* (see plate 41). It is not certain, however, which of these manuscripts is the earlier and whether they were both executed by one artist or were both copied from a third manuscript.

FOLIOS 19V–20
A double page with marginal illustrations showing the exodus from Egypt. From right to left, the Israelites are depicted as armed soldiers on horseback, in carriages, and on foot. In the top left-hand corner a bear appears from behind a tree to prevent the Israelites from going through the land of the Philistines on their way to Canaan.
JERUSALEM, SCHOCKEN LIBRARY, MS. 24 087

SPECIFICATIONS: Vellum, 42 leaves, $10\frac{1}{8} \times 7\frac{1}{8}$ ins (25.5 × 18 cm.). Written in square Ashkenazi script, 13 lines to the page, the instructions in a smaller script. Three full-page paintings of preparations for Passover eve. Marginal illustrations to all text pages. Initial words, some in panels in gold, and red, green, and blue ink. Unbound.

PROVENANCE: The German Museum in Nuremberg, MS. 2121. 1958, the Schocken Library, Jerusalem.

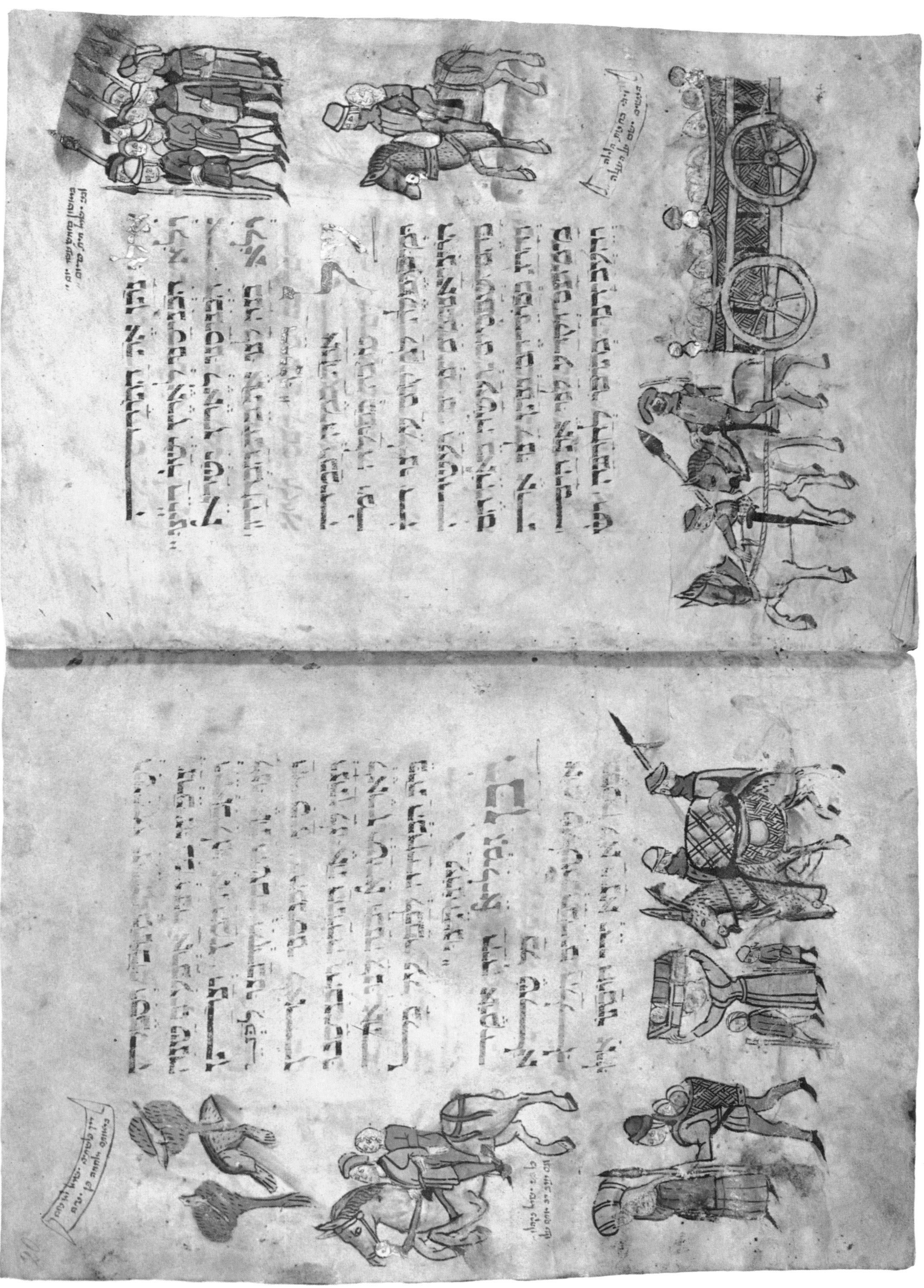

PLATE 41

Yahuda Haggadah

Haggadah of German rite for Passover eve
Southern Germany, mid-15th century

The illustrations of the *Yahuda Haggadah* are almost identical to those of the *Second Nuremberg Haggadah* (see description to plate 40). It also contains two full-page illustrations depicting the preparations for Passover (fols. 1v–2), as well as textual, biblical and ritual illustrations in the outer margins of all pages. The selection of scenes, the style, the colors and the inscription of interpretative verses within the illustrations are also similar. However, it is not certain which of these two *Haggadot* is earlier, whether they were painted by the same artist, copied one from the other, or both copied from an antecedent manuscript.
Judging by its style, this manuscript was executed in southern Germany in the middle of the 15th century. The appearance of some archaic motifs in the architecture, clothing, and decoration and the primitive character of the illumination make it clear that the artist of the manuscript was not a master craftsman.

FOLIO 22
A family seated around a *seder* table and raising their wine cups, illustrating the passage *lefikhakh* ("Therefore it is our duty to praise and laud").
JERUSALEM, ISRAEL MUSEUM, MS. 180/50

SPECIFICATIONS: Vellum, 40 leaves, $9\frac{1}{8} \times 6\frac{3}{4}$ ins (23 × 17 cm.). Written in square Ashkenazi script, 13 lines to the full page. The instructions written in smaller script. Modern, wooden binding with 19th-century brown leather back and two leather straps and metal clasps.

PROVENANCE: 1899, Rosenbaum Antiquariat, Frankfort. Professor Dr. Victor Goldschmidt of Heidelberg (20th century). Purchased by Mr. Heinrich Eisemann, London, from Goldschmidt's widow. Professor A. S. Yahuda. Given to Bezalel National Art Museum in 1955 by his widow, Rachel Ethel Yahuda.

אל'א את אותנו גאל עמהם
שנ' ואותנו הוציא משם
למען הביא אותנו אל הארץ
אשר נשבע לאבותינו:
כל אחד יגביה
לפיכך
אנחנו חייבים להודות להלל

PLATE 42

Joel Ben Simeon Haggadah

Haggadah with commentary by R. Eleazar of Worms
Germany and North Italy, mid-15th century

This *Haggadah* must be one of the earliest illuminated manuscripts of the workshop of the scribe-artist Joel b. Simeon. The sides and lower margins of most pages have illustrations of two types—German and Italian. They are in color but are unframed, with scenes and single figures. Illumination of the German type appears in the first, and part of the second quire, as well as in the last two quires (out of a total of six). In illustrations of this German type, the figures are typically large and stocky, animated in their facial expression rather than in their gestures. They are painted in softly modeled colors, characteristic of the Middle Rhine in the second quarter of the 15th century. The panels of this type are in vivid blue or burnished gold, and the initial words or letters are done in either gold or solid colors.

Illustrations of the second type are characteristically Italian. They are found in part of the second quire, as well as in the third and fourth quires. The figures of the Italian type are in pen drawing and wash colors. They are slender, and some are seen in profile. The initial-word panels are colored in green or lilac, with the decoration in lighter shades on darker grounds of the same color. Most of the decorations consist of foliage scrolls which cover the entire panel, formed either by short, thick acanthus leaves, or by slim, oval, bladder-shaped leaves. Some scrolls are heavy and look like folded ribbons. Many have grotesque human and animal heads, with a few dragons, rabbits and dogs. The marginal commentary is sometimes figurated in human or animal shapes. The illustrations include many ritual and text pictures, and some biblical ones.

This *Haggadah* is the most outstanding and controversial work in the large group of manuscripts attributed to Joel b. Simeon, called Feibush Ashkenazi of Bonn or Cologne, 11 of which bear a colophon to this effect. Six of these manuscripts are dated between 1449 and 1485. Among those related to this *Haggadah* in their style are the *Second New York Haggadah* (JTS ms. 555 of 1454); the *siddur* in the British Museum (Add. 26957) of 1469; the *Washington Haggadah* of 1478, Library of Congress (pl. 50); the unsigned *Parma Haggadah* (Bib. Palat. ms. 2998); and the six single leaves of Temple Implements in New York (JTS, ms. 0822).

It is generally assumed that Joel b. Simeon must have emigrated to northern Italy as early as 1452, since the Italianate *maḥzor* of 1452 formerly in the Library of Turin (since destroyed) was written in Cremona. An early date, shortly before that of the *Second New York Haggadah* of 1454 has been assumed for Add. ms. 14762 partly because of the still apparent links to Germany as seen in the illumination. Conversely, some German elements also remain in the art of the Italian type.

From the rhymed colophon at the end of the *Haggadah*, it appears that Joel b. Simeon was the artist. That he was the only artist, however, is not certain, mainly because of the two distinct styles of the manuscript. In other manuscripts, he calls himself "scribe" or "scrivener," rather than "painter" or "artist."

FOLIO 6

An initial-word panel with marginal illustrations including a Passover table for the opening text of the *Haggadah*.

LONDON, BRITISH MUSEUM, ADD. MS. 14762

SPECIFICATIONS: Vellum, 49 leaves, $14\frac{7}{8} \times 11$ ins (37.5×28 cm.). Written in square Ashkenazi script, mostly 12 lines to the page. The commentary in cursive Ashkenazi script in the margins. Painted marginal illustrations decorated in figurated initial-word panels of two styles. Part of the commentary in figurated script, outlined and completed in colored pen drawing. Fifteenth-century, dark-brown Morocco binding. The upper cover in elaborate cuir ciselé illustrating St. Michael with a lance and uplifted sword, astride a prostrate devil. To the left are Adam and Eve, standing naked on a wheel of fortune.

COLOPHON: Folio 48v. Verse in the outer margin. The first letters of each line form an acrostic of the name Joel: "My heart prompts me to answer him who might ask who designed this: I am one Feibush called Joel . . . for Jacob Mattathias, may he live for ever, ben R. S."

PROVENANCE: Purchased by the British Museum from Messrs. Payne and Foss in 1844.

הא
לחמא עניא דאכלו אבהתנא
בארעא דמצרים כל דכפין
ייתי וייכל כל דצריך ייתי
ויפסח השתא הכא לשנה
הבאה בארעא דישראל השתא

PLATE 43

Darmstadt Haggadah

Haggadah of German rite
Germany, Middle Rhine, second quarter of the 15th century

The *Darmstadt Haggadah* contains many full-page illustrations and panels, mostly of ritual nature. Besides those of *seder* tables, the best known illustration in this *Haggadah* is the picture of damsels being instructed by elderly male teachers (pl. 43). It is therefore plausible to infer that the manuscript was executed for a woman, as this type of presentation is unusual. None of the most common text illustrations are to be found in this *Haggadah*; nor are there many other ritual illustrations, and no biblical ones. The manuscript can nevertheless be regarded as one of the richest in its profusion of illustrations and in the style of its figures. At the end of the manuscript are two full-page illustrations which have no relation to the text: one is a stag hunt scene, which is a common allusion to the persecuted Jewish nation (fol. 57v); the other (fol. 58) depicts the fountain of youth, showing old and crippled men and women climbing the steps of the fountain and coming out younger and healthier. The main divisions of the text have large initial-word panels, and the entire page is framed by illustrations of a ritual nature. According to a monumental full page inscription, the manuscript was written by Israel ha-Sofer b. Meir of Heidelberg. There is no proof however, that the script and the illumination of the *Darmstadt Haggadah* were done by the same hand, even though the scribe was known to have been an expert bookbinder, and Meir b. Israel Jaffe of Ulm (copyist of the *First Cincinnati Haggadah*—see plate 45), who was possibly the scribe's son, is known to have tooled the leather binding of the Pentateuch for the City Council of Nuremberg in 1468. In fact, the manuscript seems to have been illuminated by several artists of the same school in the Middle Rhine around the second quarter of the 15th century. This provenance can be recognized in the figure style as well as the grotesques and foliage scrolls. The dark colors used by the artist on some of the pages point to either the Italian or Netherlands-gothic influences.

FOLIO 37V
A full-page border decoration and initial-letter panel for "Pour out Thy wrath." The illustrations depict female pupils with their teachers and a Passover *seder* table at the bottom of the page.
DARMSTADT, HESSISCHE LANDES- UND HOCHSCHULBIBLIOTHEK, COD. OR. 8

SPECIFICATIONS: Vellum, 59 leaves, $14 \times 9\frac{3}{4}$ ins (35.5×24.5 cm.). Written in square Ashkenazi script, 15 lines to the page. Many initial-word and initial-letter panels in gold and colors, some within completely framed leaves (fols. 2v, 4v, 5, 6, 7, 10v, 11, 25v, 27, 27v, 28v, 31, 37v, 48v, 51v) and scattered illustrations of ritual or instructional nature. Two full-page, unrelated illustrations. Fifteenth-century German, blind-tooled, brown leather binding.

COLOPHON: Fol. 56v "Israel b. Meir of Heidelberg."

PROVENANCE: Seventeenth and eighteenth-century owners' inscriptions in Italian script. In 1788 the *Haggadah* was in the Baron Hüpsch collection. Upon his death in 1805 it came into the possession of the Hofbibliothek in Darmstadt.

ש
פוך חמתך על הגוים
אשר לא ידעוך ועל
הממלכות אשר בשמך

PLATE 44

Siddur of the Rabbi of Ruzhin

Siddur of German rite for daily use, Sabbaths, and festivals, including the *Haggadah* and *Pirkei Avot*
Southeast Germany, c. 1460

This small-format *siddur* was intended for personal rather than communal use, since it does not include a large selection of *piyyutim* as in the large-sized *maḥzorim* from Germany. The decoration of the manuscript consists of initial-word panels to the different prayers, with thick, full, border decorations to the opening pages of the main divisions. Most pages of the *Haggadah* have text illustrations in the borders (fols. 151v–187v). Some illustrations are in framed miniatures with landscape backgrounds. Others are painted figures and edifices on a ground of plain, naked vellum. The illustrations of the *Haggadah* are mainly ritual, with a few biblical illustrations, within the miniature. The main decoration consists of scrolls, colored, fleshy leaves, flowers, birds, and animals, all of which are typical of the south German style after the middle of the 15th century. The heavy human figures and busts emerging from flowers resemble the east German schools of Austria and Bohemia.

The manuscript has no colophon, but it contains names of contemporaries of the scribe and the patron. On folio 10v, in the memorial benedictions, "My father, Rabbi Gershon ben Isaac," is written in red.

In the 19th century, up to 1850, the *siddur* was in the possession of the famous ḥasidic rabbi, Israel Friedman of Ruzhin.

FOLIO 296v
"Night of the Vigil": Initial-word panel and decorated border.
JERUSALEM, ISRAEL MUSEUM, MS. 180/53

SPECIFICATIONS: Vellum, 365 leaves (+ five leaves which were partly cut and not foliated: 51 bis, 124 bis, 151 bis, 227 bis, 274 bis), $7\frac{3}{8} \times 5\frac{3}{4}$ ins (18.5 × 14.5 cm.). Written in square Ashkenazi script, 14 lines to the page, which leave a very wide margin. In the margins of folios 3v–61 are additions in smaller script up to 45 lines per page. Initial-word panels to the different prayers, with full border decorations to the main divisions. Border text illustrations to the *Haggadah* (fols. 151v, 187v).

PROVENANCE: Fol. 151: a list of births from 1661 to 1688. R. Moshe Ephraim inherited the *siddur* from his uncle, R. Abraham Dov of Avrinna (?), who received it as a gift from R. Joseph (18th century). On folio 1, there is a customs seal of Satanow containing the Royal Polish Eagle with the inscription "Satanow Kómora." Next to it a signature: "Pietrawski GDDRmmy 3 dbr 1790." In the 19th century (up to 1850) it was in the possession of the ḥasidic rabbi, Israel (Friedman) of Ruzhin. Acquired by the Bezalel National Art Museum in 1951 from the Friedman family of Borósh.

PLATE 45

First Cincinnati Haggadah

Haggadah of German rite
Southern Germany, c. 1480–90

The *Cincinnati Haggadah* is one of the most typical Ashkenazi illuminated manuscripts in both text and illustration. Beside initial-word and initial-letter panels in its main divisions, many marginal text illustrations adorn the pages. They depict preparations for Passover eve, ritual scenes of the Passover eve *seder*, including some literal text illuminations, and biblical and eschatological scenes. Iconographically, this *Haggadah* is similar to such earlier 15th-century *Haggadot* as the *Joel ben Simeon Haggadah* in the British Museum (see description to plate 42); but stylistically it is definitely German. The stocky figures wearing benign expressions, heavy folding drapery, very detailed furniture and interior design, and stage-like attempts at three-dimensional landscapes are all evidence of the Italianate south German style of the late 15th century.

The date of the manuscript has been in doubt since 1927, when B. Italiener, who first studied the text, suggested 1400. A. L. Mayer, studying the illumination, placed it between 1420 and 1430. However, in 1940, F. Landsberger established that the scribe of the *Cincinnati Haggadah*, Meir b. Israel Jaffe of Heidelberg, and Israel b. Meir of Heidelberg, the scribe of the *Darmstadt Haggadah* of c. 1430 (see plate 43), were father and son. Taking this, and the style of the manuscript, into consideration, he suggested a more likely date of 1480 to 1490 for the *Cincinnati Haggadah*. Still debatable is the question of whether the scribe, Meir b. Israel Jaffe, is also the artist of the manuscript and whether the colored bands framing the pages of the entire manuscript were executed by the original artist or added during the 16th century.

The scribe was also known as an expert bookbinder and leather tooler whose name is signed on the Pentateuch he bound for the Nuremberg City Council in 1468, when his name is mentioned in a decree issued by the council permitting him to reside in the city.

FOLIO 1V

Search for leaven on the evening before Passover eve. A man brushes crumbs from a cupboard into a bowl with a feather.

CINCINNATI, HEBREW UNION COLLEGE

SPECIFICATIONS: Vellum, 69 leaves, $13\frac{3}{8} \times 9\frac{7}{8}$ ins (33.8 × 25 cm.). Written in square Ashkenazi script, nine lines to the page. Various initial-word and initial-letter panels. Textual illustrations in the borders and within the panels. Each page is framed by a wide decorated border.

COLOPHON: Fols. 68v, 69: "I, Meir the scribe, son of Israel Jaffe the scribe (may his repose be honorable) of Heidelberg, wrote this work (?) in token of esteem for R. Ens-chen (?), the Levite, of Schiffermuehl (?) son of Aaron, the Levite".

PROVENANCE: Fol. 69: A shield bearing the inscription of an owner in 1559, Taeublein, daughter of Rabbi Issachar. Her name is illustrated by a little dove. In the left-hand corner, another owner's transcription of 1560, "Madame Leah, the daughter of Rabbi Moses, presented the manuscript to her son-in-law, Abraham, son of the deceased, Jacob, in Huerben." Fol. 1: In 1689 the *Haggadah* was in the possession of Eliezer b. Moses, Mainz Kanstatt.

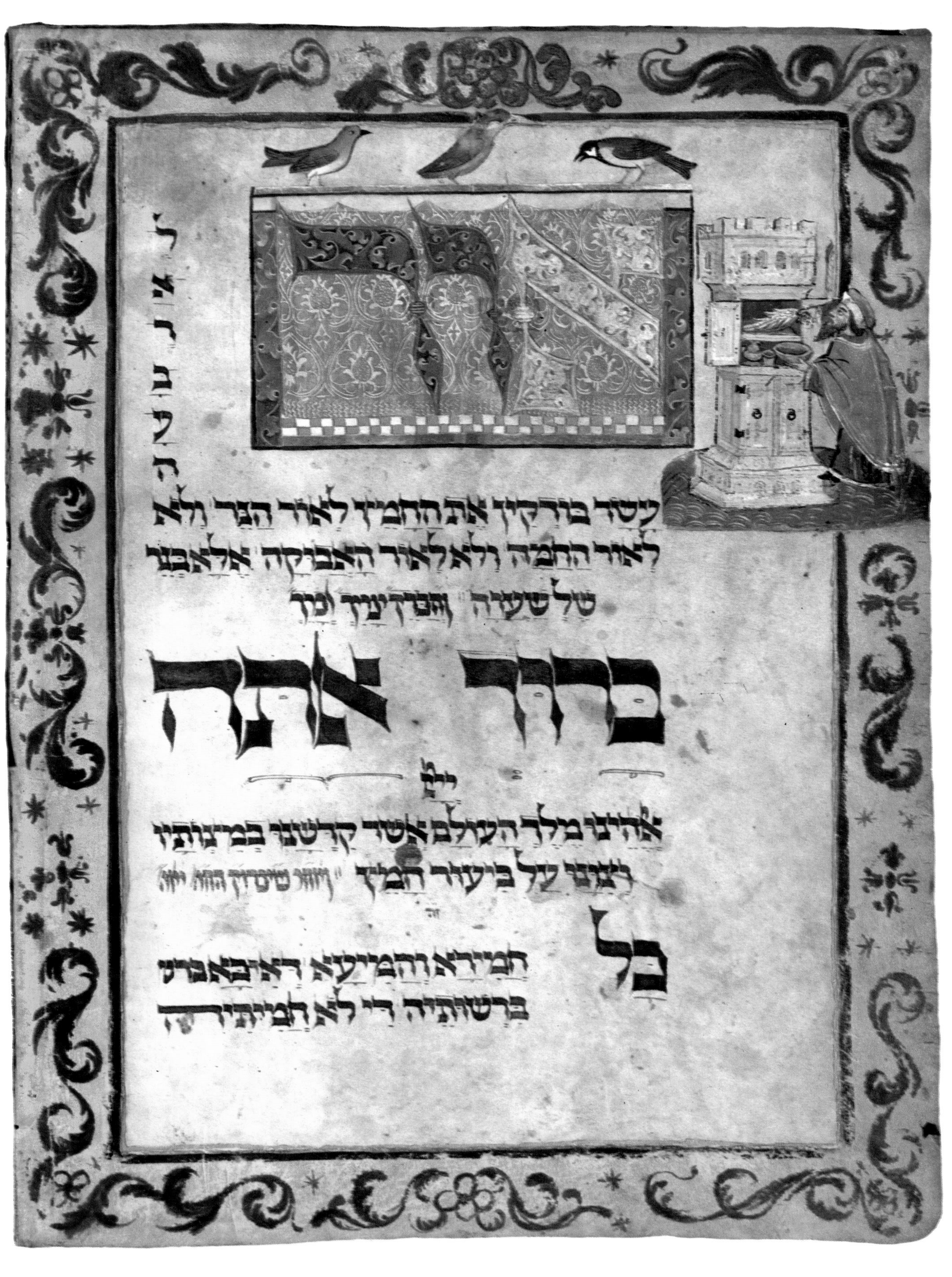

אור

לארבעה

עשר בודקין את החמץ לאור הנר ולא
לאור החמה ולא לאור האבוקה אלא בנר
של שעוה ומברך וכך

ברוך אתה
יי
אלהינו מלך העולם אשר קדשנו במצותיו
וצונו על ביעור חמץ

כל
חמירא וחמיעא דאיכא
ברשותיה די לא חמיתיה

PLATE 46

Bishop Bedell Bible

Bible with masorah magna and parva
Italy, Rome, 1284

The *Bishop Bedell Bible* is one of the earliest surviving examples of Italian Hebrew illumination. It is an important specimen both as an illuminated Bible and as an example of dated Roman illumination of the late 13th century. There are two types of ornamentation in this three-volume manuscript: illustrations painted with colors and gold, and pen drawings in ink and color. The two frontispieces (fols. Iv and II) are painted with different shades of blue, pink, vermilion, green, and burnished gold, most of which has peeled off. The rest of the decoration is in ink and wash of yellow, red, lilac, and green.

The opening pages of the main books of the Bible have large arches encompassing the entire text of the page. The openings of other books have smaller arches on top of one text column. All of these arches are round and have a rectangular framed top.

The titles of the books are written in red in the tympanum of the arches, and the initial words are in ink between the capitals. Two of the three wider arcades at the beginning of the three volumes of the manuscript (fol. 1, Genesis, and fol. 416, Chronicles) have no title, but the initial word is surrounded by a thin yellow frame with small yellow scrolls and red dots extending upward and downward from the corners of each letter.

The indicators of the *parashot* and *haftarot* are written in the margins and framed by a colored rectangle or palmette but with a long, linear stem sometimes ending in a bird's head. They have decorated tops in the shape of a gabled roof or a palmette bud.

The decorated arcades, as well as the painted frontispieces, seem to be contemporary with the script, and therefore belong to the end of the 13th century. The scribe, Abraham b. Yom Tov ha-Kohen, was active in the last two decades of the 13th century. Several works copied by him are preserved in various libraries. The punctuator, Benjamin b. Joab was similarly active. Among the codices on which he worked was a Bible (Parma, Bibl. Palat. ms. 3216) which has the same decorations as the *Bishop Bedell Bible*. The scribe, Abraham b. Yom Tov ha-Kohen may also have been the artist of this group of manuscripts, since he calls himself *ha-Meḥokek* ("the limner").

VOLUME I, FOLIOS IV–2

The two full-page frontispiece panels to the three-volumed "giant" *Bishop Bedell Bible*. On the first page is the ornamented letter, *shin*, referring to the name of the original patron, Shabbetai b. Mattathias. The gold inscription on a dark blue ground in the middle of the second page reads, in Hebrew, "Crown of Beauty, Pentateuch, Prophets and Hagiographa."

CAMBRIDGE, EMMANUEL COLLEGE, MSS. I. I. 5–7

SPECIFICATIONS: Vellum, three volumes, IV + 584 (IV + 150, 265, I + 169 respectively) 13¼ × 9¾ ins (33.6 × 24.5 cm.). Written in square Italian script, 28 lines in two columns. Two full-page painted frontispieces (fols. IV–2). Colored arcades to the openings of all books. Decorated panels to the *parashot* indicators. A 17th century English, green Morocco binding by Thomas Mearne, stationer to King Charles II. Gold-tooled fillets and cornerpieces. Emblem of Emmanuel College.

COLOPHON: Fol. 584v (end of vol. III). "Written by Abraham ben R. Yom-Tov ha-Kohen for Shabbetai ben Mattathias, completed in Rome on Thursday, 19th of Tevet 5045 A.C." (Dec. 28, 1284 C.E.). Above the colophon is a rhymed poem with the acrostic of Abraham ha-Kohen and with an allusion to Shabbetai and his son Solomon, fol. 415v (end of vol. II). In the hand of the masoreter in the margins: "Benjamin the punctuator . . . *ḥazak* [be strong]"—"Bar Joab of the family of the *Anavim*." Below it is a verse containing the name "Abraham, the limner," fol. 584 (end of text in vol. III). In the same hand, a verse expressing joy at the completion of the masorah.

PROVENANCE: Inside the front cover of vol. I, a note in an 18th century hand confirming that this is the Bible bought by William Bedell, Bishop of Kilmore and Ardagh, with the help of Rabbi Leone Modena, when Bedell was chaplain to Sir Henry Wotton at Venice between 1607 and 1610. Presented to Emmanuel College, Cambridge by Bishop Bedell during his lifetime, but lost with the rest of his library during the Rebellion in Ireland in 1641. Recovered by Dennis Sheridan, his deacon, after Bedell's imprisonment and given to the College after his death in prison.

PLATE 47

Jerusalem Mishneh Torah

Maimonides' *Mishneh Torah*
Copied in Spain, 14th century; illuminated Perugia, Italy, c. 1400

This is one of the most sumptuous manuscripts of the *Mishneh Torah*. In the absence of a colophon, it can be inferred from the script that the manuscript was copied either in Spain or southern France in the first half of the 14th century (in any case, before 1351, when the codex was sold in Avignon). The scribe's name was probably Isaac, since this name is decorated in several places in the text (e.g., fols. 58v, 250v). This manuscript was illuminated in burnished gold and lively wash colors by a skilled non-Jewish artist of Perugia, Matteo di Ser Cambio. The decorations and illustrations, which occur in the opening pages of each of the books in the manuscript and in the margins surrounding the initial-word panels in most chapters, are few in number as they occur only in the first 40 leaves of the manuscript; but they are very significant as they are the earliest survivors of the group of illustrations influenced by an earlier *Mishneh Torah*. They therefore constitute an important stage in the development of illustrations in *halakhic* manuscripts of the Middle Ages.

The text illustrations appear in 16 separate pages, some of which are unique because they illustrate precepts of Jewish law; e.g., "Thou shalt not go up as a tale-bearer amongst thy people" (Lev. 19:16). The panel (fol.18v) portrays two people conversing and pointing at a third in the opposite panel, who is assumed to be the object of their gossip. The most interesting of these illustrations depicts punishment by stoning (fol. 22v). The opening pages of main divisions of books have elaborate border decorations of scrolls, twisted, multicolored, fleshy leaves interspersed with human figures, putti, birds, animals and grotesques. Some of these borders frame the entire page.

Space was left in the rest of the book for other panels and border decorations and for an exposition of the plans of the Temple (fols. 244v, 255), and some of its implements (fols. 243v, 250v). Matteo di Ser Cambio, the artist who illuminated the first 40 pages, was famous in Perugia in the last quarter of the 14th century as an illuminator and a gold- and silversmith. He painted the opening pages of the matricula and statutes for the money changers' guild and for the merchants' guild in Perugia, the styles of which are very close to this *Mishneh Torah*. There is documentary evidence of an official relationship between Matteo and the Jewish community of Perugia.

FOLIO 32
A typical decorated opening page for the "Book of Love [of God]." The illustration in the top initial-word panel shows a man embracing a Torah scroll. In the lower margin, another man is reciting the *shema* before going to bed.
JERUSALEM, JEWISH NATIONAL AND UNIVERSITY LIBRARY, MS. HEB. 4°1193

SPECIFICATIONS: Vellum, 463 leaves, $17\frac{7}{8} \times 11\frac{5}{8}$ ins (45 × 29.5 cm.). Written in a square Sephardi script, 49 lines to the page in two columns. Nineteenth-century, light brown leather binding on wooden boards. Incised and blind tooled with geometric motifs on both covers and spine. Initial-word panels, border decorations and illustrations in the first 40 leaves of the manuscript only. Two leather straps and metal clasps.

PROVENANCE: Fol. 426v: May 6, 1351, bought by Manasseh b. Jacob of Navarre from Don Louis Samuel of La Garda, through Eliot Joseph of La Haya, who brought the codex to Avignon. On February 25, 1373 it was bought in Arles by R. Judah b. Daniel from Don Abraham Vidal of Bourriane.
Fol. 463: "1527 in Mantua;" heads a list of books bequeathed by Abraham Finzi of Rovigo to his son Menahem.
Fol. 462v: Nov. 18, 1547, sold by Manasseh Finzi's son, Abraham, in Ferrara to Don Jacob and Don Judah, the sons of Don Samuel Abrabanel, the leader of the Jewish community. Bought in 1880 by Julius Hamburger of Frankfort at the sale of Marquis Carlo Trivulzio's Library in Milan. Herman Kramer of Frankfort (20th century). Acquired in 1966 by the Jewish National and University Library in Jerusalem from Mr. Solomon Flörsheim, formerly of Frankfort.
Censor: Laurentius Franguellus, Dec. 15, 1574 [in Ferrara?].

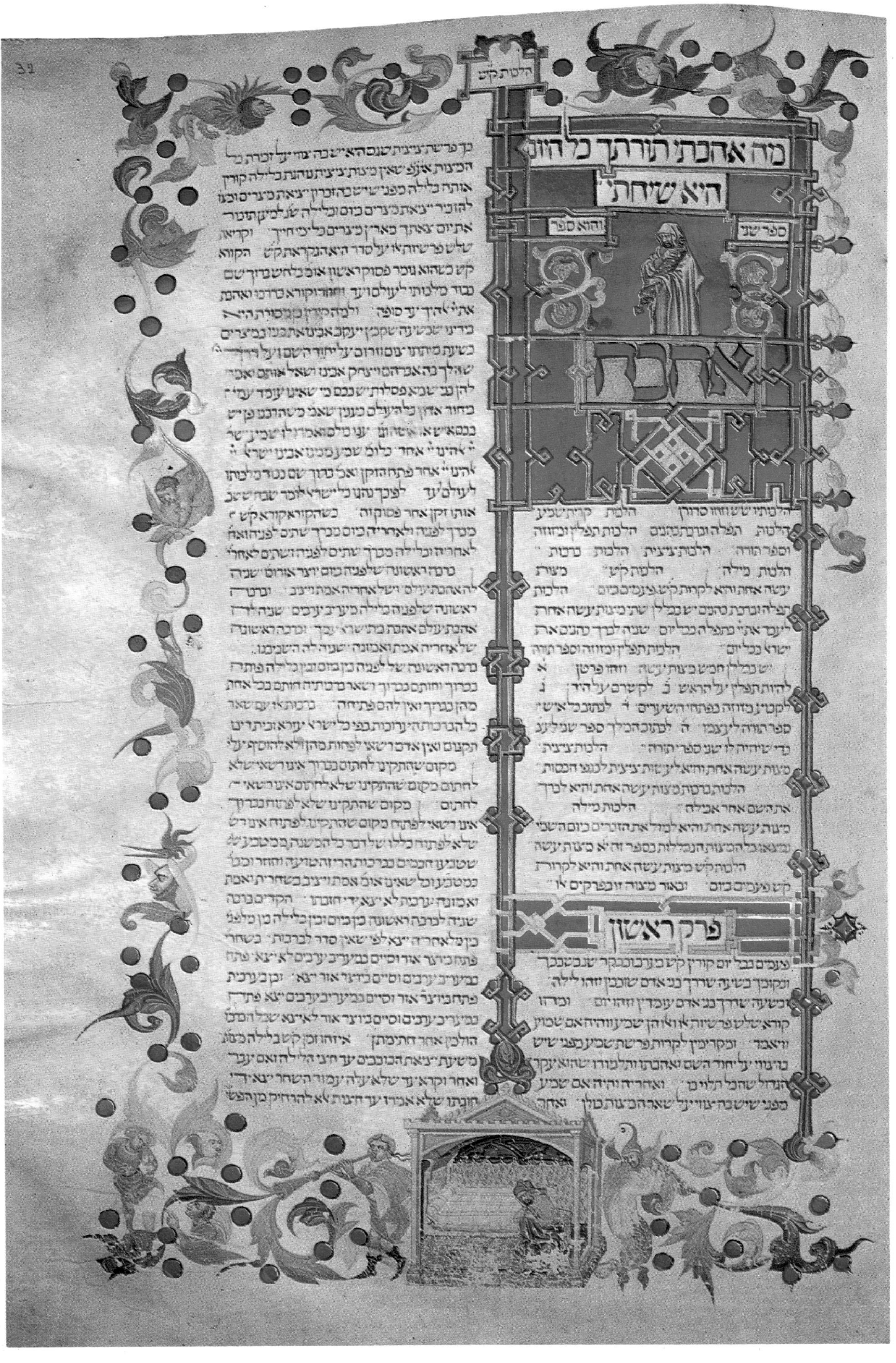
32
הלכות ק״ש
מה אהבתי תורתך כל היום
היא שיחתי
ספר שני
והוא ספר
אהבה
פרק ראשון

PLATE 48

Vatican Arbaʿah Turim

Arba'ah Turim by Jacob b. Asher
Italy, Mantua, 1435

The *Arba'ah Turim* by Jacob b. Asher contains four parts, each one dealing with a different type of legal material. The opening of the four divisions is illuminated with wide borders framing the page and a large miniature above the initial word, below which the text begins. The subject of each miniature is directly related to the text.
The first book, *Tur Oraḥ Ḥayyim*, concerning the precepts of daily, private, and community life, is illustrated on its opening page (fol. 12v) by a synagogue scene with the *ḥazzan* at the ark. In the four corners of the miniature are the four symbolic beasts mentioned in the beginning of the text of this section. The opening page illustration of the second part, *Tur Yoreh De'ah* (the verso of an unpaginated folio between fols. 127–128) dealing with the cleanliness of food and the slaughtering of animals, portrays four people slaughtering and cleaning animals and birds. The third part, *Tur Even ha-Ezer*, dealing with marital laws, has a panel illustrating an elegant wedding scene (fol. 220). In the fourth part, *Tur Ḥoshen Mishpat*, a discussion of civil law, the panel depicts a court scene (the verso of an unpaginated folio between fols. 292–293).
The wide borders framing each of these four pages are composed of curling foliage scrolls interspersed with flowers, animals, and people. Some of the human figures, as, for instance, the women in prayer, are related to the text within the frame of the first part. Others, such as the four musicians in the border of the page reproduced here, are merely decorative.
The composition and interior of each of the illustrations are executed in an advanced and sophisticated manner. The coffered ceiling device was used by the artist to express depth. The elegant international gothic style of the Paduan school is quite clearly demonstrated in the style of some of the figures. The coloring is bright and shows a great knowledge of the technique used by the master artists of northern Italy at the time.
According to the colophon (fol. 440) the work was completed by Isaac the Scribe b. Obadiah in Mantua in 1435.

UNPAGINATED FOLIO
The verso of an unpaginated folio between fols. 292 and 293 is a panel illustrating a court of law (*Bet Din*) in the opening page of *Tur Ḥoshen Mishpat.*

ROME, VATICAN LIBRARY, COD. ROSSIANA, 555

SPECIFICATIONS: Fine vellum, 441 + 2 leaves (127 bis. and 292 bis.) $13\frac{1}{4} \times 9\frac{1}{4}$ ins (33.5 × 23.5 cm.). Written in cursive Italian script, 52 lines in two columns. Four illuminated pages with full borders and illustrated miniatures at the beginning of each book. Some headings and titles are decorated with blue and purple filigree work. Eighteenth-century, brown leather binding on cardboard. Inlay of green, red, and light brown leather in rectangles and rhomboids. Gold-tooled with central floral motifs. Title inscribed in gold on the outside, back cover.

COLOPHON: Folio 440: "I, Isaac Sofer b. Obadiah, completed the work within ten months in Mantua, on the third of Kislev, 5196, [Friday, Dec. 23, 1435] and I wrote it for R. Mordecai b. Avigdor . . . and I confess that I received from him all that which is due to me" (followed by signatures of scribe, owner, and witnesses).

PROVENANCE: Fol. 440: Under the colophon are two owners' signatures; one is within a rhymed poem, mentioning the scribe, patron, and composer of the poem, Judah b. Joseph b. Judah b. Isaac. Censors' signatures of 1575 and 1578. Inside the front cover, the coat of arms of Cav. Gian Francesco de' Rossi, the former owner, and a stamp of the Bibliotheca Rossiana, with its signature, Plut IX, 245.

וישב

PLATE 49

Schocken Italian Maḥzor

Maḥzor of Roman rite with laws, customs, forms of contracts
Italy, (Rome?), 1441

This Italian *maḥzor* is an unusual specimen because so few *maḥzorim* from Italy have been found and also because of its fascinating combination of styles. The script is Ashkenazi with the iconography of an Ashkenazi *maḥzor*, while the choice of *piyyutim* is of Roman rite and the style of illumination is Italian. The manuscript is profusely illuminated, with large, colored and penned initial-word panels. The openings of most of the festivals are decorated with either miniatures or marginal illustrations relating to the text, mainly following the tradition of the Ashkenazi *maḥzor* in iconography, e.g., a full-page exposition of the implements of the Tabernacle done in gold (fol. 18v). The opening pages of the different prayers also contain borders of foliage scrolls with colored curling leaves interspersed with putti, animals, birds, and grotesques. The style of the miniatures and border illustrations, like the border decorations, is on the whole of central Italian origin. The manuscript may have been decorated at the same time that it was copied by Moses ha-Sofer b. Abraham, for Joseph b. Abraham of Tivoli.

FOLIO 76
A miniature for the *Parashat Parah* (the red heifer, Numbers 19), read on one of the four special Sabbaths.
JERUSALEM, SCHOCKEN LIBRARY, MS. 13 873

SPECIFICATIONS: Vellum, 465 leaves, $15\frac{3}{8} \times 11$ ins (39×28 cm.). Written in square Ashkenazi script, 36 lines to the page. Text illustrations and initial-word panels to the openings of all festivals.

COLOPHON: A rhymed poem with the acrostic of the scribe and the patron. The colophon also includes the name of the scribe, the name of the patron, and the date, 5201 A.C., the second of Sivan (June 22, 1441).

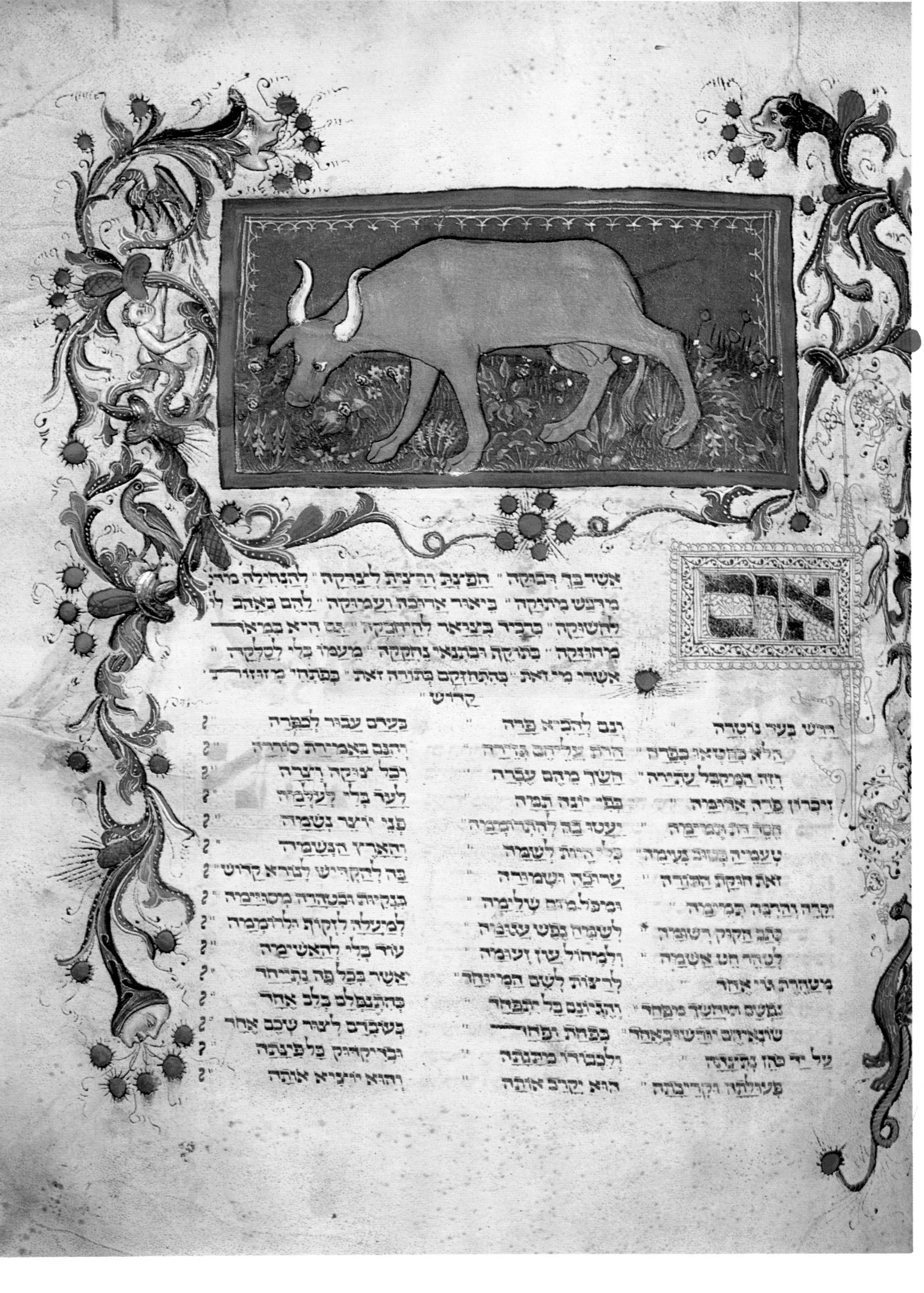

PLATE 50

Washington Haggadah

Haggadah of German rite
Italo-Ashkenazi, 1478

The *Washington Haggadah* is one of the signed and dated manuscripts of the prolific scribe Joel b. Simeon. It is illuminated entirely in Italian style, with no trace of German motifs other than the iconography. All the illustrations are placed in the margins, and are mainly ritual or literal; none are biblical, and only one (fol. 19v reproduced here) is eschatological. Beside the four sons (fols. 5v, 6v), other illustrations typical of German iconography are the cooking and roasting of the Passover lamb (fol. 15v) and a man pointing to his wife while saying "*maror zeh*" (fol. 17). An interesting literal illustration is that of a man in the attire of a wanderer carrying a satchel and a lance, illustrating the passage beginning with "Come out and learn" (fol. 7v).

The style of the manuscript is central Italian with elongated figures. The initial-word panels are decorated with cabbage-leaf motifs which were common at the time in majolica earthernware of central Italy. The filigree work on the side of initial words is typical of Florentine pen work, with profiles of expressive masks woven into the patterns.

Joel b. Simeon, called Feibush Ashkenazi of Bonn, reached Italy in the middle of the 15th century and opened a workshop for copying and illuminating manuscripts. In this manuscript, Joel b. Simeon calls himself (fol. 34v) the humblest of scribes, stating that "the work was completed on the 25th of Shevat, 5238" (May 29, 1478). Landsberger's assumption that there were two Joel b. Simeons, one at the beginning and one at the end of the 15th century, cannot be substantiated, especially since the *First Nuremberg Haggadah* has no date.

FOLIO 19V

The coming of Elijah on Passover eve at the moment when the door is being opened for him upon the recitation of "Pour out Thy wrath." The illustration is symbolic not only of national redemption, but also of personal redemption of each participant in the *seder*. Seated behind Elijah on the donkey are the father of the family and his son, while the mother and the daughter are seated on the tail of the donkey, with the small servant hanging on to the end of the tail.

WASHINGTON, LIBRARY OF CONGRESS

SPECIFICATIONS: Vellum, 14 leaves, $9\frac{1}{8} \times 5\frac{7}{8}$ ins (23 × 15 cm.). Written in square Ashkenazi script, 13 lines to the page. Many painted initial-word panels and several marginal illustrations to the text.

COLOPHON: Fol. 34v: "The work was completed and enow [Ex. 36:7]. This occurred today, the 25th of Shevat in the year 5238 [May 29, 1478], thus speaketh he of little consequence among the scribes, Joel b. Simeon, may his memory be blessed."

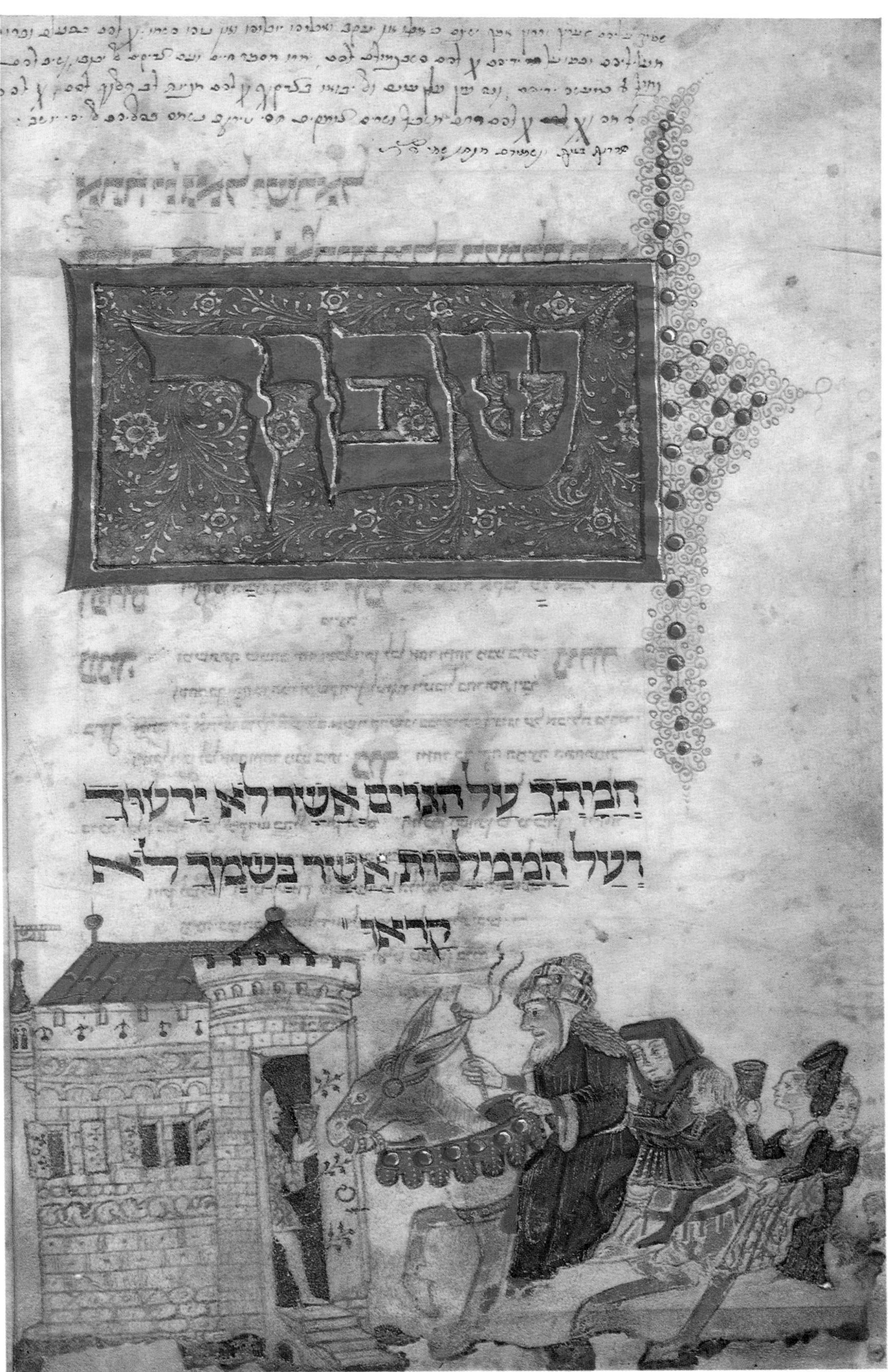
שפוך
חמתך על הגוים אשר לא ידעוך
ועל הממלכות אשר בשמך לא
קראו

PLATE 51

Cambridge Medical Miscellany

Medical and Philosophical treatises
North Italy (Padua?), 15th century

Illustrated medical treatises were widespread among the Jews of Europe in the 14th and 15th centuries. Most of these manuscripts were not illuminated, however, and the illustrations that were included were of a technical or diagrammatic nature. Only during the 15th century did the illuminated medical book come into fashion in Italy. The *Canon of Avicenna* (see plate 54) is one of the most sumptuous examples of such a work. Another one, less lavish but interesting from a textual and illustrative point of view, is this miscellany of medical treatises.

The illumination of this manuscript is composed of miniatures painted on top of the opening page of each of the books (in the case of the larger books, at the openings of their main divisions). Most of the miniatures depict physicians with patients, sometimes related to the books they illustrate. One of the seven miniatures illustrating the text of this miscellany is a decorated diagram (fol. 259v). The panel reproduced here depicts a physician treating a female patient by bloodletting. Behind the miniature is a hanging drapery, giving the picture a stage-like effect.

The style of the figures is quite advanced, revealing the then modern knowledge of modeling and natural gestures. The old archaic element in the miniature is the decorated, diapered background. The title of the treatise is written in large letters under the framed panel. The text itself is not framed. The stocky figures resemble illuminated Latin manuscripts of a Ferrarese type, although not necessarily from Ferrara itself. The bright orange, red, green, and blue colors may point to a Paduan origin for this manuscript.

FOLIO 211

A doctor bleeding a patient. A miniature illustrating a treatise by an unknown author on the "Days when bleeding is prohibited according to the wise men of the gentiles."

CAMBRIDGE UNIVERSITY LIBRARY, MS. Dd 10. 68

SPECIFICATIONS: Vellum, 621 leaves, $10\frac{5}{8} \times 8\frac{5}{8}$ ins (27 × 22 cm.). Written in cursive Italian script. Seven painted miniatures illustrating the text at the openings of the seven separate books. Some frames around major items in the text for emphasis. Seventeenth-century, red binding with blind-tooled scrolls, birds, and the name of Isaac Faraji written in Hebrew.

PROVENANCE: Presumably from the collection of Hebrew books brought together in Italy by Isaac Faraji. This collection was purchased for £500 by Parliament in 1648 through the bookseller, George Thomason, for the University of Cambridge.

מרצו	הוא ניסן	יום ח׳	בכנסתו		ויום ג׳	ביציאתו	
אפרילי	הוא אייר	יום ו׳	בכנסתו		ויום י״א	ביציאתו	
מיי	הוא סיון	יום ג׳	בכנסתו		ויום ז׳	ביציאתו	
יוניו	הוא תמוז	יום ו׳	בכנסתו		ויום ט״ו	ביציאתו	
לוליו	הוא אב	יום י״ג	בכנסתו		ויום י׳	ביציאתו	
אגשטו	הוא אלול	יום ח׳	בכנסתו		ויום כ׳	ביציאתו	
סיטימברי	הוא תשרי	יום ג׳	בכנסתו		ויום י׳	ביציאתו	
אוטוברי	הוא מרחשון	יום א׳	בכנסתו		ויום י׳	ביציאתו	
נובימברי	הוא כסליו	יום ה׳	בכנסתו		ויום ז׳	ביציאתו	
דיצימברי	הוא טבת	יום ז׳	בכנסתו		ויום י׳	ביציאתו	
ינרו	הוא שבט	יום א׳	בכנסתו		ויום ג׳	ביציאתו	
פיברו	הוא אדר	יום ד׳	בכנסתו		ויום ג׳	ביציאתו	

PLATE 52

Rothschild Siddur

Siddur of Roman rite for the entire year
Italy, Florence, 1492

A beautifully illuminated *siddur* containing prayers for the entire year (according to Italian usage this would be called a *maḥzor* which includes the daily as well as the festival prayers). This is an example of illuminated liturgies which became fashionable by the end of the 15th century in central and northern Italy. The illustration of such a work depended on earlier 14th- and 15th-century traditions which had set the basic divisions of the prayer book used privately by rich members of the community. Each of the main divisions of the daily prayers, prayers for the Sabbath, the different festivals, family feasts, and also private festivals—like marriage ceremonies, circumcision, etc.—were all included in this type of work. Some of these manuscripts are of considerable size, though the very fine vellum used for their execution made them light and easy to carry about.

The decoration of the *Rothschild Siddur* starts with a symbolic representation of eternity (fol. 2). There are two concentric circles, the outer of which is an arrangement of the eternal cycle of the signs of the zodiac. The inner circle depicts six opposing conditions of life, one leading into another: love, leads to richness, which leads to pride, which leads to hatred, which leads to poverty, which leads to meekness, which leads again to love, and so the cycle begins again.

A second full-page illustration (fol. 4) depicts two wild men supporting a shield on which is displayed the badge of the Norsa family of Mantua and Ferrara.

The text of the *siddur* begins on folio 16 on a framed page with an illustration of *Keter Malkhut* ("royal crown") on top of the page and the above-mentioned coat of arms below. The main decorations of the *Rothschild Siddur* appear on the opening pages of the different sections. In most cases, they are initial-word panels with some added illustration next to them, and the entire page is framed either by painted scrolls or by pen-drawn and wash-colored light decorations. In some cases, there are additional painted miniatures, some of which illustrate the text. The illumination of the manuscript was executed in at least three different techniques, not necessarily by the same artist in the same atelier, or at the same time. According to the colophon, it was copied in Florence in 1492 by Abraham b. Judah of Camerino for Joab b. Elijah of Vigevano of the Gallico family. The linear and wash-color illumination is typical of late 15th-century Florentine art. The other kind of painted illumination can also be found in and around Florence at about the same time. The figure style is reminiscent of the Italian art of Joel b. Simeon (see pls. 42 and 50). In addition to the many coats of arms of the Norsa family, there are also a few smaller escutcheons depicting a cock, the badge of the Gallico family (e.g., fol. 93).

FOLIO 139

Moses receiving the Tablets of the Law at Mount Sinai, while the Israelites stand behind a fenced mountain. Angels from heaven are blowing horns, and Mount Sinai is covered with flames. This is a marginal illustration to the mishnaic tractate *Avot*.

NEW YORK, JEWISH THEOLOGICAL SEMINARY

SPECIFICATIONS: Vellum, at least 470 folios, $11\frac{1}{4} \times 8$ ins (28.5×20.3 cm.). Written in a cursive Italian script, about 30 lines in one, two, or three columns to the page. Two fully-decorated pages (fols. 2 and 4) and many full framed pages with initial-word panels and some text illustrations to the main divisions of the prayerbook.

COLOPHON: "Written by Abraham b. Judah of Camerino in Florence in 1492 for Joab b. Elijah of Vigevano of the family of Gallico."

PROVENANCE: Formerly in the collection of Baron Edmond de Rothschild (1845–1934) of Paris. Presented to the Jewish Theological Seminary by his grandson.

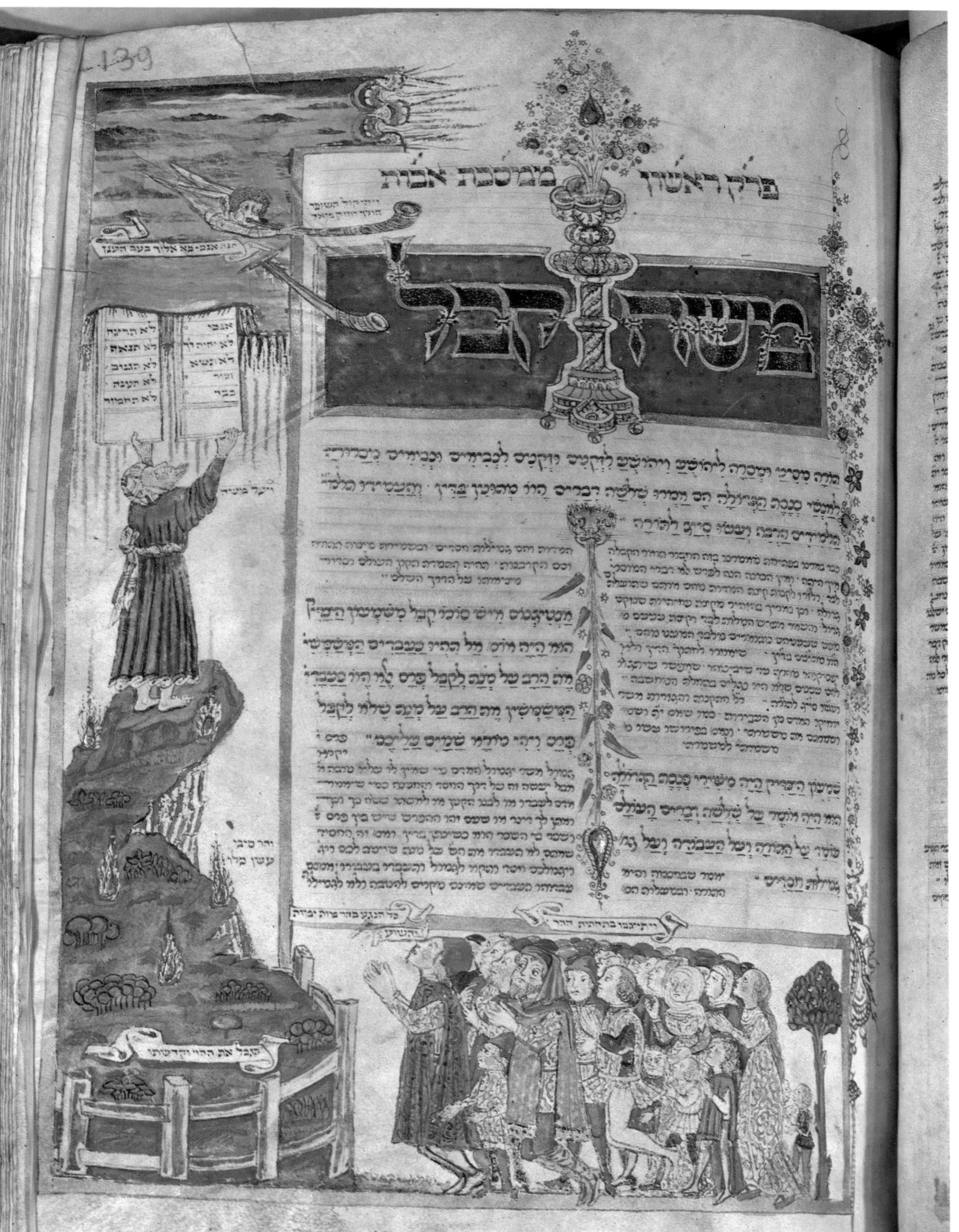
פרק ראשון ממסכת אבות
משה קבל
תורה מסיני ומסרה ליהושע ויהושע לזקנים וזקנים לנביאים ונביאים מסרוה
לאנשי כנסת הגדולה הם אמרו שלשה דברים הוו מתונים בדין · והעמידו תלמי'
תלמידים הרבה ועשו סייג לתורה
אנטיגנוס איש סוכו קבל משמעון הצדי'
הוא היה אומ' אל תהיו כעבדים המשמשי'
את הרב על מנת לקבל פרס אלא הוו כעבדי'
המשמשין את הרב על מנת שלא לקבל
פרס ויהי מורא שמים עליכם
שמעון הצדיק היה משירי כנסת הגדולה
הוא היה אומר על שלשה דברים העולם
עומד על התורה ועל העבודה ועל גמ'
גמילות חסדים
אנכי
לא יהיה לך
לא תשא
זכור
כבד
לא תרצח
לא תנאף
לא תגנוב
לא תענה
לא תחמוד
כל הנוגע בהר מות יומת
ויתיצבו בתחתית ההר
יהושע

PLATE 53

Pesaro Siddur

Siddur of Roman rite
Italy, Pesaro, 1480

The *Pesaro Siddur* is a typical north Italian *siddur* of the late 15th century. In many ways, its plan of illustration is similar to that of the *Rothschild Siddur* (pl. 52). Its decoration is more delicately illuminated in a unified style executed by one artist throughout the manuscript. As in the other *siddurim*, the opening pages of the main divisions of the prayers are decorated by initial-word panels and wide framing borders. There are, however, fewer text illustrations in this *siddur* than in the Rothschild manuscript, and these are always on the lower side of the framing border, usually within a roundel framed by a wreath. Examples of these illustrations are Moses receiving the Tablets of the Law as an illustration to the Mishnah tractate *Avot* (p. 233); a stag in a landscape for the Song of Songs (p. 295); a seated king for Esther (p. 309); Moses on Mount Sinai for the "Great Sabbath" before Shavuot, according to the Italian usage (p. 333); and a green *sukkah* for the feast of Tabernacles (p. 759).
As in the *Rothschild Siddur*, the *Haggadah* is not illustrated. The colophon (pp. 842–3) is surrounded by a border with a rabbit in one of the roundels. The style of the decorations is Ferrarese, with large flowers and interwoven, colored leaves surrounded by filigree pen work and large gold dots. The figure style also shows a pronounced Ferrarese influence. It is possible that the manuscript may have been illuminated in Pesaro by a Ferrarese artist.

PAGES 758–9
Two decorated pages with the final prayers for the Day of Atonement and the beginning of the feast of Tabernacles. The framing border at the bottom of the page contains a green *sukkah* within a green wreath held by two naked puttis. In the top border is an illustration of a stag lying in a meadow.
LETCHWORTH, S. D. SASSOON COLLECTION, MS. 23

SPECIFICATIONS: Fine vellum, 850 pages, $7\frac{1}{8} \times 5\frac{1}{4}$ ins. (18 × 13 cm.). Written in square Italian script, 30 lines to the page. Decorated full-page framing borders to the openings of sectional prayers, some with text illustrations. Many other foliage and floral decorations in the margins of the text and next to initial-word panels. Eighteenth-century, red Morocco binding, gold tooled with silver frames, buckles, and clasps. Gilt edges goffered.

COLOPHON: Pp. 842–3. Abraham b. Mattathias of Treves the Frenchman, completed the work on the *maḥzor* in Pesaro, on Tuesday, eighth of Iyyar, 5240, (April 17, 1480) for Elia b. Solomon of Ravenna.

PROVENANCE: Owned by the Perugia family in the 16th century. Acquired by D. S. Sassoon in 1904.

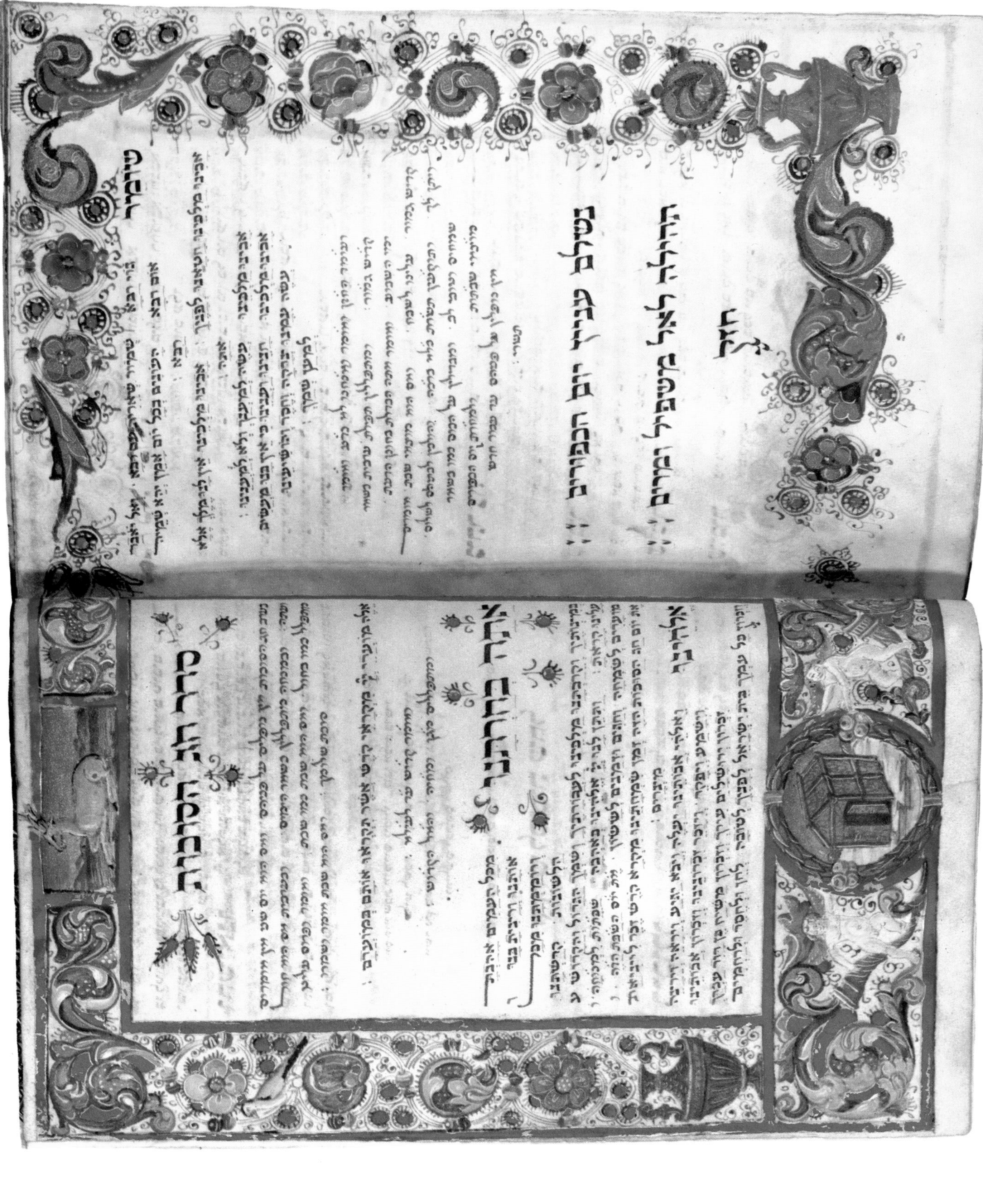

PLATE 54

Canon of Avicenna

Ibn Sinna's Canon (medical treatise)
Italy, Ferrarese, 15th century

The first chapter of each book contains a page with a decorative framed border illustrating the contents of that particular book. The chapters of the manuscript are not in the right order because of incorrect binding. This explains the fact that the introduction appears on folio 448v. The style of the illustrations and the decorations is Ferrarese of the late 15th century, which is characterized by the foliage scrolls interspersed by flowers, animals, birds, dragons, and grotesques. The landscape and the figure style is also Ferrarese in its depth and volume. The castle in the background of folio 448v is similar to a Renaissance Ferrarese castle.

In Book One the illustrated page (fol. 23v) contains a miniature showing a physician teaching his pupils the various medications; other liberal arts are portrayed in the lower borders; in two of the framing borders, the 12 signs of the zodiac are depicted within roundels. In Book Two the page (fol. 38v) has a miniature of a pharmacy on a typical Italian Renaissance street. Naked men displaying different illnesses are portrayed in the borders. In Book Three the page (fol. 317v) has a miniature illustrating the story of a queen who was murdered by the poison poured into her ear. The two margins contain illustrations of court scenes and hermits. Book Four deals with the different kinds of fevers and the page (fol. 126v) has a miniature illustrating two rooms in which sick people are lying in bed. One patient is being attended by a physician whose horse and servant are awaiting him outside; the other is shown after having been visited by a physician who is leaving the room. Below the miniature, on the right is an additional small miniature depicting a lawyer reading the will of the deceased, who is lying in bed. In one border, there are crowned personifications seated within an interlacing scroll.

FOLIO 448V

The introduction to the entire manuscript is found on this page. The half-page miniature shows a madman in prison being haunted by creatures like a dragon, snake, crab, and scorpion. A hermit gathers herbs, which he gives to a woman to administer to the madman. The smaller miniatures illustrate a man being bitten by a snake and death taking its toll of man regardless of his station in life. The meaning of the other miniature on this page is unclear.

BOLOGNA, UNIVERSITY LIBRARY, MS. 2197

SPECIFICATIONS: Vellum, 631 leaves, 17 × 11½ ins (43 × 29 cm.). Written in square and cursive Italian script. Fully-framed and decorated borders for the opening of each of the chapters and the introduction, each with one large miniature illustrating the text.

PROVENANCE: Fol. 1: Many owners in the 16th and 17th centuries. In 1587, the manuscript belonged to the physician (Jehiel) da Pesaro who later converted to Christianity as Vitale Medici. Francesco Maria, Grand Duke of Tuscany, offered him 200 ducats for the manuscript, but Vitale would not sell it. Vitale became a Dominican Friar and the manuscript thus became the property of the Dominican Convent in Bologna. In 1796, the French carried it off to Paris. In 1815, the Pope retrieved the manuscript after the fall of Napoleon. The manuscript remained in the Medical Faculty of Bologna until Pope Pius IX donated it to the Library of the University.

אמר
השר אבו עלי בן סינא
הספר הראשון

PLATE 55

Vercelli Tur Even ha-Ezer

Fragment of *Arba'ah Turim* by R. Jacob b. Asher
Italy (Mantua?), late 15th century

This single page from the *Tur Even ha-Ezer* is attached to a manuscript of legal treatises which were written by Nethanel b. Levi Trabot in Ferrara, 1457 (colophon, fol. 392v). However, the date is not applicable to this page since it was definitely bound in the manuscript at a later period.

The illustration is of a delicately painted wedding scene, which includes the dancing bride and groom and a band of musicians within an arcade. The initial word is written in gold in a floating scroll held by two putti. The entire page is framed by delicate foliage scroll.

The style of the decoration and the figures is undoubtedly Mantuan of the second half of the 15th century.

FOL. 13V
Marriage scene illustrating the opening of *Tur Even ha-Ezer*.
VERCELLI, SEMINARIO VESCOVILE

SPECIFICATIONS: Vellum, 1 leaf, $13\frac{3}{8} \times 9\frac{7}{8}$ ins (33.7 × 24.9 cm.). Written in cursive Italian script.

PLATE 56

Rothschild Miscellany

Miscellany
Northern Italy, Ferrara (?) c. 1470

This manuscript contains over 50 religious and secular books copied in both main and border texts. The religious books include Psalms, Proverbs, the book of Job, a *siddur*, a *mahzor*, and many legal books. Among the secular books are chronicles and historical books, and philosophical and moral treatises either in original Hebrew or translated into Hebrew. This sumptuous book lacks a colophon, but it was undoubtedly the work of several scribes. The name Moses b. Jekuthiel ha-Kohen is mentioned in the Sabbath benedictions (fol. 106) and may be the name of the patron for whom this rich manuscript was written.

The work contains over 300 text illustrations to the various books. Those relating to the biblical and secular books are executed as framed miniatures, either on a full page or within text pages. The illustrations within the miniatures usually have a landscaped background. In the prayerbooks the illustrations without a painted background are usually found within the text, but the framed initial-word panels are decorated, for the most part, by landscapes.

The *Haggadah* (fols. 155v–166) is the most profusely illustrated section of the manuscript. Its well-worn look clearly shows that it was the most used part of the book.

On folio 471 there is a calendar of the lunar cycle starting from 1470, which is evidence that the manuscript was not executed prior to this date.

Almost every page in the manuscript is decorated or illustrated in gold and rich colors, perhaps best described as the style of Ferrara of the second half of the 15th century. They can be favorably compared to those in the *Bible of Borso d'Este* (Modena, Este Lib., MS. V. 12). The stylistic differences between the different parts of the manuscript can be accredited to the work of at least three artists.

FOLIO 65

The Wealth of Job: a full page miniature of a rural landscape that depicts various agricultural and pastoral activities. Inscribed above the border in gold letters, *le-Iyyov la-mishneh* ("and the Lord gave Job twice as much as he had before," Job 42:10).

JERUSALEM, ISRAEL MUSEUM, MS. 180/51

SPECIFICATIONS: Thin vellum, 473 leaves, $8\frac{1}{4} \times 6\frac{5}{8}$ ins (21 × 16 cm.). Written in Italo-Ashkenazi square and cursive script in black and gold. Square script in the main text (Psalms, Proverbs, and Job), 28 lines to the page. The *mahzor* in 27 lines. Cursive script in the main text 35–36 lines per page. In the upper and lower margins, up to 60 lines to the page. Modern vellum binding on wooden boards.

PROVENANCE: From 1832 to c. 1855 in the library of Solomon de Parente in Trieste. Rothschild Library in Paris, MS. 24. The manuscript was stolen from this library during the Nazi occupation and was offered for sale at the Jewish Theological Seminary in New York. The librarian, Alexander Marx recognized it, and it was recovered. As a gesture of gratitude, the Rothschild family agreed to allow the manuscript to remain in the Seminary until 1952, when it was returned to them. Presented anonymously to the Bezalel National Art Museum in 1957.

לאיוב למשנה

PLATE 57

Sefer ha-Ikkarim

Joseph Albo, *Sefer ha-Ikkarim*
Central Italy, 15th century

In this remarkable illustrated manuscript of the philosophical classic *Sefer ha-Ikkarim* ("Book of Dogmas") by Joseph Albo, each of the four chapters and the introduction (fols. 1, 9, 31, 59, 106) is decorated by a similar initial-word panel. In all of them, the initial word is written in gold on a floating scroll carried by putti in a landscape. The entire page is framed by delicate white scrolls interspersed with putti and some cartouches, medallions, and small miniatures. The decoration within the roundels and miniatures is composed mainly of animals, birds, and putti. No text illustrations are found in the illumination. The intricate white scrolls with tiny leaves are typical of Florentine illumination in the second half of the 15th century. The depth of the landscapes within the initial-word panels is achieved by means of several stage-like backdrops.

FOLIO 1

Opening page of the manuscript: Within the top part of the wide framing border are two centaur-putti. In the outer border are partridges, a lion, putti, butterflies, and a deer. In the middle of the lower border are two putti holding a green wreath, within which a coat of arms seems to have been painted at one time; a segment of a moon can still be seen. A hound and a hare, birds, and putti are interspersed between the scrolls. In the initial-word panel are four putti, four trees, and two castles on either side of the scroll.

ROVIGO, BIBLIOTECA SILVESTRIANA, MS. 220

Vellum, 1 + 178 + 1 leaves, $14\frac{1}{4} \times 9\frac{7}{8}$ ins (36 × 25 cm.). Written in cursive Italian script, 37 lines to the page. Five fully-framed illuminated pages and initial-word panels to the introduction and the opening pages of the main sections of the book. Blue, purple, green, yellow, and red filigree work in all chapter numbers, sometimes extending to the borders. Eighteenth-century, brown leather binding on wooden boards, gold-tooled with a central motif. Fan motif in the corner, and double, rectangular frame.

COLOPHON: The scribe wrote the name "Solomon" within the text itself (e.g., fols. 104, 140, 176).

PROVENANCE: Many censors' signatures of the 16th and 17th centuries. Several passages are erased, crossed out, or damaged by the censors.

למה
הקדמה

PLATE 58

Bibliothèque Nationale Portuguese Bible

Bible with masorah magna and parva, and other masoretic treatises
Written and partly illuminated in Lisbon (Portugal), other illuminations in Florence (Italy), end of 15th century

This is a complete and sumptuous manuscript of the Bible, like the three-volume *Lisbon Bible* in the British Museum (pl. 20). The script is Portuguese, as is the arrangement of the additional masoretic treatises. The scribe intended the manuscript should have illuminated pages to all openings of the books of the Bible, like those of the *Lisbon Bible*, and space was left for them. However, only two of 18 intended opening pages were illuminated in the Portuguese style, (fols. 9v to Genesis, and 374v to Chronicles). The foliage and feathery scrolls framing the single column text—interspersed with birds and animals, and the spread peacock, long necked dragon and lion in the lower border are typical of this style. Although the manuscript has no colophon, it must be dated later than the *Lisbon Bible* of 1483 from which the grammatical treatise of Ben Asher was copied incorporating even its mistakes.

Seven other illuminated opening pages were executed in Italy—probably in Florence—before the end of the 15th century in the work-shop of Attavante degli Attavanti (fols. 1 opening page, 40v Exodus, 67 Leviticus, 83v Numbers, 113 Deuteronomy, 137v Joshua, and 251 Isaiah). The opening pages to Joshua and Isaiah, which were written in single columns, are decorated with a deep stage-like arcade, surrounded by wide framing borders. The initial word, in gold, is in the tympanum of the arch, surrounded by putti. The arch rests on columns between which a landscape can be seen. The floor of the arcade is tiled. The framing borders are decorated by foliage motifs, grotesques, animals, and birds emerging from vases. Within the borders there are some cartouches depicting animals within landscapes.

The entire opening page (fol. 1) is decorated with gold scrolls on alternating red, blue, or green ground. In the middle is a green garland of fruit surrounding a bright red ground, in which are precious stones, scrolls, and heads of two putti. The four other opening pages, painted in the Florentine style, have an initial-word panel within one of the two text columns, decorated with foliage scrolls, geometrical interlacing and putti holding a tablet. The entire page is framed by decorated borders leaving scroll-like spaces for the masorah. The borders are decorated like the arcaded pages with foliage motifs, animals, birds, putti, grotesques and wild men. The two styles of illumination can possibly be explained if the manuscript was written in the 1490's in Lisbon and illumination started at a date close to 1496–97—when the Jews were expelled from Portugal—and was not completed. Its owner may then have brought the manuscript to Italy where a new attempt was made to illuminate it but even then it was not completed. The personal manner of Attavante degli Attavanti (court illuminator to Matthias Corvinus, king of Hungary) is evident in the combination of the deep stage-like arcade, the putti playing with monkeys, the delicate landscapes with buildings or animals in the foreground, the decorative motifs emerging from vases, and especially the four combined red precious stones and wild men. The style of the "Geronomite Bible," executed by Attavante in collaboration with the brothers Gherardo and Monte del Fora for Emanuel, king of Portugal (now in Lisbon National Library) is very similar. This Bible was executed between 1494 and 1497 in Florence, where some opening pages of our manuscript were apparently added.

FOLIO 251
Opening page to the book of Isaiah fully decorated with deep stage-like arcade. On the tiled floor are putti playing with a monkey.

PARIS, BIBLIOTHEQUE NATIONALE COD. HEB. 15

SPECIFICATIONS: Vellum, 524 leaves, $12\frac{5}{8} \times 9\frac{3}{4}$ ins (32 × 24.7 cm.). Written in square Sephardi script, 28 lines in two columns. Nine fully framed decorated pages to the title page and to openings of books. Nine folios with spaces left around text for illuminations (folios 153v Judg., 169 Sam., 207 Kings, 278 Jer., 312v Ezek., 346 Hos., 416 Ps., 448v Job, 463 Prov.).

PROVENANCE: Folio 324v: sale inscription stating that Manasseh b. Jekuthiel of Tivoli sold the Bible to the physician R. Elhanan for the sum of 47 ducats on the 28th of Tammuz 5264 (July 10th, 1504). Other entries from 1529. Number LIX in the library of Henry IV.

חזון ב ר״פ וסימנהון חזון ישעיהו בן אמוץ ר״ס ספרא חזון
עבדיה׳ ׃ תכו ב׳ וסימנהון והם תכו לרגלך על מה תכו עוד תוסיפו ׃

חזון

ישעיהו בן אמוץ אשר חזה על יהודה וירושלם
בימי עזיהו יותם אחז יחזקיהו מלכי יהודה׃ שמעו
שמים והאזיני ארץ כי יהוה דבר בנים גדלתי
ורוממתי והם פשעו בי׃ ידע שור קנהו וחמור
אבוס בעליו ישראל לא ידע עמי לא התבונן׃ הוי
גוי חטא עם כבד עון זרע מרעים בנים משחיתים
עזבו את יהוה נאצו את קדוש ישראל נזרו אחור׃
על מה תכו עוד תוסיפו סרה כל ראש לחלי וכל
לבב דוי׃ מכף רגל ועד ראש אין בו מתם פצע
וחבורה ומכה טריה לא זרו ולא חבשו ולא רככה
בשמן׃ ארצכם שממה עריכם שרפות אש אדמתכם
לנגדכם זרים אכלים אתה ושממה כמהפכת זרים׃
ונותרה בת ציון כסכה בכרם כמלונה במקשה
כעיר נצורה׃ לולי יהוה צבאות הותיר לנו שריד
כמעט כסדם היינו לעמרה דמינו׃

טריה ב׳ בתרי לישנ׳ וסימנהון וימצא לחי חמור טריה׳ פצע וחבורה ומכה׳ ׃
ורוממתי ב׳ א׳ מל׳ וא׳ חס׳ וסימנהון בנים גדלתי ורוממתי׳ ורממתי עור׳ דין חס׳ ׃
כעיר ב׳ וסימנהון כמלונה במקשה כעיר נצורה׳ כעיר שחברה לה יחדו׳ ׃

PLATE 59

Hamburg Halakhah Miscellany

Isaac Düren, *Sha'arei Dura* and *Hilkhot Niddah* with commentary; Meir of Rothenburg, *Berakhot*
Italy, Padua 1477

The *Hamburg Halakhah Miscellany* is a small manuscript containing treatises on dietary laws and laws pertaining to women. Three sections of the book (fols. 3v, 75v, and 93v) are decorated with full page miniatures and the last two are part of initial-word panels. The miniatures depicting figures within a landscape are related directly to the text. The first miniature (fol. 3v) dealing with dietary laws, depicts a man seated under an arch inspecting a chicken; (also marginal illustration of a man slaughtering a deer, fol. 6). In the landscape are four rabbits. The second miniature (fol. 25v), an opening page to the laws on menstruation is divided horizontally into two parts. On top is the initial-word panel and at the bottom a marriage ceremony within a mountainous landscape. The third miniature (fol. 93v), an opening page and a large initial-word panel to Meir of Rothenburg's list of benedictions, starts with those on partaking of fruits depicting, in the lower part of the panel, a youth climbing a ladder to pick fruit from a tree.
The illumination of this manuscript was executed by two different artists. One, a less accomplished artist who painted the miniatures on folios 3v and 93v and two initial-word panels (fols. 44 and 50). The second, better, artist painted the miniature (fol. 75v) reproduced here, the marginal illustration on folio 6, as well as a band on the outer and lower margins of folio 4, framing the general outline of the ten chapters of *Sha'arei Dura*. The first artist was a somewhat inferior draughtsman. His figures are small and resemble Florentine pen drawings. The work of the second artist resembles Venetian art, though it could be Paduan. His drawings are good, his modeling is sure, and his landscapes have depth, even in the unframed marginal illustration. The first colophon of this manuscript (fol. 118v), at the end of the *Benedictions*, states that the manuscript was completed in Padua in 1477, a likely date and origin for the style of the more accomplished artist. The other artist may have been his disciple, or a contemporary of Florentine origin, working in Padua.
A second colophon from 1492 (fol. 121v) at the end of the shortened version of the *Benedictions* indicates that it must have been added to an existing manuscript.
A full-page opening to the treatise on the laws on menstruation, divided horizontally with the initial-word panel on top, and a miniature below. It shows a marriage ceremony, set within a landscape. The bridegroom is placing a wedding ring on the bride's finger. The groom has a white circle—the Jewish badge—on his elegant coat, and a dog is seen behind him. On the right-hand side of the landscape is a mountain shaped like a seated figure of a woman, holding the left arm across the lap.

FOLIO 75V

SPECIFICATIONS: Vellum, 1 + 122 + 1 leaves (foliated in Hebrew alphabet), 6 × 4½ ins (15.2 × 11.5 cm.). Written in cursive Italian script, 18 lines in the main text and 36 lines in the commentary in the outer borders. A short version of the *Benedictions* was copied in 1492 at the end of the book (fols. 119–122). Three painted full page miniatures and initial-word panels (fols. 3v, 75v, 93v), one marginal illustration (fol. 6) and one decoration (fol. 4), two painted initial-word panels (fols. 44, 50). The Commentary is written in geometrical shapes. Eighteenth-century, blind-tooled, parchment binding.
HAMBURG, STAATS- UND UNIVERSITÄTSBIBLIOTHEK, COD. HEB. 337 (SCRIN 132)

COLOPHON: Fol. 118v; "The scribe Menahem b. Jekuthiel ha-Kohen Rapa, completed in the year 5237 [1477] in Padua . . ." Fol. 121v: "The shortened 'Benedictions by *MaHaRaM*' [= Meir of Rothenburg] were completed on Tuesday, 23rd of I Adar 5252 [1492]."

PROVENANCE: Fol. 1: Obituary and birth notes of the Rapa family, the family of the original scribe: 5239 (1479), 5365 (1505), the manuscript was given as a present to his son in 1531. Fol. 120: Censor's signature 1613.
The manuscript was still in the possession of the Rapa (= Rapaport) family in 1701, when more obituaries were inscribed.

PLATE 60

Frankfort Mishneh Torah

Maimonides' *Mishneh Torah*
North Italy (Mantua?) 15th century

This is another example of an illustrated *Mishneh Torah*, about one hundred years later than the *Jerusalem Mishneh Torah* (pl. 47). Unfortunately, no comparative iconographical study can be carried out, since both manuscripts are incomplete and their text illustrations do not correspond. No more than the first 40 leaves of the *Jerusalem Mishneh Torah* were illuminated. Only part of the books 7–14 of the Frankfort manuscript have survived, and mostly incorrectly bound. The manuscript starts with book 8 which deals with the sacrifices in the Temple (fol. 1), but continues with book 7, chapter 5 (fol. 17). The illustrations are therefore not in the right sequence.
The illumination of the manuscript consists of six, large, miniature title panels illustrating the text, at the beginning of each of the existing book openings. The text illustrations are shown within a landscape and a decorated ground, on which the title is written in gold, such as: Sacrifices in the Temple (fol. 1-Book 8); preparations for Passover meal (fol. 93-book 9); dead man in a tent (fol. 106v–book 10); and the Court of the Sanhedrin (fol. 298-book 14). The title of almost every chapter has a text illustration in the margin, or within the title panel. The most interesting ones depict legal matters, using contemporary costumes, buildings, and customs. The style of the illuminations points to the second half of the 15th century, though Müller and Von Schlosser dated it to the middle of the 15th century. H. Swarzenski and R. Schilling also pointed out its relation to the style of Mantua. The heavy figures with modeled drapery, and the heavily painted landscapes are typical of this school. In the absence of a colophon, only the style can help in dating and placing the manuscript.

FOLIO 1
An historiated title panel for the "Book of Sacrifices," depicting two priests performing the sacrifice outside the Temple. The Temple is represented, as in many medieval paintings, by an octagonal domed building. This resembles the Dome of the Rock, built on the site of the Jerusalem Temple.
NEW YORK, PRIVATE COLLECTION (formerly Frankfort, Municipal Library, ms. Ausst. 6)

SPECIFICATIONS: Vellum, 347 leaves, $8\frac{3}{8} \times 7$ ins (22×17.6 cm.). Written in cursive Ashkenazi script, 46 lines to the page, with square script for titles and initial words. Six large title miniatures, for openings of the books, smaller painted initial-word panels mostly with text illustrations. The manuscript was cropped by a binder and at least one marginal illustration was cut out (fol. 190). Bound in calf leather with gold tooling in the first half of the 19th century.

PROVENANCE: The manuscript was incorrectly bound and badly cropped in the beginning of the 19th century, and the first part of books one to seven are missing. Up to World War II it was in the Municipal Library of Frankfort; it is now in a private collection in New York.

שאלו שלום ירושלים ישליו אוהביך׃ ספר שמיני והוא ס

ספר

הלכותיו תשעה. וזהו סדורן. הלכות בית הבחירה. הלכות כלי המקדש והעובדים בו. הלכות ביאת המקדש. הלכות איסורי מזבח. הלכות מעשה הקרבנות. הלכות תמידין ומוספין. הלכות פסולי המוקדשין. הלכות עבודת יום הכפורים. הלכות מעילה׃

הלכות בית הבחירה

פרק ראשון

יש בכללן שש מצות. שלשה מצות עשה. ושלשה מצות לא תעשה. ופרטן כך׃

וביאור מצות אלו בפרקים אלו׃

מצות עשה לעשות בית ליי׳ להיות מקריבין עליו קרבנות. וחוגגין אליו שלש פעמים בשנה. שנ׳ ועשו לי מקדש. וכבר נתפרש בתורה משכן שעשה משה רבינו

Notes

References to books and articles which appear in L. A. Mayer, *Bibliography of Jewish Art* (1967), are quoted by referring to their number (e.g., Mayer, 2680).

Catalogues of manuscripts are not listed in the Mayer Bibliography and are therefore abbreviated thus:

Margoliouth, Cat = G. Margoliouth, *Catalogue of the Hebrew and Samaritan Manuscripts in the British Museum*, 3 vols. (1899, 1905, 1909–15; reprinted 1965).

Leveen, Cat = J. Leveen, *Introduction, Indexes, Brief Descriptions of Accessions and Addenda and Corrigenda* (1935); vol. 4 of the above catalogue by G. Margoliouth.

Neubauer, Cat = A. Neubauer, *Catalogue of Hebrew Manuscripts in the Bodleian Library and the College Libraries of Oxford* (1886), 2 vols. (1886–1906).

Zotenberg, Cat = H. Zotenberg, *Catalogue de manuscrits Hébreux et Samaritains de la Bibliothèque Impériale* (Paris, 1866).

For other abbreviations see Mayer, p. 17.

[1] The problem of rabbinical laws and idolatry is dealt with extensively by E. E. Urbach (Mayer, 2680, 2681). See also J. Gutman (Mayer, 993).

[2] Goodenough (Mayer, 880), vol. 3, fig. 854.

[3] Yale University Art Gallery: cf. Goodenough (Mayer, 880), vol. 3, fig. 959.

[4] The synagogue was excavated during 1932–34 by Comte du Mesnil du Buisson of the French Academy, under the direction of Yale University, and was reconstructed in the National Museum in Damascus; see Kraeling (Mayer, 1344).

[5] The problem of early Hebrew illuminated manuscripts was dealt with quite extensively as early as 1901. Joseph Strzygowski has assumed the existence of a Jewish biblical cycle of pictures in Hebrew illuminated manuscripts which served as prototypes for Early Christian Greek and Latin illumination like the *Alexandrian World Chronicle* and the *Ashburnham Pentateuch*. During the past 15 years, many papers have been devoted to the question of the existence of Hebrew illumination in antiquity. The most important studies are: Leveen (Mayer, 1496); C. Roth (Mayer, 2207); K. Weitzmann (Mayer, 2775, 2776A); C. R. Morey, *Early Christian Art* (1958), 71, 78, 151; Nordström (Mayer, 1900, 1901); Hempel (Mayer, 1071, 1073); and J. Gutmann, who has recently (1966) summed up the "Present State of the Question" (Mayer, 2972).

[6] *Targum Jonathan* and other Midrashim; see Kraeling (Mayer, 1344), 177–8, pls. LXVII–LXVIII.

[7] Paris, Bibliothèque Nationale, Nouvelles Acquisitions Latines, 2334, folio 22v; see J. Gutmann (Mayer, 990), 65–66; idem (Mayer, 2972), 40, fig. 8.

[8] The quotation in the Talmud refers to a *baraita* which is a pronouncement by the rabbis of the Mishnah, though not an integral part of the Mishnah. This dates the story to the late first or second centuries C.E.: see Leveen (Mayer, 1496), 3.

[9] The story of the gold-written Septuagint is repeated by Philo and Josephus. There is no basis for the assumption that the family Beit Hagirah, in the time of the Second Temple, were illuminators; see P. Romanoff, "A Family of Illuminators in the time of the Second Temple" (JQR, 26 (1935), 29–35). The material collected here can prove only that the Beit Hagirah family were *katevanim umanim*, that is artist-scribes or calligraphers; see Leveen (Mayer, 1496), 6.

[10] Naméyi (Mayer, 1835).

[11] General characteristics of Hebrew illumination and its history can be found as early as 1778 in Tychsen (Mayer, 2674); D. Kaufmann, in: Müller (Mayer, 1792), 255–311; M. Steinschneider (Mayer, 2524), 24–27; idem (Mayer, 2523), 326 ff.; G. Margoliouth (Mayer, 1638); Frauberger (Mayer, 742); E. N. Adler (Mayer, 24, 25); R. Wischnitzer (Mayer, 2811); Landsberger, in: C. Roth (Mayer, 2232), 377–454; J. Gutmann (Mayer, 2970) is the most recent study.

[12] An example of an outmoded manuscript is the "Sister" to the *Golden Haggadah* [pl. 9] in the British Museum (MS. Or. 2884), which is iconographically related to the *Golden Haggadah* [pl. 8] and reveals an Italo-French style in its drawings.

[13] Other Spanish examples are the *First Kennicott Bible* (1476) [pl. 17], by the artist Joseph ibn Ḥayyim, and the works of the Ashkenazi scribe Joel b. Simeon who headed a workshop of scribes and illuminators in Germany and Italy in the second half of the 15th century, [pls. 42 and 50].

[14] See J. Hillgarth and B. Narkiss (Mayer, 1096), 316–20.

[15] On Jewish distortion of human figures in the south of Germany, see B. Narkiss in *Maḥzor Lipsiae* (Mayer, 1222A), 103, and H. L. C. Jaffé in: *The Birds' Head Haggadah*, introductory volume (1967), 66–72.

[16] See Ameisenowa (Mayer, 58), 21–45.

[17] *Tosafot* to Babylonian Talmud, Yoma, 54b.

[18] For examples see plates 4, 14, 28, 34, 35, 49, 50.

[19] J. Gutmann (Mayer, 2969), 24 n.43; B. Narkiss, in: *Maḥzor Lipsiae* (Mayer, 1222A), 98, 107; idem, in: *The Birds' Head Haggadah*, introductory volume (1967), 94.

[20] See Müller (Mayer, 1792), pls. IV, 2, 3V; C. Roth (Mayer, 2235), 27, fol. IV, 2, 3V.

[21] See Millard Meiss, "Italian Style in Catalonia and a Fourteenth Century Catalan Workshop", in: *Journal of Walters Art Gallery*, 4 (1941), 45–87; F. Wormald (Mayer, 2900); R. Edelman (Mayer, 360).

[22] On medieval materials and techniques in general see D. V. Thompson, *The Materials and Techniques of Medieval Painting* (1956), 23–30.

[23] See Thompson, *op. cit.*, 27.

[24] See C. Bernheimer (Mayer, 265). On artistic aspects of Hebrew paleography see L. Blau (Mayer, 296).

[25] See Thompson, *op. cit.*, 81–82.

[26] See Thompson, *op. cit.*, 74ff.

[27] Paris, Bibliothèque Nationale, Cod. héb. 20, fol. 69.

[28] S. Goitein (Mayer, 848A), 169★–72★.

[29] R. Hoering, *British Museum Karaite Manuscripts . . .* (1899).

[30] British Museum, MS. Or. 9880; see M. Gaster (Mayer, 800).

[31] M. Derenbourg, "Manuel du Lecteur, d'un auteur inconnu", in: *Journal Asiatique*, 16 (1870), 309–550.

[32] See Pinsker, *Likkutei Kadmoniyyot*, 1 (1860), 32; D. Fürst, *Geschichte des Karäerthmus* (1862); H. Graetz, *History of the Jews*, 3 (1949), 207; idem, in: MGWJ, 20 (1871), 1–12, 49–59; B. Clare, in: *Tarbiz*, 14 (1942/43),

156–73; 15 (1943/44), 36–49; A. Dothan, in: *Sinai*, 41 (1947), 280–312, 350–62.

33 See P. Kahle (Mayer, 2003). The manuscript was given as a present to the Karaite synagogue in Jerusalem by the patron of the manuscript, Jabez b. Solomon the Babylonian (p. 583). It also has Karaite formulas at ends of books, such as *Dirshu Adonai be-Himazo* ("Seek God where He is") on p. 581.

34 For carpet pages of Korans from the tenth to the twelfth centuries, see Ettinghausen (Mayer, 670).

35 See Pinder Wilson and Ettinghausen (Mayer, 2003); also Ettinghausen (Mayer, 669).

36 For example, British Museum, MS. Or. 2363, fols. 67v–68 and 238v–240 (Persia, 12th cent.); MS. Or. 2348, fols. 76–76v and 151–152v (Yemen, 1469).

37 See British Museum, MS. Or. 1476, fol. 43–43v.

38 See British Museum, MS. Or. 2363, fol. 73v.

39 See description and bibliography of pl. 3.

40 Oxford, Bodleian Library, MS. Heb. 2807; other similarly decorated *ketubbot* are in Cambridge University Library, T.-S. 12.453; T.-S. 16–19; T.-S. 8/90; T.-S.K. 10.

41 Kaufmann (Mayer, 1235).

42 See F. Spalding, *Mudejar Ornament in Manuscripts* (1953).

43 British Museum, MS. Or. 2887.

44 Paris, Bibliothèque Nationale, MS. Lat. 4670A.

45 Letchworth, S. D. Sassoon Collection, MS. 499.

46 Letchworth, S. D. Sassoon Collection, MS. 487.

47 Oxford, Bodleian Library, MS. Can. Or. 77.

48 Dublin, Trinity College, MS. M.2.5.

49 Paris, Bibliothèque Nationale, Cod. héb. 592.

50 An illustration of two human-headed dogs can hardly be regarded as text illustration; see British Museum, Harley MS. 5649, fol. 159v.

51 New York, Hispanic Society of America, MS. B.241.

52 Jerusalem, Jewish National and University Library, Hebrew Manuscripts, 4°, 790; see bibliography to pl. 5.

53 Lisbon, National Library, MS. 72; see bibliography to pl. 6.

54 Paris, Bibliothèque Nationale, Cod. héb. 7, fols. 12v–13; see Zotenberg, Cat, no. 7.

55 An earlier Bible of the same type, from Toledo (1277), is in Parma, Biblioteca Palatina, MS. 2668; see G. Tamani, "Elenco dei manoscritti ebraici miniati e decorati della 'Palatina' di Parma," in: *La Bibliofilia*, 70, no. 1–2 (1968), 46. For other representations of implements see Nordström, "Some miniatures in Hebrew Bibles," in: *Synthronon*, 2 (1968), 89–105, where other references can be found.

56 For the other page of the *First Leningrad Bible* see Stassof (Mayer, 2515), pl. 2. Other medieval representations of square-branched *menorot* are quite common. Two of them are reproduced here [pls. 23B and 24], both from France from the end of the 13th century. In the *British Museum Miscellany* (Add. MS. 11639) there is a second picture of a square-branched *menorah* on folio 522v. From Spain as well, there are pictures of square-branched *menorot*. In a plan of the Second Temple executed in 1306 in Soria by the artist Joshua b. Abraham ibn Gaon, attached to a Spanish Bible codex (Oxford, Bodleian Library, MS. Kennicott 2, fols. 2v–3), there are traces of a *menorah* of this type. In another Bible, which was illuminated by Joshua ibn Gaon in 1301 (Paris, Bibliothèque Nationale, Cod. héb. 20, fol. 54), a marginal text illustration of a square-branched *menorah* was painted. The reason may have been to avoid a true replica of the round-branched Temple *menorah*, or perhaps to distinguish between the Tabernacle and the Temple *menorot*. See B. Narkiss, "Joshua ibn Gaon's Plan of the Temple," in: *Proceedings of the Fifth World Congress of Jewish Studies*.

57 See J. Gutmann, "When the Kingdom Comes," in: *Art Journal*, 27 no. 2 (1967/68), 172, figs. 9–11.

58 Letchworth, S. D. Sassoon Collection, MS. 368; see bibliography to pl. 16.

59 British Museum, MS. Or. 2201, fol. 2. Probably not an original part of the manuscript, and possibly of an earlier date.

60 Oxford, Bodleian Library, MS. Kennicott 2, fols. 2v–3; see C. Roth (Mayer, 2205), 365–8; B. Narkiss, *op. cit.*, note 48.

61 Paris, Bibliothèque Nationale, Cod. héb. 1314, fol. 3v.

62 See description of pl. 16.

63 Paris, Bibliothèque Nationale, Cod. héb. 20, fols. 2, 7v, 8.

64 Paris, Bibliothèque Nationale, Cod. héb. 21, fol. 1.

65 As for instance in the *Kennicott Bible* of 1476 (Oxford, Bodleian Library, MS. Kennicott 1); and perhaps also in the *Cervera Bible* of 1300 (Lisbon, National Library, MS. 72).

66 Paris, Bibliothèque Nationale, Cod. héb. 1314, fol. 5v.

67 British Museum, MS. Or. 2626–28; see description of pl. 20.

68 New York, Hispanic Society of America, MS. B. 241; see description of pl. 21.

69 Lisbon, National Library, MS. 72; see description of pl. 61.

70 The flock of chickens motif on fol. 442v, is repeated in the *Kennicott Bible*; see T. Metzger (Mayer, 1728B).

71 Oxford, Bodleian Library, MS. Kennicott 1, fol. 447; see description and bibliography to pl. 17.

72 For example, a French Bible in Cambridge University Library (Add. MS. 468), which has many text illustrations.

73 Letchworth, S. D. Sassoon Collection, MS. 82; see C. Roth (Mayer, 2205), 367.

74 For example, *Shem Tov Bible* (MS. Sassoon 82), fol. 501; *Cervera Bible* (Lisbon, MS. 72), fols. 118v, 448v.

75 Dublin, Trinity College, MS. M.2.6.

76 Paris, Bibliothèque Nationale, Cod. héb. 20.

77 For illustrations from the *First Kennicott Bible* see C. Roth (Mayer, 2221).

78 C. Roth (Mayer, 2229), 661.

79 For example, British Museum, Add. MS. 15250, fol. 8; 15252, fol. 116v.

80 For example, Paris, Bibliothèque Nationale, Cod. héb. 1314, fols. 52v–53; and British Museum, MS. Or. 2201, fols. 34v–35.

81 For example, the *Psalter of St. Louis*, Paris, Bibliothèque Nationale, MS. Lat. 10525; see J. Porcher, *French Miniatures* (1960), 44–47.

82 For example, the *Paris Psalter*, Paris, Bibliothèque Nationale, MS. Gr. 139; see H. Buchthal, *The Miniatures of the Paris Psalter* (1938).

[83] See S. B. Freehof, "Home Rituals and the Spanish Synagogue," in: *Studies in Honor of A. A. Neuman* (1962), 222–6.

[84] For example, the *Dragon Haggadah* in Hamburg, Staats- und Universitätsbibliothek, Cod. héb. 155; see description to pl. 22.

[85] As in the *Golden Haggadah*, British Museum, Add. MS. 27210, fol. 5.

[86] As in the *Sarajevo Haggadah*, fol. 20.

[87] As in the *Kaufmann Haggadah*, Budapest, Hungarian Academy of Sciences, MS. A422, fol. 9v.

[88] For example: *Haggadot* in *siddurim*, S. D. Sassoon Collection, MS. 59 and 1017; Cambridge, University Library, Add. MSS. 514, 1214, and 1203; Paris, Bibliothèque Nationale, Cod. héb. 592, and 637.

[89] See M. Metzger, "Two fragments of a Spanish 14th century Haggadah," in: *Gesta*, 6 (1966), 25–34.

[90] For example, Letchworth, S. D. Sassoon Collection, MS. 417; British Museum, Harley MSS. 5689–5699.

[91] For example, Letchworth, S. D. Sassoon Collection, MS. 1047; Cambridge, University Library, Add. MS. 1493; British Museum, Harley MS. 7586B; Paris, Bibliothèque Nationale, Cod. héb. 689.

[92] See bibliography to pl. 18.

[93] Oxford, Bodleian Library, MS. Poc. 376.

[94] Paris, Bibliothèque Nationale, MS. Esp. 30.

[95] See bibliography to pl. 23, especially Leveen, and Metzger.

[96] Paris, Bibliothèque Nationale, Cod. héb. 36; see bibliography to pl. 24.

[97] For example, Dublin, Trinity College Library, MS. F.6.4; London, Lambeth Palace, MS. 435; Oxford, Bodleian Library, MS. Laud Or. 174, which belonged to the Abbey of Bury St. Edmunds.

[98] Oxford, Bodleian Library, MS. Bodl. Or. 621, fol. 1v.

[99] For example, Jerusalem, C. Roth Collection, MS. 301; Oxford, Bodleian Library, MSS. Arch. Seld. A.5., and Can. Or. 30; Manchester, John Rylands Library, MS. Heb. 31.

[100] For example, Cambridge, Trinity College, MS. F.12.70–71 (possibly from Avignon, 1419).

[101] For example, Cambridge, University Library, MS. 3127, dated 1399; British Museum, MS. Or. 10733.

[102] Oxford, Bodleian Library, MS. Hunt 54; and MS. Marshall Or. 41.

[103] For example, Paris, Bibliothèque Nationale, Cod. héb. 1181 (a medical treatise, dated 1487); and 1136 (Avicenna Code, Vilialon, France, dated also 1487).

[104] Good examples are: The *Aich Bible* of c. 1240, and the *Graduale* of St. Katharinenthal of 1312; see E.J. Beer, *Beiträge aus oberrheinischer Buchmalerei* (1959; and A. Boeckler, *Deutsche Buchmaterei Voragotischer Zeit* (1959).

[105] Paris, Bibliothèque Nationale, Cod. héb. 5, of 1298; Oxford, Bodleian Library, MS. Can. Or. 91, 1304; Hamburg, Universitätsbibliothek, MS. Levi 19, of 1300.

[106] Darmstadt, Hessische Landes- und Hochschule, Cod. Or. 13.

[107] *Maḥzor Leipzig*, Universitätsbibliothek, MS. V. 1102; vol. I, fol. 51v; Oxford, Bodleian Library, MS. Laud 321, fol. 51; *Maḥzor Worms*, vol. I, fol. 57; Dresden, A. 46a, fol. 82.

[108] *Maḥzor Leipzig*, vol. I, fol. 53v; Bodleian Library MS. Laud 321, fol. 53; MS. Adler 476, Bamberg 1279; MS. Mich. 617, fol. 21, dated 1258; *Maḥzor Worms*, vol. I, fol. 59.

[109] *Maḥzor Leipzig*, vol. I, fol. 59; Bodleian Library, MS. Mich. 617, fol. 26; *Maḥzor Worms*, vol. I, fol. 64v.

[110] *Maḥzor Leipzig*, vol. I, fol. 64v; Budapest, Academy of Sciences, A. 384, fol. 103v; *Maḥzor Worms*, vol. I, fol. 72v.

[111] *Maḥzor Leipzig*, vol. I, fols. 85–87; Budapest, A. 384, pp. 284–89, fol. 133; *Maḥzor Worms*, vol. I, fols. 95v–97v; MS. Mich. 617, fols. 49–51.

[112] *Maḥzor Leipzig*, vol. I, fol. 130v; British Museum, MS. Add. 22413, fol. 3v; *Maḥzor Worms*, vol. I, fol. 151.

[113] *Maḥzor Leipzig*, vol. I, fols. 26v, 54, 66; Bodleian Library, MS. Laud 321, fol. 184; MS. Reg. 1, fol. 207v; *Double Maḥzor* Breslau, fol. 46v.

[114] *Maḥzor Leipzig*, vol. II, 74v, 85, 164v; MS. Mich, 617, fol. 48; Tübingen, Or. Fol. 388, fol. 69; *Maḥzor Worms*, vol. II, fol. 72v; *Double Maḥzor*, Breslau, fol. 89.

[115] For instance: MS. Sassoon 511, p. 17, circa 1502.

[116] Darmstadt, Hessische Landes- und Hochschule, Cod. Or. 8.

[117] Other South German illuminated *Mishneh Torah* manuscripts are: Budapest, Academy of Sciences, MS. Kaufmann A. 78 of 1310; Oxford, Bodleian Library, MS. Arch. Seld. B2; Nuremberg, Protestant Archive, MS. 18–12 of 1389; MS. Sassoon 1043 of 1355; see B. Narkiss, in: *Kirjath Sepher*, 43 (1967/68), 298.

[118] MS. Opp. 154; Peachy and Alesander 162—related in style to Parma MS. 2895 and Fürstenberg MS. 242; also Bodleian Library MS. Can. Or. 59.

[119] For example: Israel Museum, MS. 180/55, from Florence, late 15th century.

[120] Parma, Biblioteca Palatina, MS. Parm. 3216 (MS. De'Rossi 1261), and in a *Moreh Nevukhim* (1283) British Museum, MS. Harl. 7586A.

[121] British Museum, MS. Add. 26968, fol. 340v; other manuscripts executed for this patron are: MS. Or. 2736, *Siddur* of 1390; and Bodleian Library, MS. Can. Or. 81 (Rashi's commentary on the Pentateuch, Pisa 1396).

[122] Parma, MSS. De'Rossi, 180, 197, 326, 475, 1135, 1147; MS. Sassoon 405; British Museum, MSS. Add. 15421, 21967, 26974; Bodleian Library, MS. Opp. Add. 4°38; MS. Mich. 489; MS. Can. Or. 5, and 79; see C. Bernheimer, *Paleografia Ebraica* (1924), 263–4, 266, 278.

[123] See C. Roth, *The Aberdeen Codex of the Hebrew Bible* (1958).

Glossary

A.C. (Lat. "*anno creationis*"): the "year of creation"; the reckoning from the creation of the world according to the Jewish calendar.

afikoman: piece broken from the middle of three *mazzot* used in the *seder* ceremony on Passover eve.

aggadah (Heb. "tale" or "lesson"): name given to those sections of rabbinic literature which contain homiletic expositions of the Bible, stories, legends, folklore, anecdotes, or maxims. In contradistinction to *halakhah*.

A.H. (Lat. "*anno hegirae*"): "in the year of the hegira [flight]" of Muhammad to Medina; date at which Muslims set the beginning of their time reckoning.

amora (pl. *amora'im*): title given to the Jewish scholars in Palestine and especially Babylonia in the third to sixth centuries. These scholars were responsible for the *Gemara*.

aravah (Heb. "willow"): one of the *arba'ah minim* ("four species") used on Sukkot ("festival of Tabernacles") together with the *etrog*, *hadas*, and *lulav*.

arba kanfot (Heb. "four corners") or *tallit katan* (Heb. "small prayer shawl"): smaller form of the *tallit* which is worn perpetually under the outer garment by male Jews.

arba parashiyyot (Heb. "four portions"): special portions which are read on the Sabbaths preceding Passover.

Arba'ah Turim: codification of talmudic decisions and later commentaries, compiled by Jacob b. Asher (c. 1270–1343).

Ashkenaz: since the ninth century, a term applied to Germany.

Ashkenazim: term applied to the Jews of Germany and thereafter to their descendants, wherever resident. In contradistinction to Sephardim.

baraita (pl. *beraitot*) (Aram. "external"): teaching or a tradition of the *tanna'im* that has been excluded from the Mishnah and incorporated in a later collection.

bar mitzvah (Heb. "one who is obliged to fulfill the commandment"): ceremony marking the initiation of a boy at the age of 13 into the Jewish religious community and into observance of the precepts of the Torah. The central feature is the calling-up of the boy to the reading of the Law in the synagogue.

behemoth: legendary creature who will engage in mortal combat with leviathan at the end of time, and is destined to be served as a delicacy at the feast of the Righteous.

blood libel: false allegation that Jews murder Christians in order to obtain blood for Passover or other rituals.

C.E.: "Common Era"; Jewish designation for the Common Christian calendar (A.D.).

"*Dayyeinu*" (Heb. "it would have sufficed us"): refrain of a hymn in the Passover *Haggadah*.

Ein ha-Kore: Ashkenazi handbook for guidance in the correct reading and cantillation of the Torah.

etrog: one of the *arba'ah minim* ("four species"). A fruit of the citrus family used on Sukkot ("festival of Tabernacles") together with the *lulav*, *hadas*, and *aravah*.

feast of the Righteous: legendary feast which will take place at the coming of the Messiah at which the Righteous will partake of the flesh of the leviathan, the *behemoth*, and the *ziz*.

Four Cups: four cups of wine, symbolizing the four promises of redemption, drunk during the Passover *seder* ritual.

Four Sons (Midrash of): part of the Passover *Haggadah*, in which a reference is made to four types of children: the wise, the wicked, the simple, and the one who does not know how to ask questions.

Gemara (lit. "completion" or "learning"): traditions, discussions, and rulings of the *amora'im*, both commenting on and supplementing the Mishnah, and forming part of the Babylonian and the Palestinian Talmud.

genizah: depository for used sacred books. The best known was discovered in the synagogue of Fostat, (Old Cairo).

hadas (Heb. "myrtle"): one of the *arba'ah minim* ("four species") used on Sukkot ("festival of Tabernacles") together with the *etrog*, *lulav*, and *aravah*.

haftarah (pl. *haftarot*): designation of the portion from the prophetical books recited after the reading from the Pentateuch on Sabbaths and Holy Days.

Haggadah: ritual recited in the home on Passover eve at the *seder* table.

halakhah (pl. *halakhot*): an accepted decision in rabbinic law. Also refers to those parts of the Talmud concerned with legal matters. In contradistinction to *aggadah*.

Ḥanukkah (Heb. "dedication"): feast of Lights; an eight-day celebration commemorating the victory of Judah Maccabee over Antiochus Epiphanes and the subsequent rededication of the Temple (165 B.C.E.).

ḥaroset: symbolic food made from apple, nuts, and wine eaten at the Passover *seder* ritual.

ḥazzan (Heb. "cantor"): precentor who intones the liturgy and leads the prayers in the synagogue.

Karaite: name given to members of a Jewish sect which rejected the Oral Law. Originating in the eighth century.

kerovah (pl. *kerovot*): religious poem incorporated in the Eighteen Benedictions, written for Sabbaths and festivals as well as Purim and fast-days.

ketubbah (Heb. "a written document"): wife's marriage contract specifying the obligations and sums she is entitled to receive in the event of divorce or the death of her husband.

kinah (pl. *kinot*): dirge over the dead. In the Middle Ages, the name was applied to a special type of dirge for the Ninth of Av.

Leviathan: legendary sea-monster which rules over the sea. At the onset of messianic times, leviathan will come up onto the land where it will engage in mortal combat with *behemoth*. Its flesh will be placed before the pious at the feast of the Righteous.

lulav (rabbinic Heb. "sprout"): one of the *arba'ah minim* ("four species"). Name applied to the palm-branch used on Sukkot ("festival of Tabernacles") together with the *etrog*, *hadas*, and *aravah*.

mahzor: festival prayer book.

maror: bitter herb eaten at the *seder* ritual on Passover eve.

Marrano(s): Jews (and their descendants) who were forcibly converted to Christianity in Spain and Portugal in the Middle Ages, but continued secretly to observe Jewish rituals.

masorah: body of traditions regarding the correct spelling, writing, and reading of the Hebrew Bible.

masorah magna: long lists of variant readings of the Bible written in the margins of the text.

masorah parva: short notes of variant readings of the Bible written in the margins of the text.

masoretic: in accordance with the masorah.

masorete: scholar of the masoretic tradition.

mazzah: unleavened bread eaten during the Passover festival.

megillah (pl. *megillot*) (Heb. "a scroll"): scroll; especially the Scroll of Esther. (See also Scrolls, The Five).

menorah: seven-branched oil lamp used in the Tabernacle and Temple.

Midrash: method for the interpretation of Scripture by finding new meaning in addition to the literal one. Also the name for collection of such rabbinic interpretations.

mikveh (lit. "a gathering" or "collection," especially of water): ritual bath for the immersion of persons and objects according to certain laws of the Jewish religion.

Mishnah ("learning", "repetition"): collection of statements, discussions, and biblical interpretations of the *tanna'im* in the form edited by Rabbi Judah ha-Nasi.

Mishneh Torah: Hebrew compendium of Jewish law written by Moses b. Maimon (Maimonides; 1135–1204).

Moreh Nevukhim: "Guide of the Perplexed," a philosophical and theological treatise by Moses b. Maimon (Maimonides; 1135–1204) completed in 1190.

nakdan (pl. *nakdanim*): experts in the Middle Ages who provided biblical manuscripts with vowels and accents.

parashah (pl. *parashot*) (Heb. "section," "portion"): subdivision of the Pentateuch.

parnas (Heb. from *parnes* "to foster," "support"): chief synagogue functionary, originally vested with both religious and administrative functions.

piyyut (from Greek *poietés*): form of Hebrew liturgical poetry which began in Palestine, c. 300–500 C.E.

Purim: festival held on the 14th or 15th day of Adar in commemoration of the delivery of the Jews of Persia through Mordecai and Esther from destruction by Haman.

Rabbanite: name given by the Karaites to their opponents who accepted the precepts of Jewish law which are contained in the Mishnah and Talmud.

Scrolls, The Five: comprehensive name for five works of the biblical Hagiographa read on special occasions: The Song of Songs (Passover), Ruth (Shavuot), Lamentations (Ninth of Av), Ecclesiastes (Sukkot), Esther (Purim).

seder (Heb. "order"): ceremony observed in the Jewish home on the first night (outside Israel, first two nights) of Passover, when the *Haggadah* is recited.

Sepharad: since the Middle Ages, a term applied to Spain.

Sepharadim: term applied to the Jews of Spain and thereafter to their descendants, wherever resident. In contradistinction to Ashkenazim.

Seleucid calendar ("*anno seleucide*"): reckoning used in Babylonian documents (including those of Jewish community).

Shavuot (Pentecost, feast of Weeks): second of the three annual pilgrim festivals commemorates the receiving of the Torah at Mount Sinai.

Shema (Heb. "hear . . . [O Israel]"), Deut. 6:4: Judaism's confession of faith, proclaiming the absolute unity of God.

siddur: daily prayer book in distinction to the *mahzor*, which contains the festival prayers.

sidrah (pl. *sidrot*): section of the Pentateuch read in the synagogue on the Sabbath. There are 54 such divisions, this arrangement permitting the reading of the entire Pentateuch annually.

Special Sabbaths: four Sabbaths preceding Passover on which special portions are read. The Sabbaths have received their names on the basis of these special sections.

Sukkot ("Tabernacles"): the last of the three annual pilgrim festivals.

sura: chapter of the Koran.

tallit (lit. "prayer shawl"): four-cornered prayer shawl with fringes (*ẓiẓit*) at each corner, worn during the morning prayers by adult males.

Talmud: compendium of discussions on the Mishnah by generations of scholars and jurists in many academies over a period of several centuries. The Palestinian (or Jerusalem) Talmud: compiled 350–400 C.E., mainly contained the discussions of the Palestinian sages. The Babylonian Talmud, the redaction of which was completed in the eighth century, incorporated the parallel discussions in the Babylonian academies. This codex became the most important Jewish legal source-book.

tanna (pl. *tanna'im*) (lit. "one who repeats" or "teaches"): rabbi quoted in the Mishnah or *baraita*.

Targum: Aramaic translation of the Bible.

tefillin: phylacteries; small cases containing passages from the Scripture and affixed on the forehead and arm by male Jews during the recital of morning prayers in accordance with Deuteronomy 6:8.

Tosefta (Aram. "addition," "supplement"): name of a collection of teachings and traditions of the *tanna'im*, closely related to the Mishnah. Like the Mishnah it is divided into six orders or divisions whose names are identical with those of the Mishnah's divisions.

Tur Even ha-Ezer: one of the four divisions of the *Arba'ah Turim*, dealing with personal and family matters. (See *Arba'ah Turim*).

Urim ve-thummim: sacred means of divination, attached to the breastplate of the high priest, and used by the early Hebrews.

yeshivah: Jewish traditional school devoted primarily to the study of the Talmud and rabbinic literature.

ẓaddik (Heb. "righteous man"): appellation given to a person outstanding for his faith and piety.

ziz: legendary king of the birds. As monstrous in size as leviathan, his ankles rest on the earth and his head reaches to the sky. Like leviathan and *behemoth*, a delicacy to be served to the pious at the end of time.

ẓiẓit (Heb. "fringe"): threads intertwined with blue cord. The Bible commands the wearing of *ẓiẓit* on the corners of garments. Now worn on the *tallit* and the *tallit katan*.

Bibliography to Plates

[1] Stassof (Mayer, 2515), 8, 12, pls. I–IV, 12–14, 22[1]; Harkavy (Mayer, 1047); P. Kahle, *Masoreten des Westens*, (1927), 58–59; N. Allony, "An autograph of Sa'id ben Farjoi of the ninth century," in: *Textus*, 6 (1968), 106–17.

[2] Stassof (Mayer, 2515), 8, pls. VII and VII*; A. Harkavy and H. L. Strack, *Katalog der hebräischen Bibelhandschriften der kaiserlichen öffentlichen Bibliothek in St. Petersburg* (1875), 263–76.

[3] H. Yalon, "An Oriental Manuscript of the portion *Shelaḥ Lekha* written in 1106", in: *Kirjath Sepher*, 30 (1954/55), 257–63 (Hebrew).

[4] Margoliouth, Cat, 1 (1899), 63–65, no. 89; R. Ettinghausen (Mayer, 670A).

[5] A. Harkavy, in: *Ḥadashim gam Yeshanim*, 1 no. 6 (1886), 5; A. Yelin, in: *Mizraḥ u-Ma'arav*, 1 (1919), 24–26; Sotheby and Co., *Sale Catalogue* (Dec. 11, 1961), lot 114, pl. 2; I. Joel, in: *Kirjath Sepher*, 38 (1962/63), 122–32; B. Narkiss, *Hebrew Illuminated Manuscripts from Jerusalem Collections*, The Israel Museum, Exhibition Catalog no. 40 (1967), no. 2; C. Sirat and M. Beit-Arié, *Manuscrits médiévaux en caractères hébraïques* (1969) (specimen of vol. I, no. A8).

[6] C. Roth (Mayer, 2221, 2229) idem, *Gleanings* (1967), 316–9; H. Schirmann, *Hebrew Poetry in Spain and Provence* (Heb.), 2 (1956), plate opp. p.417; Schwartz (Mayer, 3009C).

[7] Italiener (Mayer, 1147), 25, 272–4; *Synagoga*—Recklinghausen (Mayer, 2074), no. B.21; *Synagoga*—Frankfort (Mayer, 730), no. 91.

[8] Margoliouth, Cat, 2 (1905), 200–2, no. 607; Müller (Mayer, 1794), 103–4, pl. 4; Frauberger (Mayer, 742), 47, fig. 46; Leveen (Mayer, 1496), 99–104, pls. 31–32; J. Dominquez Bordona, "Minatura," in: *Ars Hispaniae*, 18 (1962), 135–43, figs. 170–5; C. M. Kaufmann, "Vidal Major," in: *Aachener Kunstblätter*, 29 (1964), 109–38; J. Gutmann (Mayer, 2969), 21, 23; B. Narkiss, in: *The Golden Haggadah* (1969), introductory volume.

[9] Margoliouth, Cat, 2 (1905), 202–3, no. 608; Müller (Mayer, 1792), 109–10; J. Gutmann (Mayer, 2969), nos. 26, 33; S. B. Freehof, "Home Rituals and the Spanish Synagogue," in: *Studies in Honor of A. A. Neuman* (1962), 222–6.

[10] Müller (Mayer, 1792); C. Roth (Mayer, 2235–2237); J. Gutmann (Mayer, 2969), nos. 30, 41 (see also Mayer's index, s. v. *Sarajevo Haggadah*).

[11] D. S. Sassoon, *Ohel Dawid*, 1 (1932), 303–4.

[12] Margoliouth, Cat, 2 (1905), 197–8, no. 605; Müller (Mayer, 1792), 108–9; Wischnitzer (Mayer, 2810).

[13] Müller (Mayer, 1792), 95–102, pls. I–III; C. Roth (Mayer, 2227); H. Rosenau (Mayer, 2160); *Manchester Exhibition* (Mayer, 1632), case 2, no. 2, pl. 4; Gutmann (Mayer, 2969), nos. 38–40.

[14] Margoliouth, Cat, 2 (1905), 198–200, no. 606; Müller (Mayer, 1792), 105–6, pl. IV2; C. Roth (Mayer, 2227); Rosenau (Mayer, 2160); J. Gutmann (Mayer, 2969), nos. 26, 30, 38.

[15] Müller (Mayer, 1792), 187–99, pls. XXXI–XXXV; Radojčić (Mayer, 2061); Scheiber (Mayer, 2302); B. Narkiss: *Kirjath Sepher*, 34 (1958/9), 71–79; 42 (1966/7), 104–7.

[16] D. S. Sassoon, *Ohel Dawid*, 1 (1932), 6–14, no. 368; Leveen (Mayer, 1496), 109–13, pls. XXXIV–XXXVI.

[17] B. Kennicott, *Vetus Testamentum Hebraicum* (Oxford, 1776); Neubauer, Cat, 1 (1886), no. 2322; Wischnitzer (Mayer, 2809); Leveen (Mayer, 1496), 114–7, pls. 39–41 and frontispiece; C. Roth (Mayer, 2205, 2221, 2229); idem, *Gleanings* (1967), 298–319.

[18] *Copenhagen Catalog* (Mayer, 1736), no. 83; *Stockholm Catalog* (Mayer, 1736), no. 83; *Paris Catalog* (Mayer, 1736), no. 6; *Strasbourg Catalog* (Mayer, 1736), no. 63; Wormald (Mayer, 2899); R. Edelmann (Mayer, 630); *Synagoga*—Recklinghausen (Mayer, 2074), no. B.51; *Synagoga*—Frankfort (Mayer, 730), no. 149; R. Edelmann, *Hebraica from Denmark* (1969), no. 1; Millard Meiss, in: *The Journal of the Walters Art Gallery*, 4 (1941), 45 ff.

[19] Margoliouth, Cat, 2 (1905), 102–4, nos. 486–7; B. Narkiss, "An Illuminated Manuscript of the *Mishneh Torah* in the Jewish National and University Library, Jerusalem," in: *Kirjath Sepher*, 43 (1967/68), 298.

[20] C. D. Ginsburg, "A Manuscript of the Old Testament," in: *Athenaeum* (March 31, 1883), 409; Ginsburg, *Introduction to the Massoretico—Critical Edition of the Hebrew Bible*, (1897), 707–14, no. 48; Margoliouth, Cat, 1 (1899), 33–35, no. 62; Leveen, Cat, 184; idem (Mayer, 1496), 113 f., pls. XXXVI–XXXVIII.

[21] *Catalogue de Vente de la succession de feu M. D. Henriques de Castro Mz.* (Amsterdam, April 26–27 and May 1–10, 1899), lot 475, pp. 44–48, and plate.

[22] M. Steinschneider, *Katalog der hebräischen Handschriften in der Stadtbibliothek zu Hamburg* (1878), 39, no. 91.

[23] Margoliouth, Cat, 3 (1909–15), 402–27, no. 1056; Leveen (Mayer, 1496), 72–85; Frauberger (Mayer, 742); Ameisenowa (Mayer, 57); C. Sirat, in: REJ, 2 (1961), 19; Morel-Payen, *Les plus beaux manuscrits et les plus belles réliures de la bibliothèque municipale de Troyes* (1935); M. Metzger, "Les illustrations bibliques d'un manuscrit hébreu du Nord de la France (1278–1340 environ)," in: *Mélanges offerts à René Crozet* (1966), 1237–53.

[24] Zotenberg, Cat, no. 36; *Israël à travers les âges*, Exhibition Catalog, Petit Palais, Paris (1968), no. 544 and plate.

[25] M. L. Gengaro et al., *Codici decorati e miniati dell' Ambrosiana, ebraici e greci* (Milano, 1959), 19–34, pls. I–XXIII; Ameisenowa (Mayer, 55); P. D'Ancona (Mayer, 556); B. Narkiss (Mayer, 1222A), 99; idem, in: *The Birds' Head Haggadah*, introductory volume (1967), 90–104, pls. 5, 6, 25–29; J. Gutmann, "When the Kingdom Comes," in *Art Journal*, 27 no. 2 (1967/68), 168–75.

[26] S. Rothschild (Mayer, 2246); Wischnitzer (Mayer, 2846, 2876); D. Goldschmidt (Mayer, 857); E. Roth (Mayer, 2239); B. Narkiss (Mayer, 1222A), 91, 93, 105; M. Beit Aryeh, in: *Leshonenu*, 29 (1965), 27–46, 80–102; B. Narkiss, *Hebrew Illuminated Manuscripts from Jerusalem Collections*, Israel Museum, Exhibition Catalog no. 40 (1967), no. 5.

[27] Neubauer, Cat, 1 (1886), 828–9, no. 2373; Wischnitzer (Mayer, 2846), 29f, fig. 20; C. Roth (Mayer, 2232), 396, fig. 196; Ameisenowa (Mayer, 58), 40, pl. 18a; B. Narkiss (Mayer, 1222A), 104–5.

[28] *The Birds' Head Haggadah* (1967), introductory volume ed. by M. Spitzer, with contributions by E. D. Goldschmidt, H. L. C. Jaffe, and B. Narkiss, and an

introduction by Meyer Shapiro. For further bibliography see pp. 123, 124.

29 Ameisenowa (Mayer, 53); Wischnitzer, in: MGWJ, 75 (1931), 69–71; idem, in: JQR, 25 (1934/35), 303–6; E. E. Urbach, *The Tosaphists* (Heb., 1955), 106–7, 275; E. Roth (Mayer, 523).

30 D. Kaufmann, in: Müller (Mayer, 1792), 282 ff.; E. Moses (Mayer, 1781, 1782); F. Landsberger (Mayer, 1438); J. Gutmann (Mayer, 992); F. Landsberger, in: C. Roth (Mayer, 2232), 397–9, fig. 197 and frontispiece; E. Roth (Mayer, 523), no. D. 73, color plates I, II, fig. 26; Wischnitzer (Mayer, 2847); B. Narkiss, "An Illuminated *Mishneh Torah* Manuscript in the Jewish National and University Library in Jerusalem," in: *Kirjath Sepher*, 43 (1967/68), 285–300 (Hebrew).

31 F. Landsberger, in: C. Roth (Mayer, 2232), 399, and color plate opposite.

32 T. J. Pettigrew, *Bibliotheca Sussexiana*, 1 (London, 1827), 14–16, no. 3, pls. 1–5; Margoliouth, Cat. 1 (1899), 48–49, no. 74; Leveen, Cat, 184; Leveen (Mayer, 1496), 107 ff., pl. XXXIII.

33 Müller (Mayer, 1792), 114–120, pls. VII–X; Leveen (Mayer, 1496), 94 ff.; B. Narkiss, "A Tripartite Illuminated Mahzor from a South German School of Hebrew Illuminated Manuscripts Around 1300," in: *Papers of the Fourth World Congress of Jewish Studies*, 2 (1968), 129–33, figs. 30–33.

34 Margoliouth, Cat, 2 (1899), 285–8, no. 662.

35 S. Z. Offenhausen, *Theriaca Judaica* (Hanau, 1675), translated into German by Johan Wulfer (Altdorf, 1681); Andrea Wurfel, *Historische Nachrichten von der Judengemeinde Nürnberg* (Nuremberg, 1755), 97–105; B. Ziemlich (Mayer, 2933); N. Brüll (Mayer, 393), 115–8.

36 G. B. De' Rossi, *Manuscripti codices hebraici bibliothecae J. B. De Rossi* (Parma, 1803), no. 440, 1 and 2; L. Mortara Ottolenghi (Mayer, 2990A), 66–68, nos. 20, 21, pl. IV; idem, "La decorazione del codice biblico ebraico della Biblioteca Berio di Genova," in: *Quaderni dell' Università di Genova* (1967); G. Tamani, "Elenco dei manoscritti ebraici miniati e decorati della 'Palatina' di Parma," in: *La Bibliofilia*, 70 no. 1–2 (1968), 47–48, no. 4.

37 Margoliouth, Cat, 1 (1899), 53–56, no. 80; Leveen, Cat, 184, add. 56a.

38 B. Narkiss, *Hebrew Illuminated Manuscripts from Jerusalem Collections*, The Israel Museum, Exhibition Catalog no. 40 (1967), no. 9.

39 M. Steinschneider, *Katalog der hebräischen Handschriften in der Stadtbibliothek zu Hamburg* (1878), no. 86; Italiener (Mayer, 1147), 10, 34, 180 ff.; Fooner (Mayer, 723), 221; J. Gutmann (Mayer, 992), 21; *Synagoga*—Recklinghausen (Mayer, 2074), no. B. 30; *Synagoga*—Frankfurt (Mayer, 730), no. 99; *Monumenta Judaica* (Mayer, 523), no. D. 30.

40 Müller (Mayer, 1792), 125–70; pls. XVI–XXVI; J. Gutmann (Mayer, 992); idem (Mayer, 2969), no. 34; B. Narkiss, *Hebrew Illuminated Manuscripts from Jerusalem Collections*, The Israel Museum, Exhibition Catalog no. 40 (1967), no. 11.

41 D. Kaufmann (Mayer, 1236); M. Narkiss (Mayer, 1866); J. Gutmann (Mayer, 992); idem (Mayer, 2969), no. 35; B. Narkiss, *Hebrew Illuminated Manuscripts from Jerusalem Collections*, The Israel Museum, Exhibition Catalog no. 40 (1967), no. 12.

42 Müller (Mayer, 1792), 120–5, pls. XI–XV; G. Warner, *Descriptive Catalogue of the Illuminated Manuscripts in the Library of C. W. Dyson Perrins* (1920), no. 124; C. Bernheimer, (Mayer, 265), 353–5, pls. 27–29; Italiener (Mayer, 1147), 194–211, pls. 4–6; E. Munkacsi (Mayer, 1818), 6, 25, 66; A. Marx (Mayer, 1662, 1663); M. Fooner (Mayer, 723); Lansberger (Mayer, 1431, 1433, 1435); C. Roth (Mayer, 2193); Sotheby and Co., *Dyson Perrins Sales Catalogue* (Dec. 9, 1958), lot 33, pls. 37–38; *Synagoga*—Recklinghausen (Mayer, 2074), no. B. 35; *Monumenta Judaica* (1964), nos. D.68 and 70; M. Lehrs, *Geschichte und kritischer Katalog des deutschen, niederländischen und französischen Kupferstichs im XV*, Jahrhundert, 2 (1908); 9 (1934); M. Steinschneider, *Die hebräischen Handschriften der K. Hof-und Staatsbibliothek in München*, (1895), 1; M. Geisberg, *Der Meister E. S. und Israel van Meckenem* (1924); O. Mitius (Mayer, 1760); M. J. Husung (Mayer, 1130); O. Kurz (Mayer, 2981); A. and W. Cahn, "An Illuminated Haggadah of the fifteenth century," in: *The Yale University Library Gazette*, 41 no. 4 (1967), 166–176, pls. 177–82.

A LIST OF MANUSCRIPTS SIGNED BY OR ATTRIBUTED TO JOEL BEN SIMEON:

A. Dated manuscripts

1. *Siddur* of 1449. Parma, Biblioteca Palatina, MS. Parm. 3144 (MS. De' Rossi 1274), (signed by the "scribe Joel ben Simeon, called Feibush of Bonn.").

2. *Mahzor Cremona* of 1452. Formerly Turin, Royal Library; destroyed by fire. (Signed by "Joel ben Simeon. . . Feibush of Bonn.").

3. *The Second New York Haggadah* of 1454. N.Y., Jewish Theological Seminary, MS. 555. (Signed by the "scrivener Joel ben Simeon, called Feibush Ashkenazi of Cologne on the Rhine, who wrote, punctuated and painted it.")

4. *Siddur* of 1469. London, British Museum, Add. MS. 26957. (Signed by the "scrivener Joel ben Simeon.")

5. *Washington Haggadah* of 1478. Library of Congress. (Signed by "the humblest of scribes Joel ben Simeon.")

6. *Commentary on the Psalms*, Modena 1485. Parma, Biblioteca Palatina, MS. Parm. 2841 (Signed by "the scrivener Joel ben Simeon Ashkenazi, for Manuel ben Isaac of Modena.")

B. Undated manuscripts

7. *The Second Nuremberg Haggadah*. Jerusalem, Schocken Library (formerly: Nuremberg, National Museum, MS. 2170b). (Signed by "the scribe Joel ben Simeon"). The manuscript was incorrectly dated to 1492 by Müller, to 1410 by Fooner, to 1400 by Landsberger, and to after 1454 by Italiener (the last by interpreting the name Proyna mentioned in the manuscript, as Brünn, from where the Jews were expelled in 1454. It should be noticed that Joel was already in Cremona by 1452.)

8. *Haggadah*. London, British Museum Add. MS. 14762. (Signed "Feibush called Joel, [who] painted it").

9. *The First New York Haggadah*. New York, Jewish Theological Seminary, MS. 75048. (Signed by the "scribe Joel ben Simeon.")

10. *Implements of the Temple*, six leaves. Ibid., MS. 0822. (Signed by "Joel the painter called Feibush.")

11. *Haggadah.* Cologne and Geneva, Martin Bodmer Collection (formerly: Malvern, Dyson-Perrins Collection MS. 124). (Signed by the "scribe Joel ben Simeon called Feibush Ashkenazi of Cologne on the Rhine.")

C. Attributed manuscripts

12. *Haggadah.* Parma, Biblioteca Palatina, MS. Parm. 2998 (MS. De' Rossi 111).

13. *Haggadah.* Stuttgart, Württembergische Landesbibliothek, Cod. Or. 4°, 1.

14. *The Murphy Haggadah:* Yale Univ., Heb. MS.+143.

[43] A. Schmidt (Mayer, 2322, 2323); D. Simonsen (Mayer, 2463); B. Italiener (Mayer, 1147); A. Boeckler (Mayer, 328); A. Marx (Mayer, 1662, 1663); F. Landsberger (Mayer, 1431); *Synagoga*—Recklinghausen (Mayer, 2074), no. B.34; *Synagoga*—Frankfort (Mayer, 730), no. 105; E. Roth (Mayer, 3003A); *Monumenta Judaica* (Mayer, 523), no. D.61.

[44] B. Narkiss, *Hebrew Illuminated Manuscripts from Jerusalem Collections*, The Israel Museum, Exhibition Catalog no. 40 (1967), no. 10.

[45] B. Italiener (Mayer, 1147), 166–74, pls. 1–3; F. Landsberger (Mayer, 1431); E. Roth (Mayer, 3003A); J. Gutmann (Mayer, 2969), no. 38.

[46] Margoliouth, Cat, 3 (1965), no. 906; J. Leveen, *Hebrew Bible in Art* (1944), 72–117; M. R. James, *The Western Manuscripts in the Library of Emmanuel College* (1904), 5; C. Roth, "Leon de Modena and his English correspondents," in: *Transactions of the Jewish Historical Society of England*, 17 (1953), 41; N. Alony, "Hebrew Manuscripts in Cambridge Libraries," in: *Aresheth*, 3 (1961), 406 (Heb.); H. Vogelstein and P. Rieger, *Geschichte der Juden in Rom*, 1 (1896), 278, 332–3, 387–8, 438; Zotenberg, Cat, no. 176; G. B. De' Rossi, *Manuscripti codices hebraici bibliothecae J. B. De Rossi* (Parma, 1803), nos. 221, 1261; P. J. Burns, *Dissertatio Generalis* (Brunswick, 1783), 378–9; B. Kennicott, *Biblia Hebraica* (Oxford, 1810), no. 94; G. Burnet, *The Life of William Bedell* (Dublin, 1736), 16–17; E. S. Shuckburgh, *Two Biographies of William Bedell* (1902), XIX (Milan) (Mayer, 2990A), 44–45, pl. 2.

[47] D. Kaufmann, "Zur Geschichte einer Handschrift," in: *Jüdisches Volksblatt*, no. 52 (1863) (see *Allgemeine Zeitung des Judenthums*); idem, "Un manuscrit du Mischné Tora," in: REJ, 36 (1898), 65–74; R. Schilling and G. Swarzenski (Mayer, 2318); W. Bombe, "Documente und Regesten zur Geschichte der Peruginer Miniaturmalerei," in: *Repertorium für Kunstwissenschaft*, 33 (1910), 1–4, 114; H. Frauberger (Mayer, 735), fig. 23; idem (Mayer, 738), figs. 6, 11; idem (Mayer, 742), figs, 34, 35; Wischnitzer (Mayer, 2847), 48–52; B. Narkiss, "An Illuminated *Mishneh Torah* Manuscript in the Jewish National and University Library in Jerusalem," in: *Kirjath Sepher*, 43 (1967/68), 285–300 (Hebrew); idem, "An Illuminated Maimonides Manuscript," in *Ariel*, no. 21 (1968), 51–59 (Eng.).

[48] E. Munkacsi (Mayer, 1818), 34–40, pls. VI–IX; idem (Mayer, 1814).

[53] D. S. Sassoon, *Ohel Dawid*, 1 (1932), 289–93, pl. 38.

[54] E. Munkacsi (Mayer, 1818), 73–78, pls. XXXIII–XXXVII.

[55] M. Brizio, *Catalogo delle cose d'Arte e di Antichità d'Italia* (1933), 161–3, 3 reproductions.

[56] B. Narkiss, in: *Haaretz* (May 15, 1957); I. Levi, in: REJ, 89 (1930), 281–92; Müller (Mayer, 1792), 199–207, pls. XXXVI–XXXVIII.

[57] E. Munkacsi (Mayer, 1818), 52–56, pls. XVII–XXI; G. Mazzatinti, *Inventario dei manoscritti della Biblioteca Rovigo* (1893), 4, no. 5.

[58] Margoliouth, Cat, 1 (1899), no. 15; Frauberger (Mayer, 742), 37, fig. 27; P. d'Ancona, *La miniatura fiorentina dei secoli XV–XVI*, 1 (1914), 100–1, pl. XCIX.

[59] M. Steinschneider, *Katalog der hebräischen Handschriften in der Stadtbibliothek zu Hamburg* (1887), 172–3, no. 353; *Synagoga*—Recklinghausen (Mayer, 2074), no. B.45; *Synagoga*—Frankfort (Mayer, 730); *Monumenta Judaica* (Mayer, 523), no. D.77.

[60] Frauberger (Mayer, 742), fig. 27; Stadtbibliothek, Frankfort, *Katalog der ständigen Austellung*, no. 6; Wischnitzer (Mayer, 2847); Müller (Mayer, 1792), pls. 37, 38; R. Schilling and G. Swarzenski (Mayer, 2318), 329–41, no. 214, plates 77, 75; Bezalel Narkiss, in: *Kirjath Sepher*, 43 (1967/68), 298.

Index

(Numbers in italics indicate main entires).

תם ונשלם שבח לאל
בירושלים השלמה במדינת ישראל
לראש הסולם העליתי האמור
אני משה בן אריה המוציא לאור

ער"הש תש"ל